SEEDS
OF CHANGE
THE LIVING TREASURE

The Passionate Story
of the Growing Movement to
Restore Biodiversity and Revolutionize
the Way We Think About Food

KENNY AUSUBEL

HarperSanFrancisco
A Division of HarperCollinsPublishers

A Tree Clause Book

Harper San Francisco and Seeds of Change, in association with the Rainforest Action Network & ReLeaf, will facilitate the planting of two trees for every one tree used in the manufacturing of this book.

FIRST PAPERBACK EDITION

Library of Congress Cataloging-in-Publication Data
Ausubel, Ken.
    Seeds of Change: the living treasure: the passionate story of the growing movement to restore biodiversity and revolutionize the way we think about food/Kenny Ausubel. —1st ed.
        p. cm.
      ISBN 0–06–250008–2 (pbk.: acid-free paper): $18.00
      1. Seeds of Change. Incorporated. 2. Food crops—Seeds. 3. Food crops—Heirloom varieties. 4. Seed technology. 5. Cookery.
I. Title.
SB117.35.N6A9 1994
631.5'21—dc20   92-56185
                                                          CIP

94 95 96 97 98 HAW 10 9 8 7 6 5 4 3 2 1

This edition is printed on acid-free paper that meets the American National Standards Institute Z39.48 Standard.

Photography by Jim Bones
Graphite drawings by Helen Beck
Illustrations by Kathleen Edwards
Cover & Book Design by Driscoll Design Group

CONTENTS

This is really not a gardening book. Perhaps the roots of our environmental problems actually stem from gardening clichés, so let us prune our blooming metaphors, root out sprouting banality, and let lie fallow forever the fertile fields of vegetating platitudes. For now is not the time to plant seeds of hype, nor reap flowering nonsense. Let us cultivate our language and be rid of the warmed-over cabbage from last year's garden plot. You'll find here only a couple of comparisons between gardening and life—unavoidable, organic, germane. If you find more, please get a shovel and heap them onto the rot of the compost bin.

After many fascinating years of roaming around the ideas and personalities in this book, I am grateful to have had the chance to put it down on paper. My thanks to Harper San Francisco for making it possible, and to my astute editor Barbara Moulton for encouraging me to bring my own voice into it, which I would not have otherwise done. Special thanks also to Tom Grady.

My thanks go to a circle of people who made essential contributions: Steven Schmidt was seminal in midwifing this book, acting wisely throughout as an agent, enzyme, mentor, and friend. The Seeds of Change team and company supported me in this endeavor. Alan Kapuler generously brought his heart and life's work to the story presented here. Nina Simons, my incredible "tantrapreneurial" partner, capably and bravely ran the business of Seeds of Change while I stole the time to write, and was mainly responsible for bringing together the chefs and recipes presented here.

Hope Atterbury diligently sought out important original research for the investigative portions of this book; her enthusiasm and effectiveness gracefully supported the editorial process. Howard Shapiro coordinated all the wonderful artwork of Jim Bones and Helen Beck, and brought great heart to the project. Jim Bones not only created some of the most remarkable images we've encountered but also poured his soul into the project. Helen Beck stretched her limits to create her magnificently felt drawing of plant spirit.

Thanks to the Seeds of Change "Book Club," whose advance editing saved the unwitting Barbara Moulton from ever actually seeing first drafts: Steven Schmidt, Nina Simons, Hope Atterbury, Howard Shapiro, and Jeff Klein.

Thanks to Rich and Julie Pecoraro, who shared their devotion and incredibly hard work for life and this project. To Gabriel Howearth for spreading the word and bringing people together. To Emigdio Ballon for his remarkable patience, caring, and devotion to all life. Many happy thanks to Linda, Kusra, Elyrea, and Dylana Kapuler and Peace Seeds for the fine work they have all done these many years. Thanks to Susan Van Auken, Julie Spelletich, Jill Perez, and Linda Kapuler for the farm's recipes.

Thanks to dear friend Josh Mailman, whose capital serves, whose vision has begun to revolutionize the way global business operates. To brother Greg Pardes, for his perpetual emotion, perseverance, and unconditional support, and to his partner and my sister, Patricia Murray, for vacuuming the etheric after hours, and to ReSeal. To Jeffrey Bronfman, the height of admiration and appreciation for his vision, love, and courage. Very special thanks to Jenane Patterson and John Ross for nourishing the original Seed of Change. To Barbara Whitestone, thanks and respect for her excellent ongoing work and brave integrity in greening business. To J. P. Harpignies, long-term thanks for his exceptional generosity and keen insight. To Suzanne Jamison for her selfless dedication and consideration. To Jim Dreyfous for his irreverence and support. To Stephen Badger, for being born at the right time. To Arthur Jacobs for his unshakable confidence and support. To Jeff Klein, for sliding into home in the bottom of the ninth . . .

Deep admiration to the land stewards at the Seeds of Change farm: Lee Gearheart, Susan Van Auken, Jim Orlando, Carlos and Jill Perez, Will Hoeller. And also to some of our other original organic seed growers: John Sundquist, Alan and Cheryl Venet, J. J. Haapala, Mark and Margie Wheeler, Craig Thomas.

Many thanks to the team at the warehouse and fulfillment center: Jody King, Mary Pennington, Cindy Ray, James Townsend, Bud Weiser. And to the many seasonal folks who return each year with the cycles.

Thanks to Andre and Jyoti Ulrych for their seminal commitment to the land and a healthy food system. Thanks to Paul Hawken and Will Raap for showing their belief in Seeds of Change at an early, precarious, and crucial time. Thanks to Seth Roffman for providing a visual history and for his dedication to documenting native agriculture in the Southwest.

Special thanks to some of our corporate and organizational partners for exploring the edge of cooperation with us: Joseph Koster, Linda Poit, and Michael Segundo at ReSeal; Bill and Pat St. John of Bio-Remediation Services and BioTechniques; Horst Rechelbacher and Nan Upin of the Aveda Corporation; Dr. Hugh Riordan of the Garvey Center for the Improvement of Human Functioning; Kathleen Harrison of Botanical Dimensions; Mark Blumenthal and the American Botanical Council; John Perkins, Bob Graham, and Jerry Hildebrand of Katalysis; Gary Nabhan, Mahina Drees, Bret Bakker, and Native Seeds/SEARCH; Robert Henrikson and the Earthrise Trading Company; Greg Steltenpohl, Stephen Williamson, and the Odwalla juice company; Carolyn Garcia and the Rex Foundation; Bob Weir and the Further Foundation; the Social Venture Network; Yvonne Frost and Oregon Tilth; Alysa Gravitz and Coop America; Whitney Laughlin and Southwest College Horizons; John Schaeffer and the Real Goods Company; Dr. John and Nancy Jack Todd of Ocean Arks International; Dr. Steven King, Lisa Conte, and Shaman Pharmaceuticals; Doug Kepler and Damariscotta; Cary Fowler, Pat Mooney, and RAFI; Kent and Diane Whealey and Seed Savers Exchange; Dr. Jason Clay and Cultural Survival; Claudine Schneider and the Artemis Project; Anthony and Ardath Rodale and the Rodale Institute; John Domont and Lifelight Studios; Andrew Ungerleider, Kate Priest, and Natural Nectar; Tonia and Alan Gould and Old Santa Fe Trail Books; Jim and Betsy Turner and Healthy Harvest; Gary Hirschberg and Stonyfield Yogurt; Gordon Roddick and the Body Shop.

So many people have supported the project at various times, and we thank them all: Chris Bird; Peter Tompkins; Bruce Mace; Sally Sloban; Cynthia Jurs; Donna Boner; Victor di Suvero; Joshua Smith; Olaf Brentmar; Dori Dean; Brando Crespi; Gene and Karen Martineau; Carol Moldau and Martin Edmunds; Dr. James Duke; Jacki Adams and Patrick Johnson; Dan Dunlap; Nancy Pfister; Brian Enwright; Luke Gatto; Andrea Nasher; Daniel Wood; Rusty Dobkins; Greg Howearth; Bob and Dee Smith; Michael Stranahan; Charlie Walters; Michael and Darlene Wilenta; Dr. Greg Cajete; Petuuche Gilbert; Paul Poncho; Maggie Banner; Richard Deertrack; Suzanne Shown Harjo; Dr. Sheldon Hendler; Dr. Andrew Weil; Pamela Kelly and Steve Witt; Sandy Gooch; Brian Agar; Terry Gips; Jack Doyle; Jim Hightower; Tom Hayden; Dr. Rosita Arvigo; Dr. Dennis McKenna; Terence McKenna; Anna Edey; Beth and Charles Miller; Steve Lett; Mazatt Galindo; Liz Rymland; Chris Shea; Darby Long; DeWayne Youts; Mark Bennett; Steve Dentali; Debbie Reid-Goldman; Michel Herrygers; Isabel Lizarazu; Linda Grey; Reavis Moore and Eliza Gilkyson; Moonstar Rinkel; Deborah Nuzzi; Jim Nelson; Jack Copeland; Larry Herschman; Bill and Laurie Benenson; Robert Strozer; Frank Morton; Dr. Sarangamat Gurusiddiah; Zuleikha; Curtis Showell; Glenn Downs; Noel Perry; Michael Klein; Ben Dover.

Special thanks also to my brother Jesse for his early advice to make the book personal, and to my mother Anne for her lineage of wonderful writing and wit. Remembrance to my father, who loved learning and teaching, and taught me inspiration.

INTRODUCTION
SEEDS
OF CHANGE
THE LIVING TREASURE

Though I do not believe that a plant will spring up where no seed has been, I have great faith in a seed. Convince me that you have a seed there, and I am prepared to expect wonders.

Henry David Thoreau,
The Dispersion of Seeds

ising over the Rocky Mountains onto the ancient Rio Grande valley, the rich New Mexico sun triggered the solar cell on a small box wired to a fence post. The black box began to chirp, dispersing its sound over the organic plants in the most elaborate vegetable garden I had ever seen. The cameraman was pleased with the "magic hour" shot, and the soundman had definitely gotten an earful of the audio waves. I wrapped the scene and walked with master gardener Gabriel Howearth to scout the next location.

Gabriel, a lean, long-haired hippie, led me through the wonderland of gardens. He was testing a fertilizing system called Sonic Bloom, which I had come to film. Sonic Bloom used a combination of sound frequencies along with a natural fertilizer sprayed on the plants' leaves. The inventor of Sonic Bloom, Dan Carlson, had developed the idea after reading the groundbreaking book *The Secret Life of Plants*, in which one of the authors, Chris Bird, described experiments showing the potent effects of sound on plants. Gabriel explained that the theory behind Sonic Bloom corresponded to a Native American concept called the "hour of the wolf," the darkest moment just before daybreak, when symphonies of crickets, cicadas, and birds resound across the land to stimulate the plants to drink the morning dew.

I would be filming Dan Carlson and Chris Bird later that day. I had met Chris several months earlier in 1985 in Washington, D.C., while researching a film I was producing, *Hoxsey: How Healing Becomes a Crime*. The feature-length investigative documentary followed the disturbing story of how organized medicine and the federal government may have obstructed or actually suppressed valuable unorthodox cancer treatments. At the center of the controversy was the seemingly innocuous Hoxsey tonic, an herbal remedy ridiculed and vilified by organized medicine as an antiquated, worthless folk elixir and touted by supporters as a life-saving remedy.

As part of my research, I had interviewed Dr. James Duke, a world expert on plant medicine at the United States Department of Agriculture near Washington. He cited evidence that seven of the nine Hoxsey herbs had individually shown anticancer or antitumor activity in controlled laboratory studies. Dr. Duke, an open-minded, gentle scholar, pointed out that plant medicine is the foundation of modern pharmacology; plants provide the basis for half our pharmaceutical drugs. But during most of the twentieth century, he noted, plants have been subordinated to the status of a primitive, archaic tradition inferior to synthetic laboratory creations.

Back at my home in Santa Fe, I received a call from Chris, who asked if I would be available to document an unusual garden on an Indian pueblo near Santa Fe. I had only recently moved back to town from a small organic farm in the country, and I was suddenly struck by how entwined with plants my life had become. It seemed an anomaly for a city boy raised mainly in Manhattan whose parents had grown up in the wilds of Brooklyn. I had never felt any affinity for plants until I moved to New Mexico in 1974 and my then wife started working as a botanical illustrator for a local herbalist. I eventually channeled my growing interest into making a film, *Los Remedios: The Healing Herbs*, about the active use of herbs as folk medicine in the Southwest.

To my further surprise, a family history revealed to me that my father's name, Ausubel, is actually a version of an ancient Hebrew word that means marjoram, an herb long used in temple ceremonies. My father's side of the family lived for several generations on the border of Greece and Turkey, where they were pharmacists, that is, herbalists.

When my wife and I moved to the small organic farm in the country outside Santa Fe in 1976, I was intent on learning the basics of living on the land and farming organically. Although I never got very good at gardening, I came to love it, and when we moved back to Santa Fe, I missed it. The prospect of filming a garden was enticing.

The pond on the Seeds of Change farm with the foothills of the Mogollon Mountains and the Gila Wilderness behind.

I arrived at San Juan pueblo just after dawn on a misty summer morning. Here along the Rio Grande, huge cottonwoods had harbored generations of Pueblo farmers escaping the summer sun after tending their cultured fields. The ancient river valley was a cradle of agriculture in North America, a sacred garden where Pueblo legends honored fifty thousand years of living with the land.

Gabriel's gardens were overwhelming in their sheer variety of unusual plants. A sensory overload of colors and scents radiated a quality of magical vibrancy to match the clear light of New Mexico. Gabriel was attentive, articulate, and hypnotically obsessed with the garden. As he walked the rows, he displayed an intense personal relationship with each plant.

I spent many days observing Gabriel and his garden, and he introduced me to the remarkable collection of plants he had managed to gather from garden to garden over his many years of tenant farming in the West. While attending the University of California at Santa Cruz, he worked for the legendary master gardener Alan Chadwick and emerged as a master organic gardener himself. Chadwick encouraged his students to get out into the Third World to see how traditional agricultural life is really lived. During winters away from an Oregon farm, Gabriel apprenticed with Mayan Indians in Mexico to learn traditional farming methods, and backpacked into the remote Ecuadorian Andes to live with local tribes. In the course of his wanderings, he gathered traditional seeds, which indigenous peoples consider the very precious gift of life and lineage.

Aware of his work with native seeds, San Juan pueblo hired Gabriel for a project to help revive native agriculture. In a scant three acres, he was now growing an astonishing three hundred kinds of rare and unusual vegetables, herbs, and flowers. His unique mosaic contained a greater diversity of plants than farmers grow in the entire Midwest farm belt.

The garden had ten kinds of quinoa, the sacred grain of the Incan civilization. The tall golden heads rocked in the breeze, each carefully recorded for particular traits and adaptability here in the north. Over lunch, I found quinoa a truly delicious nutty dish, a fluffy light meal loaded with nutrition.

"The garden is where you take the time in your life to tune in and listen. It just takes being still long enough, opening your heart, opening your spirit up to what the plants have to tell you. Many times at the beginning stages, it'll come in the form of an insect or a butterfly or something that will come to you consistently. It's for us to create a sanctuary in our garden that allows for that interaction to occur. We all are capable of being an open channel to gentleness, and a garden is one of the most sacred places to do that."
Gabriel Howearth

Looking through the ancient cottonwoods into the fields of the Seeds of Change farm.

A stand of tall plumes flaming brilliant scarlet into the turquoise New Mexico sky was equally compelling. Gabriel was growing a dozen varieties of amaranth, the sacred grain of the Aztec society, which all but disappeared after the Spanish conquest. Amaranth is also very high in nutrition, and it made an excellent bread we shared in the shady relief of the afternoon.

I researched my way through Gabriel's garden bite by bite. The experience was my firsthand introduction to biological diversity. Not only did I discover amazing new foods and plants but multiple varieties of each one. It was astonishing to contemplate how limited my previous view of food plants had been.

As I filmed Gabriel, I also found him an intelligent advocate of organic gardening. He observed the simple truth that the health of the soil is the basis of good growing, and that disease often represents imbalances or deficiencies in the soil. He drew a parallel with the body's immune system. He was convinced that good soil management practices virtually eliminate the need for poisonous chemicals. He believed deeply in working to achieve a natural balance, using beneficial insects to offset "pests," for example. He also used flowers to attract unwanted pests, creating small habitats for their use to keep them away from the other plants. He made his own foliar fertilizing sprays from herbs and seaweed.

Gabriel revealed to me that, despite an increasing national organic movement, the seeds used to grow organic food are not themselves grown organically. Not only are they raised using conventional chemical methods, sometimes they are then coated with a pesticide or chemical fertilizer prior to sale. For years Gabriel had raised virtually all his own foods, including the organic seeds to grow them. He pointed out that the lack of organic seeds, the first link in the food chain, was a major gap in the organic cycle. Even as an organic gardener, I had never noticed that the seeds, the crucial predetermining point of the entire growing cycle, were tainted.

After a summer of field trials, Gabriel found measurable improvements in the flavor, size, and vitality of the plants raised with Sonic Bloom. That summer had also brought the Rio Grande valley a biblical plague of grasshoppers that destroyed many farms completely and severely damaged the rest. The exception was Gabriel's San Juan garden, which was not badly hurt. Other farmers came to investigate and were impressed by the results of natural farming methods.

San Juan had hired Gabriel to help find ways to restore native farming on the pueblo. The Pueblo people's lands remain relatively intact, though diminished, and the cultures of the various groups maintain a tribal continuity uncommon in the United States. The fact that they were relatively peaceful, sophisticated agrarian societies may have inclined the Spanish not to destroy them and the later Americans not to banish the Pueblo people to distant reservations, as they did most other Indian peoples in the United States.

But after World War II, many more people from San Juan were compelled to enter the wage economy off the pueblo, and farming declined dramatically. The pueblo was now exploring ways to assist people to stay on the land to farm, either commercially or for self-reliance. Pueblo Governor Herman Agoyo was determined to preserve these deep traditions from extinction.

Gabriel put the word out in the pueblo to look for seeds. People started to show up with seeds found tucked away in yellowed envelopes and dry adobe walls. Among them was James Chancellor, a thirty-five-year-old San Juan native who was inspired by the project to start gardening for the first time. He brought out some beautiful seeds that he found stored in an old clay pot. They turned out to be the sacred red corn of San Juan, which hadn't been grown in forty years. The event resonated powerfully throughout the pueblo and marked a profound spiritual homecoming. I was deeply moved by the experience of filming James with the red corn in his garden, seeds in his hand and grateful tears in his voice.

I filmed Gabriel many times over the coming weeks, as well as a stream of professional visitors to this singular garden. Chris Bird perched in front of the camera against the colorful backdrop of endangered plants to deliver a gruff warning against the ongoing extinction of these invaluable native seeds on which humanity has relied for hundreds and thousands of years.

"Good seeds, good soil, and good water. If you have all these things, you are probably a good person, too. Because never when we are in the field are we screaming. When we come to work, we ask for some blessing from the Great Spirit. There is never anger in the field. Never, never, never. It is better if you make your life more filled with joy. Why? So the crops and the seeds can be happy. If you put in one seed and you are happy, the seeds will be happy too. All these connections are working according to the way you are thinking. I know that I myself have to be very happy to put one seed into the soil, because from this seed comes my food. I want to put good seeds and good energy into the soil in the Mother Earth. The Mother Earth is happy when you put this in her." **Emigdio Ballon**

He alluded to a menacing concentration of economic forces within agribusiness taking over the seed industry and throttling diversity.

At that time, few people outside a handful of professional botanists and biologists had heard the word *biodiversity*. Although I sensed the importance of what was going on in this humble garden, I had no idea that within a few years the issue of the loss of biodiversity would be a top priority of scientists around the world as an environmental emergency. A global consortium of scientific interests led by the National Academy of Sciences and the congressional Office of Technology Assessment was about to sound the alarm on a serious threat to the world's food system posed by the loss of biological diversity of seeds. Like Sonic Bloom's effect on plants, the alarm amplified the growth of an emergent movement.

I thought I was at San Juan pueblo with Gabriel to make a film. As it turned out, I was there to found a seed company. The market for organic seeds would provide the commercial window. Biodiversity, the higher purpose of the company, would seek a partnership with gardeners, who love to tend interesting and unusual plants.

Although I didn't know it at the time, a phantom team was already hovering over the garden. The biologist Dr. Alan Kapuler, a former academic science star turned seed collector, visited Gabriel, who had been his student in Oregon. Richard Pecoraro, an organic gardener and ardent seedsman, swung through for a close look with his wife and gardening partner, Julie, hoping for a chance to resume his seed-growing passion with his former Oregon associates. Emigdio Ballon, a Quechua Indian agronomist and world expert on Incan crops from Bolivia, helped diversify the quinoa and amaranth in the garden with some of the thousands of traditional seeds he brought from the south.

This team later came together to form the agricultural core of Seeds of Change, a value-driven company intent on preserving and spreading a diversity of organic seeds through the gritty, caring hands of backyard gardeners in living gardens. By the time we formed the company in 1989, the

decline of biodiversity was entering a state of permanent crisis, a species holocaust of unprecedented dimensions. Destiny has a way of plucking you out of the garden when you are needed.

Kenny Ausubel
Santa Fe, New Mexico
May 22, 1993

· T H E ·

KINDOM
THE FABRIC
OF LIFE

Today it is not enough to say, "Thou shalt not kill." Ecological thinking assumes, above all, respect and love for all living things. This is where ecological culture comes together with religion. The meaning of life, and the unique nature of life, is in its diversity. The philosophy of survival is based on the philosophy of diversity.

Mikhail Gorbachev,
address to the Global Forum
of Spiritual and
Parliamentary Leaders,
Kyoto, Japan, April 20, 1993

A powerful bald eagle surfs a swift wind current down the jagged canyon of the Gila River in southern New Mexico. The large bird, its white head bright with the summer sun's heat, hovers in stillpoint over the wild river as it leaves the cover of wilderness mountains and decides whether to enter the world of human habitation. A worker in the fields below spies the auspicious sky creature and alerts the other farmhands to its magical presence, this original symbol of the United States that today also represents an endangered species.

The eagle holds steady on this remote cusp between wilderness and civilization, surveying the unusual fields, a quilted fabric of diversity drinking precious water from the nurturing river. Finally the bird sets its strong wings to fly against the current back into the steep, safe canyons of this last southern fling of the Rocky Mountains.

As I watch the eagle disappear over a ridge dotted with piñon pine, I notice how unusual it is to experience a farm so close to wilderness. Modern farms, with their manicured, monocultural fields, tend to reflect the completeness of human intervention, the absence of wild nature, the disappearance of diversity. Yet here I am within sight of some of the largest remaining tracts of wilderness in the United States, 3 million acres of national forest, half of which is designated wilderness with no roads at all. The presence of animals and wild game is palpable. Bear and bobcat roam the Apache-pink box canyons that only a hundred years ago harbored desperadoes like Geronimo and Butch Cassidy and the Sundance Kid. Herds of deer and packs of wild javelinas scatter across the face of ancient Indian cliff dwellings in the soft sandstone canyons.

This elegant desert bioregion is biologically rich where the Rocky Mountains fuse with the upper Sonoran desert, where the brilliant, hallucinatory light casts a thousand different masks over the face of the land in a day. The land is uniquely situated within five miles of ten distinct ecozones capable of supporting probably a quarter of the world's plant families, a natural diversity unmatched except in tropical rain forests.

Last light of day in the Gila Wilderness behind the Seeds of Change farm.

THE SEEDS OF CHANGE BIODIVERSITY FARM

The extraordinary natural diversity is complemented by the astonishing diversity of cultivated plants at the Seeds of Change farm. The gardens here are a botanical ark, a genetic shelterbelt against an eroding future. They hold an inheritance, these cherished and rare plants that continue the green web of life upon which people have depended for sustenance and spirit. Many of these plants have been rescued from extinction by determined seed collectors, and the Seeds of Change team has worked further to propagate them and distribute them widely to gardeners across the country. This is a biodiversity farm, and its efforts go beyond conservation into the commercial dissemination of the world's botanical gene pool into as many hands as possible.

Richard Pecoraro and Emigdio Ballon disperse teams across the glistening fields to attend to the day's many tasks. Biology waits for no one, and the relentless cycles of gardening have trained the crews well, patterning their lives into the seasons of the earth itself. Rich, who is production supervisor for this formidable enterprise, leaps athletically across wide rows heaving large lengths of irrigation pipe like oversized drinking straws. In striking contrast to those of conventional monocultural farms, the crop rows are staggered in polycultural abundance, splattered with bouquets of unusual varieties, many recognizable only to serious botanists.

Rich knows intimately each one of the astonishing eight hundred kinds of plants growing here, and they are anything but "garden variety." Rich names some of the dozens growing in just this small patch of the 128-acre farm. Turkish Orange eggplant is a tight, bulbous sun of a vegetable with pungent flavor. The Calabash tomato, reputed to be the ugliest tomato in the world, with deep red flesh virtually falling through its misshapen stocking skin, is unsurpassed as one of the most delicious vegetables on earth,

Zinnias and sunflowers growing for seed in Oregon, late
September.

even though its irregular form and bizarre looks have eliminated it from modern vanity vegetable production. The Calabash is one of 150 varieties of tomato under study at the farm, entire societies of European folk varieties handed down through generations of survivors. These plants illustrate a family tree of discrete lineages of foods linked in genetic kinship of plant-human memory. They are known as "heirlooms," and they constitute the real legacy of life.

"I got started gardening on such a diverse note, growing a couple of hundred kinds," Rich recalls with a grin, "that I became intimately connected to diversity. As soon as I learned the plants and their names, I loved them and I knew there was an actual relationship you could have with species. I just started to love them all. They're all important."

Peering out from under the upturned brim of his battered, stained hat, Emigdio Ballon studies a long row of multicolored Indian corns. A rustle ripples through their leaves, a whisper of the cultures that worshiped them. They are striking in their variation, each with subtle but marked differences. As with snowflakes, there are no two alike, and native peoples have always prized these differences. Emigdio, a Quechua Indian agronomist, is conscious of his Incan lineage as he conducts meticulous observations in the tradition of his ancestors, who practiced some of the most sophisticated gardening ever known on earth. The native corns are called "traditionals," and before coming to the fields today, Emigdio prayed privately for the nurturing endurance of this sacred partnership between people and nature.

"My people believe that sometimes we cannot go out into the fields, if the sun or the moon is not in the right position, or if we have anger in our hearts. But today is a good day," Emigdio winks, going back to entering dense notes on his thick pad. Emigdio will send the notes he is making off to Alan Kapuler in Oregon. It is fifteen years of Alan's prior research that has made possible the invisible biological grid upon which the Seeds of Change gardens grow. As a geneticist and biologist, Alan parked his science training in the backyard, where he could observe evolution firsthand and participate in the very creation process of life itself.

"Being in an immense garden so full of bees, butterflies, ladybugs, and beneficial insects, which you don't see at all at a commercial farm, made me realize that the Seeds of Change farm was really more like wilderness than an agricultural landscape. To be able to see the same diversity in a garden that I've seen in the wilderness made me realize that there need be no barrier between wild nature and ourselves. We ourselves are just the growth, the extension, the consciousness of this beautiful earth. We're at the beginning of a phase in which we don't have to kill the plants, because we're their caretakers. I believe they may actually be using us to propagate themselves." **Jim Bones**

The plants here are all *open-pollinated*, which means that they propagate themselves in the imaginative multiplicity of sexy practices nature designed. Birds do it, bees do it, and so do butterflies, wind, animals, other plants, and people. When you are growing plants for seed, the idea is to get a true strain that holds steady to the parent. Most seed growers sternly avoid the physical presence of other related plants anywhere within miles, and they grow one kind of seed or a very few unrelated types. Usually they grow modern *hybrid varieties*, special crosses that do not reproduce true to form anyway and are in no jeopardy of intermixing.

Growing diversity in close physical proximity is the Olympics of seed gardening. Alan's genetic maps are a complex, three-dimensional, biological board game, and he loves the challenge. Some plants are separated by physical distance, or by other plants whose height prevents the migration of pollen. Yet others are timed like a sequence of fertile firecrackers set to go off at different times. Others are stationed far from plants placed deliberately distant to distract certain bugs that might favor their pollen. It is an ultimate test of botanical safe sex.

Of course, as the biologist Edward O. Wilson likes to say, "Evolution is messy," and inevitably plants connect, evolve, and adapt naturally in the dance of life. The best gardeners are the ones looking for the spontaneous mutations, the odd, unpredictable shifts that make the world new each moment and forever change the flow of history. In the end, we're all hybrids, re-creating ourselves constantly from generation to generation. Diversity is quirky and idiosyncratic, and there is a lot of it. Nature is prolific, the earth is fertile, and life is change. These are the seeds of change, and their adaptability is their strength and virtue.

The diversity in the Gila gardens represents the best efforts of this passionate band of seed savers. At the same dire time that the planet's diversity entered a genetic free fall in the latter twentieth century, it was the world's good fortune that these and other collectors spread out around the world to grab what they could and plant backyard biodiversity safely in home gardens.

As Alan Kapuler discovered early on, it turned out that a commercial seed company is actually one of the very best vehicles today to preserve diversity. There are millions of gardeners, and they cherish interesting and unusual plants. "What's that you have growing over the fence there?" Gardeners are always looking for something new to plant. Gardeners prize diversity.

When Alan started Peace Seeds in Oregon in 1975, he created the template for a company that would eventually become Seeds of Change. He founded the modest enterprise on the broadest possible conception of gathering a biological diversity of seed stocks, not just common food and ornamental plants. He was groping for the essence of diversity on a planet brimming with it. He further insisted on organically raised seeds wherever possible, or seeds wildcrafted—gathered in the wild—in healthy ecosystems. He trained himself in the rigorous discipline of seed growing, learning to maintain purity of strains. He began to investigate the true nature of the world flora and diversity. This demanding process ultimately honed Alan's insight and skills to a fine edge. When Seeds of Change came together fourteen years later, Alan brought to the company the soul of the science and the vision of the biology of diversity.

Alan also brought a world-class private seed collection, and Seeds of Change merged it with those of Gabriel and later Emigdio. The enterprise began by growing out the remarkable collections in commercial quantities to distribute to gardeners. The seeds (certified by Oregon Tilth, a recognized third-party organic certifier) are raised organically, free from toxic residues of petrochemical fertilizers, pesticides, or fungicides. Currently they are the only certified organic seeds available nationally. Purchased by tens of thousands of customers, from a mail-order catalog and from unique seed racks placed in well over a thousand stores in the United States and

Red Velvet okra growing in a
spiral.

Canada, these seeds of diversity, which till recently faced extinction, are growing again in gardens across the land.

The creation of this biologically driven company was able to occur in a rapid four years because it stood on the shoulders of the previous work of these agricultural "bioneers," biological pioneers who lit their own urgent path to the preservation of the diversity of life. They did not wait for government grants or official sanction. Nor did Seeds of Change, which took direct action on behalf of the environment by linking in a partnership with the large volunteer army of gardeners. As the company's fortunes have risen, based on restoring biodiversity, the loss of diversity in the world has reached critical proportions.

When the company began in 1989, few people had ever heard of biodiversity. Yet today more people are aware of its meaning, as the Environmental Protection Agency and many respected biologists have placed the loss of biodiversity at the very top of the red zone of environmental crises. What makes biodiversity so very important? Why have scientists like Alan Kapuler dedicated their lives to its conservation?

Biodiversity: The Stuff of Life

Alan Kapuler was waxing poetic with his wife, Linda, one evening, on the "Five Kingdoms of Life," the biologist Lynn Margulis's profound insight into evolution and the structure of cells. Linda, soft-spoken but forceful, interrupted to ask why he called them kingdoms. After all, she pointed out, there are no kings in nature. Alan, who is seldom at a loss for words, was speechless. Linda filled the gap by suggesting dropping the *g* and altering it to *kin-dom*. We're all kin, aren't we? Isn't that what biology is really about?

Indeed, in nature there are no kings, only kin. When one plant species becomes extinct, so too will the twenty to forty animal and insect species that rely on it. Life is a mysterious web of intricate interdependent relationships, and diversity is its heart. "Biological diversity is the key to the maintenance of the world as we know it," says Edward O. Wilson. Wilson, a biologist at Harvard University, is probably the foremost contemporary expert on biodiversity. "This is the assembly of life that took a billion years to evolve. It has eaten the storms—folded them into its genes—and created the world that created us. It holds the world steady."[1]

We are living today in an era of unprecedented extinctions. They are running at a thousand times the natural rate, threatening the very balance of evolution itself. About twenty-seven thousand species a year are already being lost, or seventy-four a day, three an hour. Within the next fifty years, experts predict that we will lose at least a quarter of the 250,000 known plants. Once organisms and their genes are lost, they cannot be recovered.

From a biologist's view, genes are as essential to life as food, air, and water. They are the fragile spiral thread linking our tenuous lineage between past and future. Yet it is this very fabric of the biological kindom that is disintegrating. As a result, the world's food system is treacherously perched on a rapidly eroding genetic base. The loss of genetic diversity in the food supply directly imperils the safety of crops, because their ability to adapt to resist blights, pests, and disease depends upon variation. And plants are the foundation of the world's pharmacy. The National Cancer Institute and many pharmaceutical companies have dispatched throngs of researchers to the rain forests in search of fast disappearing plants. These living entities cannot be reconstructed once lost, and we do not even know what we are losing.

"Great biological diversity takes long stretches of geologic time and the accumulation of large reservoirs of unique genes," notes Wilson. "The richest systems build slowly, over millions of years. A panda or a sequoia represents a magnitude of evolution that comes along only rarely. It takes a stroke of luck and a long period of probing, experimentation, and failure. Such a creation is part of deep history, and the planet does not have the means nor we the time to see it repeated."[2]

Life is a living, pulsing, vibrating, plasmic mystery, a spontaneous improvisation linked through time by memory encoded in genes. The seeds that carry these genes are the regenerative life form,[3] as Joseph Campbell said, the bridge that passes life through the generations. They are the fixed cellular recollection of the identity of lives in a moment and place in time. They encode the information of life's experiences.

Licorice mint and Hopi red dye amaranth growing in one of the fields at the Seeds of Change farm.

The secret of evolution is actually coevolution. Nothing has evolved in isolation. Everything has coevolved in relationship. People have coevolved in a special kinship with other organisms, especially plants, for many thousands of years, a relationship that is now declining. Although Charles Darwin believed that competition is the driving force of evolution, biology shows that cooperation is what sustains life. Mutualism is at the core of diversity. Partnership is the law of nature, and it is distinctly unwise for a symbiont to destroy its host.

Although five epochs of major extinctions have swept over the earth, the present one is the first that comes by the human hand. We are causing extinctions through widespread habitat destruction, human overpopulation, climate change, disease, and the introduction of exotic animals such as cows, goats, and rats.

The fabric of life must be seen as a whole cloth. Removing single threads unravels the tapestry. Yet we are clumsily undoing this fantastically elaborate web, an estimated 90 percent of which remains unexplored and wholly mysterious to us. In the subtle, contingent world of coevolution, the first rule of the tinkerer is to save all the pieces.

Adaptability to change is the key to survival, and change is the only constant in nature. Now that human tampering with nature has radically altered the balance of the world, change is occurring at a heightened pace. If, for example, human-induced expansion of deserts doubles by the year 2000, as it has done for the last ten years, then those plants that tolerate heat and drought will assume special new importance.

Variety is not only the spice of life, but the very staff of life. Diversity is nature's fail-safe mechanism against extinction. It provides the vast genetic pool of accumulated experiences and characteristics from which change can originate. Any banker recommends a diversified portfolio in case one stock fails. The most unpredictable future in history may be upon us, and by diminishing diversity, we are shrinking the genetic pool that is the very source of our biological options for survival.

The gene pool is the real treasure. This living treasure of seeds comprises billions of years of evolution and at least twelve thousand years of human selection for agriculture. Its loss represents the greatest threat to life on earth as we know it.

RESTORING THE FABRIC: PLANT PEOPLE

Emigdio Ballon picking gaillardia, blanket flower, with lemon balm in the background at the Seeds of Change farm in late August.

"The seeds are the core," observes Alan Kapuler emphatically, as he fills a packet with a rare variety of ginseng he got from an associate in Siberia. "The seed crops have provided us with a way to store the essence. Although politicians and kings frequently get more notoriety than anybody else, it's the common peasant who saves and keeps the seeds for the next generation."

The diversity of seeds planted today at the Seeds of Change farm is the legacy of countless generations of seed savers and collectors, farmers, gardeners, and world cultures. Like them, the Seeds of Change collectors found the fabric of their lives became inseparably interwoven with the plants. These are "plant people," as the botanist Kathleen Harrison calls them, "a sort of marriage between people and plants. They're like the birds carrying the seeds, or the animals with their seeds caught on their fur. It's that part of evolution that is moving the species around."[4]

The paths of these botanical explorers also grew together with one another, creating the social force that today is Seeds of Change. Their journey has been a very personal one.

"Many of the plants from Oregon we still have here now," Rich is reminded, stroking a small, fragrant rosemary plant he has known a long time. "A lot of the herbs are old friends. They were all there twelve years ago in Oregon. There are plants here in this ground that are stock from those first gardens that actually moved with Gabriel, with us, to certain places where we propagated them. That was our lineage, and we kept on carrying it.

"In the old times, people always put virtues to herbs," Rich reflects softly. "Rosemary gives you remembrance by the smell. In my Italian ancestors' culture, rosemaries are a special plant for remembering where you stand. Remember to smell the roses and the goodness of life. Rosemary is where I started with this work. Rosemaries were in the first gardens."

Of the five principal gardeners and collectors in Seeds of Change, four met under a gardening conjunction in Oregon around 1980, uniting the surprising lives of a First World molecular biologist, a California surfer, an Italian-American athlete, and an Iowa farm girl. The elder of the group, Dr. Alan Kapuler, arrived in the Pacific Northwest first, later to be synchronously met by Gabriel Howearth, Richard Pecoraro, and Julie Spelletich. They subsequently linked in New Mexico with Quechua seedsman Emigdio Ballon. None of them imagined that their work would merge years later in the stellium of Seeds of Change.

"It was at a community meeting of about thirty people where we all got together," Rich recalls with amusement. "We passed around one of the year's potatoes as our staff. *Papa tuberosa*, we called it. We were talking about a community garden. Alan hypnotized the room with his blazing intensity about the importance of seeds and species. Gabriel inspired us with the importance of growing our own food. I was ready to sign on right then for the team."

Rich Pecoraro, an Italian Green Thumb

Rich had only recently arrived in fertile southern Oregon, having left New York's Long Island a year before. "I discovered I was a plant person when I was nineteen," he remembers, "in Fort Collins, Colorado, which happens to be the main seed bank of the United States. I was coming out of being a baseball hero, and I realized that school wasn't for me either. I was radical and outspoken enough that I knew I might get in trouble, so I decided I'd hit the road." In Colorado, fresh from reading *The Magic of Findhorn*, he became inspired by the idea of spiritual gardening described in this classic book on the magical Scottish gardens. He took a class on biodynamics, a metaphysical system of organic horticulture devised by the Austrian philosopher Rudolf Steiner. Rich ambitiously took on two gardens.

"A revelatory beginning occurred as I was trying to make topsoil. I was looking at the soil, and I was wondering, 'How can I make this soil fine

Life emerged about four billion years ago, primarily in microbial form. Only 1.8 billion years ago did higher, multicellular organisms appear, and then macroscopic organisms about 500 million years ago. The flowering plants spread about 100 million years ago. Human beings entered the scene quite recently, anywhere from 1 million to 100,000 years ago. (E. O. Wilson, *The Diversity of Life*.)

enough to plant seeds directly in this rough ground?' So I thought, 'I'll sift the soil.' But I didn't really have a sifter, so I started making a pile. I was just playing with the dirt. I started seeing that if I keep piling the dirt, the fine stuff is going to stay at the top, and the other stuff is going to stay at the bottom. I was reveling in the fact that I'd done it just by piling dirt like a kid in a sand pile. I started calling it the parmesan that you put on the pizza, an Italian kind of green thumb."

Rich joined a community of people with a Findhorn background who chanted and sang to their plants. He switched to a vegetarian diet and exchanged baseball for yoga. He became obsessed with gardening, growing corn in hundred-foot biodynamic, double-dug raised beds. "The soil we made was so rich that the corn grew to twelve feet," he recalls with a gleam.

Wanting more commitment to gardening than the Colorado community offered, Rich headed for the gardeners' promised land of Oregon, where the potato sealed his fate. "We started by building a forty-foot community greenhouse with big raised beds. That evening we talked about commitments to the garden. There was nothing else in the world I wanted to devote my life to. That was when my interest in seeds came in, because we were working with so much diversity. It was hundreds of species. Both Alan and Gabriel were already collecting seeds, especially Alan. I would ask, 'Hey, did you hear about this seed?' Not only had Alan heard about it, he had the seed."

Alan Kapuler, a Vision of Kinship

Indeed, for the intense molecular biologist with a thick Brooklyn accent and a beret, collecting seeds was a recent endeavor, but biodiversity was an old and familiar friend. As a child growing up near the Brooklyn Botanic Garden and Ebbetts Field, where the fabled Brooklyn Dodgers played, Alan was twinly obsessed with orchids and baseball. Like a veteran sportscaster at the World Series, he could reel off lifetime home run records or the Latin names of obscure flowers with prodigious facility.

"My father and I have shared an interest in growing orchids from the time I was about eight years old when he took me to a night course at the

Brooklyn Botanic Garden," Alan relates with a characteristic sense of life's continuum. "He told me that his mother always liked to have plants in the house. A Russian immigrant who didn't speak the language well, she loved to grow flowers. My father ended up becoming a doctor because, when someone was sick and a doctor was going to come over to the house, his mother would be on her knees washing the floor, polishing the windows, cleaning every piece of furniture. Everything had to be immaculately clean and in the best condition for the doctor, crowned with flowers. If it is so important to his mother, he'll become a doctor. Her love of flowers got him interested in orchids. It was a hobby that he and I still do share. He's eighty-three now. I share it with my daughters too, so it's a multigenerational hobby. The real devotion and interest are passed on in lineages of people."

In the orchid class, Alan studied the five-thousand-plant collection of many very rare species. "It would sometimes be freezing and the rain would turn to 'black snow.' Sleet would be running against your face and the wind would be blowing. Then you would get into this greenhouse where it would be quiet and fragrant and full of colors. It was just heavenly. For the next couple of years on every Saturday I would go to the Brooklyn Botanic Garden. I would go into the orchid room and spend the whole afternoon just walking around looking at the labels and the flowers. Most of them were tiny. On a dinner table you could have two hundred pots of these little plants, and you'd have a major piece of the gene pool. It was like a treasure right there. You could take care of it and learn about it.

"I learned hundreds and hundreds of plants. I learned the names; I learned the species; I learned the flowers. When you're young, your mind is very sensitive, and it becomes idyllic. If you see it once and identify it, you never forget it."

Alan emerged quickly as a science prodigy. Because his father was a Freudian psychiatrist with an office at home, he was compelled to retreat to the basement to amuse himself quietly. There he developed a "molecule collection," which he bought cheaply from chemical supply houses. "I used to make precipitates that were brilliantly colored. I liked to make mercury salt and chromium salt. I had whole shelves filled with molecules, acids and bases. Brooklyn wasn't exactly an environment of sweetness and light, and so if I had little pieces of metallic sodium, I could take them and pop them in a puddle next to somebody. I'd walk down the street and it would be raining. I'd pop a piece of sodium, and all of a sudden there would be a little flash of smoke, and purple and yellow light would come out, and it would almost make a little explosion. People didn't know what was going on."

Alan's budding scientific path was destined to be illuminated by frequent flashes of brilliant light. He excelled at Erasmus Hall High School, where a biology teacher got him interested in looking at creatures through a microscope as an alternative to going to class. As a project, he tested the effect on his beloved orchids of a mutagenic chemical that changed the number of chromosomes in a cell. He wrote a paper on the successful experiment, and it led to his winning the Westinghouse National Science Talent Search award at the age of fifteen, one of only forty kids nationally.

"The orchids essentially got me into Yale," Alan chuckles. "They've been a steady ally." At the age of sixteen, Alan Kapuler entered Yale as its youngest student in a class of a thousand. A voracious learner, he audited multiple courses beyond the requirements. By the time he graduated, he was first in the class with the honors of summa cum laude and Phi Beta Kappa.

"I got interested in genetics and molecular biology," he observes. "Watson and Crick figured out the DNA double helix structure in 1953, and I went to college in 1958 when it was coming through." Another genetic discovery he made got him admitted into prestigious Rockefeller University at the propitious moment in the history of scientific discovery of molecular biology. "All we could do was eat, breathe, think, talk, and work science all the time, twenty-four hours a day, seven days a week, year after year.

"We were discovering how life works," Alan whispers with awe, "all the secrets that had been hidden for billions of years that are shared by all the organisms, the very reality of how the molecules that make up the cells and the bodies actually work. That was a time when the structure of the genetic code was being discovered. In the history of humanity, it was the greatest self-revelation about our common unity with all organisms. They were the mystery of the ages, and we were busy uncovering those secrets."

Alan apprenticed in bacterial and viral genetics, and later studied plant physiology and cancer-producing viruses. He obtained his Ph.D. in life sciences and published his work in the Journal of the National Academy of Sciences. But even the hermetic world of academic science was throbbing with the heat of the 1960s, and Alan's life was far from insulated.

"As I got to be more aware, I got in lots of political problems. It was the mid-sixties, and I was in trouble with authority. I was not exceptionally polite." He became involved in protests over the antiballistic missiles produced by the science establishment and wore a protest button at his Rockefeller graduation.

Following graduate school, Alan became a postdoctoral fellow at the Institute of Muscle Disease, working on viral enzymes that synthesize genetic material. He also worked with the revered A. M. Michelson, one of the great biochemists and an authority on nucleic acids, who hosted Alan for several months at his Paris lab at the Rothschild Institute. When Alan returned, he took a post as an assistant professor at the University of Connecticut, where he spent years as a researcher pioneering studies on the potential viral causes of cancer. Considered an expert on viruses, he had apprenticed several years before at the University of Wisconsin lab of Howard Temin, who later won the Nobel Prize for discovering the reverse transcriptase enzymes in viruses that cause cancer.

But to everyone's surprise, Alan Kapuler decided to leave his fast-track career at the University of Connecticut exactly three years from the date of his original contract. "Coming home one night, I heard this little voice whisper in my ear, 'You better leave—you do not want to do this anymore.' One of my pet projects was to develop a system to mutate genes, and I had some chemicals that were mutagenic. The year before I'd been to a symposium in Atlantic City, and there was a protest going on against all the people who do biological research in the biological warfare division of the U.S. government. These folks were making very, very lethal, dangerous viruses.

"We have been watching systematic genocide of the natural world. Biologically it is insane. If you were to find any species destroying its natural world at the rate and with the systematic intent that human beings have done it on this world, you would say that species is on its way to extinction, because it's insane." **Alan Kapuler**

There was a protest led by a respected professor from Rockefeller, who said, 'This is really bad business. We should not as biologists be making destructive and poisonous things. We should be working to make life better.' I was very moved by that."

Alan decided the work he was doing was too dangerous. "I realized that I didn't belong in a university anymore. It was 1970, and revolution was rising in the streets. I had to find my beloved wife and my kids, and a life that had a heart."

Alan's colleagues were shocked at his resolve to reject the privilege and security of First World science. "I left with a thousand dollars and a green van," Alan recalls existentially. "That's when I headed out for the West Coast. I thought I knew where I was going."

Alan pointed the van toward British Columbia to see his friends Julia Levy, a scientist at the University of British Columbia, and her boyfriend, the famed geneticist David Suzuki. In Canada, Suzuki and Alan filmed a sequence of programs together that preceded Suzuki's very popular TV series, "The Nature of Things." Suzuki wrote of the experience in his autobiography, "Al Kapuler, a brilliant scientist from Rockefeller, was visiting. I had first encountered Al when I went to a meeting of the Genetics Society of America in Boulder, Colorado. There I heard the lecture he gave on his undergraduate honors thesis at Yale. It was a brilliant piece of work and earned him the highest grade Yale had ever awarded. It was eventually published as a paper in the *Journal of Molecular Biology*, one of the leading journals in the world at that time. I was instantly attracted to him for his charisma and brilliance, and we became very good friends. My relationship with Al was based on a genuine sharing of new ideas. We would exchange recent information and bounce ideas off each other, wildly speculating, theorizing, projecting."[5]

After taping five half-hour segments with Suzuki about viruses and cancer, Alan agreed to return shortly to share land and pursue science based on humanitarian values. But life held other plans.

"I was on my way in the 'green toad'—one of the first Chevy vans produced that could hold a lot of stuff, a couple of friends, and a dog—to Canada to go to Sonora Island. I had been to Baja, California, where we found some big tortoise shells on the beach. I had bones of whales and a car full of incredible stuff. On the way up, I stopped by a commune on Thompson Creek Road in southern Oregon near Applegate. All across the country I'd met different people, and I always had places to stay because it was a time when there were communes and groups of people. It was a friendly time.

"At the Canadian border, a Canadian official asked, 'Do you smoke pot?' I said, 'Yeah,' because I was also at that time into yoga. One of the principles of Raja Yoga is truthfulness, so it never occurred to me not to tell the man the truth. He said, 'Oh, we can't let you into Canada. In fact, because of what you just said, you are barred from coming into Canada for five years.'

"So when I came back from the Canadian customs through American customs, they confiscated all my whale bones and all the shells of all the turtles, because, they said, 'These are endangered species. You can't have them.' They stripped my car, strip-searched me, and I ended up back in America.

"I was very perplexed about where to go. I said, 'I'd better go back to that commune where they treated me so well in southern Oregon.' They were people living on a piece of land, beginning to garden and raise kids. It was a very nice time to be alive.

"I ended up with very little money and a bunch of hungry people. I realized the first thing I'd better learn how to do is grow my own food. I'd never grown a garden. I didn't know what an onion seed looked like. All I knew was that if I planted some little onions, they'd get bigger. I started planting little onions." In that backyard, he started gardening seriously.

"One of the first things I found out about gardening is that you've got to buy your seeds. I remember being in the kitchen, cleaning squash, taking the seeds and throwing them in the compost bucket and wondering, 'Why am I doing this when in two months I'm going to go back to the store and I'm going to buy squash seeds?' I'd been working part-time to pay rent in the gladiolus fields in the mud, in the muck, in the cold weather for $1.91 an hour. There was no money to buy seeds. That's when I started saving my own seeds.

"I spent a couple of years gardening seriously and collecting seeds and beginning to learn the cycles. Then we moved out of town, up into the mountains—Linda and I did—with another couple of friends." Alan and Linda Sylvester, a gentle woman of Mormon lineage from Utah, would later marry. The two would become a close team as they managed Peace Seeds and reared three daughters.

Between his academic years and his first Oregon garden, Alan had had very little to do with plants, except orchids. He made three orchid-collecting trips to Latin America, the first during his junior year at Yale with Dr. Leslie Garay, head of Harvard's Oakes Ames Orchid Herbarium. Under a National Science Foundation grant, they journeyed for two months into the Andean wilds of Colombia researching Dr. Garay's orchid flora, identifying a prodigious diversity of the elegant flowers.

For the Brooklyn boy, the Andes were a wonderland of cloud forests. Alan was awestruck by the natural state of the Colombian orchid flora, more numerous than all the flowering plants of Oregon.

Upon his return, Alan published a scholarly article in the *American Orchid Society Bulletin* in September 1962.[6] Four years later, in 1966, the cover of the *Bulletin* displayed the new species he had discovered on his second trip. However, he wrote, "The paucity of specimens we encountered was the most striking feature of the trip."[7] Instead of orchids, he found the hoofprints of cattle. For the biologist, it was a crushing object lesson in the loss of biodiversity, an early warning signal of planetary distress that would profoundly inform his subsequent work.

The Oregon woods bore the same hoofprints, and worse. In addition to the damage caused by cattle grazing, logging had left acres of broken stumps and half-burned, half-bulldozed mountainsides. Alan and the crew decided to start cleaning up their newly adopted neighborhood. "We'd pitch a little pup tent, or actually sleep in a hollow log. We spent our days just stacking all the burned and broken pieces, and finding places with enough soil, outlining them with tree trunks and planting tomatoes, onions and carrots in the woods."

Alan quickly became curious about the structure of the natural diversity, however, and he got the books necessary to start identifying the local wild and weedy plants. "It was twenty years later, looking at the Willamette valley, this beautiful green valley filled with monocultures, that I realized that hundreds and hundreds of species are already extinct, and we have no record of them. We don't even consider them to ever have been part of the biosphere.

"I was looking for a way to have some effect. Gardening became a revelation. With a shovel and a bucket you can start to grow this stuff. You can do it yourself. You can take it in your own hands. You can go at the places that are being destroyed, or before that, and grab plants and put them in your backyard. You can do something about this."

The Kapulers moved back to the valley to pursue gardening and family life. "We'd till an acre or two—hire somebody with a tractor and till an acre or two—and then we would take shovels and go out one or two or three of us, or sometimes just myself, and bed out the whole thing. What an incredible feeling it is to lay a pattern of sculpture of life in the ground on the earth, and then plant it with flowers and fruits and vegetables. It allows you to feel part of the pulse of life."

It was in the early 1970s that he picked up the popular nickname that old friends continue to favor today. He used to walk around in the woods and eat wild mushrooms. There are several kinds of poisonous mushrooms in Oregon, as well as edible ones, and it is a precise avocation that dictates exceedingly narrow tolerances for a forager wishing to achieve longevity. His taxonomic and identification skills led to the handle "Mushroom."

So when *Papa tuberosa* passed from hand to hand at the community garden meeting, Alan Kapuler, Ph.D., was better known as Mushroom. When he spoke about the loss of species and the necessity of collecting seeds and

growing them out in backyard gardens, he was a man on fire. People in the room wondered if the heat of his passion would cook the potato. He made a huge impression not only on Rich Pecoraro but also on the other person in the room who had a seed collection, the young, idealistic Gabriel Howearth. "Who is this wild genius?" Gabriel was wondering.

Gabriel Howearth, Earth Artist

Soggy Oregon was a distant ecology from the California desert that originally connected Gabriel to plants. Gabriel felt compelled to leave the desert and the mass-culture implosion of California in 1978 in search of rich soil and a low-key lifestyle. He found land in southern Oregon and started gardening, growing his own food. Having suffered from asthma since childhood, he found his sensitivity to foods restricted his diet to an extreme degree. He had been a "fruitatarian" in California, but the thick, wet Oregon climate did not favor such a diet. He began growing a lot more greens, selling the surplus at a local coop and farmers' market.

The Chadwickian gardening he had picked up in dry California bore riotous results in the fertile black earth of Oregon. He explored his strong affinity for herbs, both growing and wildcrafting them. He began to make and sell a range of herbal tinctures, salves, and perfumes, as well as herbal dyes for weavers. He quickly became known as a practicing herbalist with the rare ability to grow elegant herb gardens.

But more than anything else, Gabriel's gardens became famous as earth art. He created a spiral garden design based on a Hopi Indian sunwheel and then a mandala garden in the form of an eight-pointed star. "I liked the geometric shapes," he recalls. "It's where I began to feel the nature spirits interact with the plants more deeply. It just felt more harmonious."

"Gabriel was the garden magician," Rich agrees. Gabriel culminated his garden artistry with the creation of an iridology garden, based on the pattern of the eye and its medical relationship to the organs of the body. He planted it in a pattern with the herbs corresponding to the parts of the body they are said to heal. Friends remember that he barely emerged from the magical garden for weeks at a time, causing a rumor that he was now operating by photosynthesis.

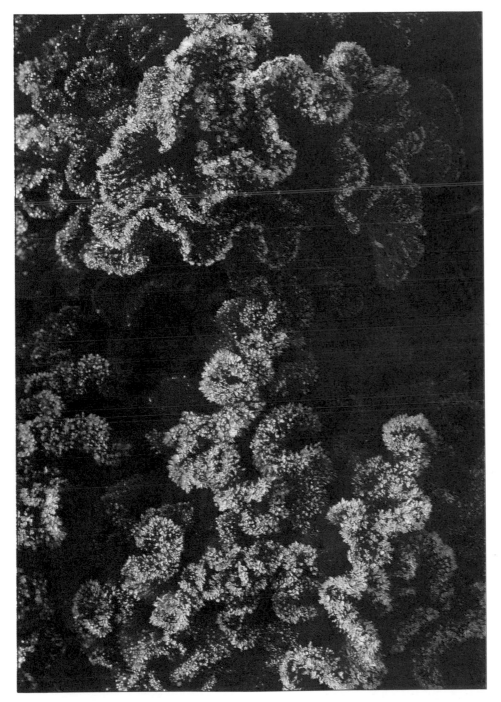

Frost on the flower of Cockscomb amaranth in late September at the Seeds of Change farm.

"Gabriel was responsible for the 'salad-arian' concept of our gardens at the time," Rich recounts. "Because Oregon is so wet, the salad greens were the thriving force. So he got into salad gardening. He and Mushroom linked up and got wildly into salad varieties. Mushroom was already collecting a lot of wild weeds at the time. Through that, we learned the importance of seed and the diversity of food, how much you can make if you put twenty ingredients in a bowl."

For Gabriel it was the conscious beginning of his work with seeds. "I began saving the key plants, the healthiest vegetables, the most vibrant herbs, and letting them go to seed. From the beginning in Baja, I had watched people tag their plants for seed, and I had done it, but on a tiny scale." As a teenager growing up near Encinitas in Southern California, Gabriel had surfed his way up and down the coast. When he surfed in nearby Baja, Mexico, he sometimes stayed and worked with the Mexican villagers in their gardens in exchange for fresh food. Isolated from the cities, theirs were large gardens for self-reliance, and they saved all their own seeds, a practice that caught his attention.

Over the years, Gabriel traveled farther south into Michoacán, Yucatan, and Guatemala among the Mayans. "I saw the seeds disappear with the cultures. I felt that if I could help preserve the seeds, then maybe the cultures could be reconstructed. It seemed very important to me to focus on the native food plants."

Gabriel introduced the first quinoa and amaranth in the Oregon community garden, where they quickly became favorites. The collector proved to be characteristically nomadic, however, and the huge gardens largely became Rich's domain. "It was only a year Gabriel was there," Rich recalls, "and half the time he wasn't there, so we took it on. By the next year he was gone up the road. We inherited this three-acre garden. Seven people maintained it and did everything by hand. There were easily 250 to 300 varieties in it."

Julie Spelletich Gets Her Fork

Rich was fiercely protective of the gardens, but during that time, another member of the team showed up, much to his pleasure. "I had heard of Gabriel and his outrageous gardens when I was in Southern California," recalls Julie Spelletich. "A good friend of mine worked with him and said to me, 'If you want to learn about gardening, go to southern Oregon. Go find Gabriel and garden with him, and you'll learn everything you need to know.' I packed up my two boxes of belongings and my bicycle, got a ride with a friend who was heading up there, and got dropped off at the community garden. That was it for me."

Julie had grown up with gardens in Iowa. Her grandmother's backyard dropped off into a ravine, which she planted with wildflowers and herbs. She used to take Julie by the hand as a child and point out her favorite plants, getting her to smell their fragrance. Her parents also had large gardens. "We had a huge patch of lilies of the valley, and I used to wait for them to burst out of the ground because they were my favorite to pick. I would just pick from that patch for hours until I had a huge bouquet. I was so proud to bring that in to my mother."

Julie had tired of school in Colorado and dropped out to visit her sister in California, where she became interested in the organic gardening movement. She fell in with a group of avid biodynamic gardeners who eventually pointed her to Gabriel and the Oregon garden.

"I just started gardening as soon as I arrived. I didn't have my pitchfork yet. I think that was when I called my parents and told them, 'This is the love of my life. I finally found what I want to do for the rest of my life. I need to borrow a hundred dollars so I can buy my Smith & Hawken fork and spade and hoe. Please send the money.' So they sent me the money.

"It was a really exciting time," Julie reminisces in the kitchen of the little white house at the Gila farm. Her two young girls swirl in and out of her arms as she speaks. "We didn't have any other responsibilities, and we had all the time in the world to garden and be fanatical and crazy. We worked all night long. I went to work with Gabriel thinking I was going to learn from this great master, but actually it was Rich and I who ended up working together."

"Because I was there every day," Rich chimes in as Julie smiles with remembrance, "you had to run into me there like the dog at the gate. We've softened way up since then. We used to chase rototillers out of the garden. We're going to hand-dig this! We'd line up with seven forks, and we'd dig really major areas of double-dug beds, at least two acres. We'd sleep under the hops trellis with the sound of the sprinkler going. They were joyous days.

"I would get myself into the dirt, and it was a homecoming for me. Finally I'm grounded on the earth. I have something for which I can use all that drive I had for athletics, and put it into something that feeds me and feeds others and actually could be a revolution—all in one. And I'm not going to get in trouble."

Within the year, Rich and Julie became a couple, and the massive harvest from the abundant gardens started pouring in along with the legendary Oregon rains. "In that first year of 1980," chuckles Rich, "we had no barns, we had no place to put anything, and we had three acres of crop to bring inside, and it was rainy Oregon. We filled the house that we were living in.

"You walked into this house, and you ducked. There were just a billion strains of chiles, strains of corns, hanging amaranth, piles of stuff. It was thirty days' straight rain in November. What do we do? There were six of us in a two-bedroom house. The whole harvest was in, and we're all living in it. How did we do it? We wheelbarrowed the pumpkins into the living room, chopped them up and finished scooping. It was torrential rains, and it would rain for days and days and days. We literally backed the truck up to the front door and processed out of it. In the kitchen there was a cider press going, and every inch of the place was strung with the harvest. It was the Ark."

Under Gabriel's entrepreneurial direction, they made products under the name Earthstar Botanicals, with modest backing from a local doctor. They grew half the gardens for produce and half for seed. Gabriel's driving interest was more in the foods. Alan was not interested in anything but seeds. For Rich, both aspects were important, but a turning point soon confronted him.

Alan Kapuler in his garden, Corvallis, Oregon.

Gone to Seed

"I found out I was really into seed on the harvest day," Rich remembers vividly. "On the harvest day in the first season, I took Gabriel's old bags of seeds. He just had piled them up, and I worked that afternoon trying to clean the seeds, not knowing what I was doing, and getting some clean seeds and putting together an inventory. I just was learning. Cleaning seeds, I loved it.

"How do you do it? We didn't have a book. We just did it. We did it and did it until we finally got it. It was so exciting, and I realized my birthday is on the seed end of the season. So to me it was the gift of the creator to be able to find out why I came into the world. I was born in the harvest moon."

Growing seed also challenged the gardening skills of this power gardener who loves to excel. "For me, growing seed was like being a finish carpenter compared with growing produce, which was like being a framer. To knock out produce was like building houses in a row. Growing seeds was getting into the fine work of agriculture. It went directly to the source, and it justified diversity."

But there was also a personal element involved. Alan Kapuler's obsession with seeds was charismatic. Seed saving was becoming seed salvation, a personal mission that was also deeply moving to Rich. "What continued to impassion me was that I loved Mushroom so much that I wanted to do it for him too. I wanted to plant and make sure we could get thirty, forty, or fifty more batches because I knew he had no money, and yet he would send me $250 checks in those years. How can we go seed to seed? It's the longest thing to do in agriculture! It definitely took a lot of camaraderie to pull this through.

"I was also quite nomadic at the time, and it was the one thing you could do. We moved around a lot, and there was nothing like carrying your savings. When you're a produce grower, you can't carry your carrots and beets around. When you're an herb grower, you can carry your little herb stash around, but that is quite cumbersome. But to be represented by carrying genetics and having it with you, it's the ancestry. It gets the most dispersion from the most consolidated. You get your work down into a box of seeds."

Rich began to collaborate seriously with Alan, whose Peace Seeds catalog started with a hundred varieties and soon escalated to several hundred. Rich's seed gardens never had fewer than fifty kinds and often more than three hundred. Virtually all of Alan's impressive offering was organically raised and hand grown. His diligence and meticulousness became legendary.

"When I completed the cycle and saved the seeds for some five thousand kinds," Alan relates matter-of-factly, "I was at step one of an education in agriculture, something I'd never known anything about. It took that much just to get into common agriculture, where I knew how to grow oats and save seeds, where I knew how to grow spinach and how the flowers pollinated, and knew squashes and which species crossed, and knew mints and which should be companions with which others—all the simple stuff that you need to know if you're going to save seeds. Every crop takes a while to do, and you have to do it a few times and make a few mistakes.

"Nothing is more compelling and more demanding than being a seedsman, using your own seeds. You find out what you've got every year all the time. You can't lie to yourself. Seeds don't lie. The genes don't lie. The grow-outs tell you how fertile, how vigorous, how homogeneous, what kinds of things are in them—what flavors, what colors. I was fortunate that I was trained in separating molecules; it was no problem to begin to learn how to separate seeds, which are just big molecules."

One thing was certain, this group was going to seed. While living on the small farm of an organic grower, Al Venet, Alan Kapuler had become completely obsessed with seeds. His molecular biologist's mind precisely held increasingly long lists of species and their Latin names. Alan's knowledge of plants was self-taught, and it was becoming formidable.

Rich Pecoraro apprenticed with Alan, learning the technical names and perfecting the craft of cleaning seeds. "I wanted to work with people who cared about seeds and life," Alan recalls. "So I got to know Rich, and when he'd say, 'I'll grow you fifty kinds of seeds,' he produced forty-five kinds of seeds. It's not easy to grow seeds. It takes extra attention. It's another couple of steps beyond gardening.

"You didn't get seeds unless you really wanted them. There are some crops you've got to grow again and again and again and again. You just do it until you get it, and there's a certain attitude that says you don't give up—because the slugs ate one batch, a fungus offed the next batch, the mice ate that one, and nobody watered them when you first transplanted. There are enough reasons why things don't work.

"But if you really want it to work, you do it with enough will and conviction, you engage it so that nature respects the engagement, and nature gives back in kind. It's demanding, but it's not unfair. In the long term, someone who believes that, understands that, and uses that becomes a very productive grower. Rich is one of those kinds. When something's going wrong, he can get there ten minutes before it happens, and make sure that it doesn't happen."

Personal Growth

For all of the group, their interest in seeds started with foods. "There are crops," beams Alan with discovery in his eyes, "we didn't know about that have been used by people for thousands of years. You don't even know how good some of the stuff tastes till you grow it in your backyard, because you're used to having stuff that was picked weeks or months before it's ripe and marketed and sent thousands of miles away. When you go get fresh stuff right out of your garden, and get lots of minerals because you treated the soil right, you realize there's another whole food system that you didn't know about."

Naturally, these diverse gardeners had their own affinities, individual inclinations to their own personal growth. They began roving across the gene pool, exploring the diversity of food plants not found in any conventional seed catalogs.

Gabriel was drawn to native food plants from indigenous peoples, as well as exotic herbs and salad vegetables. His travels to the south had opened up a world of food diversity little known at the time, an ancient diet that today is gaining recognition as a crucial source of both global nutrition and a broadened food base.

In Mexico and Guatemala, Gabriel discovered scintillating scarlet plumes gracing many local gardens, but it was a different facet of the plant that got his attention. "My inspiration came from Central American native people who carried amaranth seeds wherever they went. I saw how close this grain was to them, and when I learned how successful the Spanish were in almost wiping it off the face of the earth, it became a crusade for me to try to revive this very important grain and get it back into American diets."

He learned that amaranth had been the sacred grain of the Aztec civilization, the central food of the large, sophisticated culture whose remnants still permeate Mexico and Central America. But upon their victory, the Spanish conquistadores virtually eradicated the sacramental food. One purpose was clearly cultural domination, stripping the Aztecs of an important aspect of their identity. Another may have been more ironic. It appears that the Spanish mistook the ceremonial use of blood-red amaranth for actual blood rituals. Although the Aztecs did engage in certain blood sacrifices, these practices were far less prevalent than the Spanish believed, and amaranth suffered the consequences.

Amaranth possesses many other important traits. It falls into the new class called *leafy grains*, as its young green leaves are also edible. It has the ability to survive extreme heat. It is phenomenally prolific, producing up to 450,000 seeds from one head. It takes only four to six ounces of the grain to plant one entire acre, which in turn can produce three thousand pounds. Its productivity combined with its adaptability positions it as a grain that can feed the world. It grows in short or long growing seasons, and tolerates cool seasons as well as extreme heat. It is perhaps the most heat- and drought-tolerant of the grains. It can take alkaline soils. Gabriel went on to collect varieties growing in Nepal, Tibet, and India, where it also has a long tradition.

The National Academy of Sciences identified kiwicha, an Incan strain of amaranth, as an important food plant in its 1990 report *The Lost Crops of the Incas:* "The seeds of this amaranth, an almost totally neglected grain crop, have high levels of protein and the essential amino acid lysine, which is usually deficient in plant protein. Kiwicha protein is almost comparable to milk protein in nutritional quality, and it complements the nutritional quality of foods that normally would be made from flours of corn, rice, or wheat."[8]

"It's a great gardener's grain," Gabriel enthuses. "One head can yield half a pound to a pound. It's colorful, a great backdrop in a garden, and you can harvest it after the frost. And it's easy to harvest. One head can feed you for two or three meals." It also makes an excellent flour and can be popped for use as a breakfast cereal. Popped amaranth mixed with honey, called *alegria*, is a very popular sweet treat in Mexico.

Amaranth quickly became a favorite in the Oregon gardens. "I was strongly connected to amaranth," says Rich. "All the seeds are important for the earth's sake, but certain seeds are really important for people's sake, and we should learn to grow and care for them. The crops that have the most primary importance are these grain crops, which are seeds. They are the life force.

"I understood what the Aztecs saw when I looked straight into the head of amaranth and saw an Aztec mask. I understood the symbolism of their masks, the image of the sun god emanation. Amaranth has sustained cultures that lived for so long depending on it that they gave it mystical value. The varieties get to be twelve feet tall and make a head that's square or round, like a person's head. It's a guardian that sits up above everything else on all the fields. We've seen it cross into things that have noses and look like aardvarks. Amaranth mutates into a lot of different animal-like beings."

Alan Kapuler has had similar animistic experiences. "Frances Hoffman is a marvelous woman who was one of the founders of the Seed Savers Exchange, the nonprofit seed preservation group. A seed collector, this lady has a fantastic touch with living plants of all kinds. I went for a walk with her through the garden, and she told me stories about plants that I didn't know about. She said, 'Let me send you some interesting seeds that I've been carrying for a long time.' One of the seeds was for an amaranth that she called an elephant. She was talking about purple elephants in her garden. I had no

Amaranth protein has twice the lysine content of wheat protein, three times that of corn, and as much as milk, and it makes an excellent nutritional complement to the other grains. It can be made into many delicious foods, from popped cereal to bread. The leaves are also rich in protein, vitamins, and minerals. These vegetable amaranths may be the most popular vegetable grown in the tropics.

Nepali Red amaranth growing in the herb orchard at the Seeds of Change farm.

idea what this lady was talking about—purple elephants in your garden? It turned out that she had an amaranth that would make a tall flower spike, and when the plants got big, this long columnar flower spike would eventually start to tilt over and end up making a thing that looked like the trunk of an elephant. It would make a lot more side branches and make almost a head. When I went to her place years later, where she had some amaranth growing, the plants were five feet across and six feet tall, and they had six different heads coming out of them with long trunks. They were extraordinary. It turns out Frances had got the seeds from a woman who had got the seeds from a woman who brought them from Germany in the 1880s. Elephant Head amaranth is one of the finest heirlooms we've ever found."

The Rodale Institute Research Center in Pennsylvania, a respected institution in organic agriculture and development of new crops, began extensive testing of amaranth in the 1970s and has also helped pioneer the reintroduction of this vital grain of the Americas into the American diet and culture. In 1993, Rodale's magazine *Organic Gardening* honored this very special amaranth of the purple elephants that Frances Hoffman saved and Seeds of Change is making available to gardeners across the country, noting this whimsical heirloom's exceptional "100 percent germination in two days," a tribute to this hardy survivor.

As long ago as 1975, the National Academy of Sciences selected amaranth as one of the thirty-six "most promising world crops."[9] Along with the Rodale Institute Research Center, the National Academy of Sciences and the National Research Council have done extensive investigation of ways to reintroduce this prime food of the Americas into mainstream diets. "Together, the grain- and vegetable-type amaranths could provide many nutritious foods for the world," concludes the National Research Council study. "It took a century for the American public and the farmers to accept the soybean, and it took two centuries for Europeans to accept the potato. Within a few years, it seems likely that this ancient grain of the Americas will return to grace the modern age. Eventually it may prove to be as rich a legacy of the American Indian as maize and beans."[10]

Gabriel was also seminal in reintroducing another important grain of the Americas into the food system. Quinoa was such a sacred grain to the Incan civilization that the emperor ceremonially planted the first seed each year with a golden spike. It too is a leafy grain, a delicious nutty food that fed a highly organized empire of 15 million people and is now likely to become a primary world food.

"I was in Oaxaca, Mexico," Gabriel relates, "working with a native farmer, helping with his corn and beans. I came across a little plant in the middle of his corn patch that was a quinoa. I saw that he gave it as much respect as his corn. It had a big, beautiful golden head, and he said that he ate it with his corn."

Gabriel brought it back to Oregon, planted it, and gained one of the first quinoa seed crops in North America around 1981. Like amaranth, quinoa has "an exceptionally nutritious balance of protein, fat, oil, and starch," according to the National Academy of Sciences.[11] The Incan civilization cultivated several thousand varieties in an enormous range of microclimates, and the grain has continued to flourish among the southern Andean native cultures. In its report *The Lost Crops of the Incas*, the National Academy found the range of Incan plants to be "widely adaptable, extremely nutritious, and remarkably tasty foods. At the time of the Spanish conquest, the Incas cultivated almost as many species of plants as the farmers of all Asia or Europe (seventy species). That these traditional food crops have a possible role in future food production is indicated by the success of the few that escaped the colonial confines. The conquistadores would undoubtedly be amazed to see potatoes, tomatoes, peppers, and lima beans contributing significantly to modern Spain's cuisine. But they would see that their prejudices against oca, tarwi, quinoa, and dozens of other Inca foods are still largely in place in South America. The traditional crops are gaining more modern respect. At least some of these crops may soon become common household foods. They can be cultivated to give acceptable yields, and they offer good nutrition and interesting tastes."[12]

Noel Vietmeyer, a director of the National Research Council and a world expert on quinoa, considers it one of the principal food sources to be expanded in the 1990s to help address world hunger. Its nutritional superiority combined with its relatively easy cultivation and high productivity give it great promise. In addition, it tends to be far less allergenic than wheat, rice, and corn, to which most people have a longer exposure.

Quinoa was not optimally adapted to Oregon, however, preferring high elevations, and Gabriel later became involved in spreading the seed to more favorable locations in New Mexico and Colorado. When Gabriel left Oregon for New Mexico in 1985, the quinoa that grew so beautifully in the high-elevation San Juan pueblo garden brought him together with Emigdio Ballon, recognized around the world as an expert on Andean and high-elevation crops, who was to become another central player in Seeds of Change.

Emigdio Ballon and His Seeds of Life

A Bolivian native, Emigdio is a Quechua Indian, a gentle, genuinely modest, and astute man who probably literally has quinoa in his blood. A trained agronomist who obtained his degree in 1971 from Bolivia's University of San Simón, he headed the Andean Crops Project for four years at Bolivia's principal experimental station, specializing in quinoa, tubers, and corn. He served as a professor of Andean crops and phytopathology at Oruro University, specializing in genetics and high-altitude crops, and worked as a scientific researcher for Andean crops at Colombia's National University, where he also obtained his M.S. degree. He later served as national coordinator for a Canadian study of Andean crops.

Emigdio had been invited to the States to assist in quinoa research aimed at its ultimate mass production. Dr. Dwayne Johnson of Colorado State University and John McCamant of the Sierra Blanca Foundation brought him north in 1984. He assumed the duties of data collection, production, and selection of quinoa strains in Fort Collins, Colorado.

Born in the Bolivian high mountain village of Cochabamba, he grew up with his grandparents and his mother, who was a *curandera*, a Quechua medicine woman. His mother was also deeply involved in collecting and trading seeds. "I know every place in my country," Emigdio recalls, "because my

"If you have seeds in your pocket, you walk with life. I always have seeds in my pocket. When I go to pay, always I mix my money with the seeds, because while the seeds are growing, my money is growing too. Saving seeds is so important because I believe in life, and seeds are life." **Emigdio Ballon**

mother took me to the many Indian places collecting seeds. As a result, I became very close to plants, crops, seeds, and the land. My ancestors have been doing this same job for a long time, moving the seeds from one place to another.

"I have a very close relation with these grains because my grandpa was coming from the quinoa culture. He grew up where the quinoa grows. My grandpa lived for over a hundred years. The basic food for him was quinoa, kaniwa, amaranth, and potatoes. He was Quechua, and I believe he was a very strong person probably because of the food he was eating. He ate *macuna*, a bowl of quinoa mixed with amaranth cooked in water. You can keep it for days or even weeks and eat it when you work."

In Bolivia Emigdio was responsible for collecting almost two thousand types of quinoa. All have different characteristics: some have medicinal properties; some are good for baking bread; some have a sweet taste. "I can look at my quinoas for hours and hours and hours," Emigdio smiles, "because I can see the difference between grains." He first began sending seeds to the United States in 1974, when he shipped quinoa and fava beans to Brigham Young University in Utah. Within a few years he had sent over 750 kinds of quinoa into the country for testing, and his work has helped U.S. quinoa production to expand to meet increasing public demand for the delicious, nutritious grain of his ancestors.

Emigdio grew up with his family cultivating quinoa, corn, and potatoes in the traditional manner with an ox and a hoe. "The food was for our house supply and for trade. In my country we still often don't use money. We trade with products. Then we saved another part of the crop to give away to some people who needed it. In my culture we think life is Mother Earth and the seeds. The medicine and the food and the drink are coming from the earth. We respect the Mother Earth."

For Emigdio, seeds have a deeper significance. "You can see in my country the relation between crops and man, because usually in the pocket of Indian people you will find corn seeds, maybe mixed with money. Anytime you can ask me what I have in my pocket, and always I will have some mix of the seeds. Because the seeds are food too, and we have a saying in Spanish, *'Barriga lleno, corazón contento.'* That means that if your stomach is full, your heart is happy. If we have corn in our pocket, we are happy because we have food."

The Happy Grain

"When Emigdio first came on the crew at the Gila farm, we had a lot of corn left over from the year before," says Rich. "He popped and dry-roasted it so he could keep it in his pocket, something we didn't do. Americans are really into popcorn, but we're not into popped dry corn, this crunchy, dark, roasted-toasted corn. He did it every day and every night. That was his ritual. He'd go into the house and do the corn up in a can. He always had it, and he wouldn't get hungry. He'd work all day and just eat corn all day. I remember one night when he was in the house popping his corn. He was raised on it, and he said, 'This is what my grandfather showed me.' He told me that in the days before his grandfather died, he would put corn into his hand and say, 'As long as you have this, you have life, and don't go anywhere without it.'

"They say corn is the happy grain. Roasting his corn over the stove, Emigdio was laughing, and he was happy. Then I started laughing, and I said, 'You've got those high cheeks. You looked like a corn kernel out there, and all those smiles!' I understood right then that you really are what you eat."

In Bolivia, Emigdio points out, the Indian people have a special respect for corn; it is important that Quechua people pray when planting it. "The people believe there is a very special relationship they have with the crop, and with the Mother Earth and the Spirit, when they put these seeds in the ground." There are many corns that are used in different ways: there are toasting corns that Emigdio eats in the fields from his pocket; there are roasting corns, starch corns, dry and wet popping corns, and boiling corns.

Many of the Seeds of Change corns reflect this native diversity. In fact, until about 1900 virtually all corns in the United States were Native American varieties. These corns have almost no resemblance to the supermarket hybrid sweet corns most people know today, which were really introduced widely only in the 1930s and 1940s. "The staple corn has become one of our favorites," say Rich and Julie. "We eat corn for nutrition. We eat corn more as a staple than as an extra. Sure, we'll enjoy a super-sweet just like we'll enjoy a piece of chocolate sometimes. But we won't enjoy super-sweet every single day the way we'll enjoy standard open-pollinated good corn that we can dig into, that fills us up with quality. We'd rather have it be closer to the mainstay of our diet.

"How could we not be happy about corn?" Rich grins, lending empirical credence to the happy corn theory. "We grow all these corns from different cultures, and we have all these colors and all these kinds, all these virtues. We love the Hopi Pink corn. It makes crops all the time, and it is super-dependable. It is the best flour corn that we have. We love Black Aztec too, because the sweet starches like Aztec make great tortillas, as well as good sweet corn. Eat it while it is fresh and sweet, or let it dry and make great tortillas and posoles."

"I like how chewy the starch corns are," Julie adds. "The quality is so radically different from the quality of corn that you buy commercially. You have to cook starch corn longer. It is not a corn to cook in hot water for three minutes or eight minutes. Sometimes it takes forty-five minutes. When you eat a piece of that corn, it's really substantial nourishment. In Mexico we learned that their corn on the cob is a huge starch corn. It's not a sweet corn, but it is sweet, and when you eat it, you're full. It was our favorite. So we learned from their culture that a hardy piece of corn on the cob makes a meal."

For Gabriel too, native corns have been a botanical grail. One of his favorites is the very unusual Mandan Red. "It's earthy sweet rather than just that candy-cane sweet of hybrid corns. It's a great roasting corn, which traditionally is what most Indians grew sweet corns for. It's got a little bit of the starch and the sweet together; it's a nice property."

Red and orange Mandan, named for a tribe in the North Dakota region, is unique because it has a deep taproot. Most corns tend to have side roots that stay close to the surface, which makes them more reliant on water, and

Hopi White corn.

Fox cherry tomatoes at the first light of day at the Seeds of Change farm.

they don't stand up as well when the winds blow. The Mandan taproot can go down as much as two feet, and it helps the plant to hold against the wind better and to tolerate drought. It is able to gain more nutrients from the soil, especially deep minerals. "It seems to be a little more cold-tolerant," Gabriel recounts. "We had some corn survive twenty-two degrees. It tends to grow better in northern climates and at higher elevations."

The Mandan produces many ears from one seed. "One year the seed produced fourteen ears, which is unheard of," Gabriel boasts. "The average was six or seven ears from one seed. They make many side branches like a bush, and they produce the ears near the surface of the ground. If you have a lot of animal problems, that can be a drawback. But in that case, we have a Bolivian corn that grows to eighteen feet, and the ears don't start till about five or six feet up the stalk."

Backyard Breeding

There is one other corn that is particularly special, a "new native" corn unique to Seeds of Change. "The Rainbow Inca is definitely our favorite sweet corn, because it's one of the hardiest," Rich explains. "It's got that starch quality so that we can make great tortillas and incredible posoles. It's multicolored. Mushroom made Rainbow."

"I was saving ears of corn," admits Alan Kapuler, backyard geneticist. "I had traveled, and I'd pick up an ear of corn at one place or another. I'd go to someone's garden, and they'd have an interesting corn. For some ten years, I'd been collecting corn. I went to the box I had with hundreds of ears of corn, and I picked out a dozen ears of corn that I thought were the most lovely. They were multicolored, and there were sweet corns, starch corns, and flour corns. I had a few packs also of corns like Black Aztec corn, popular heirloom varieties grown for generations.

"I took the ears of corn and I unfurled them. There were patterns on the corn cob of who got pollinated next to one another, like a story written in the ear of corn. I liked the stories. I'd end up with an ear of corn on my desk, and I'd look at it for months or years, just to see the remarkable story that the corn had of life itself.

"I really cherished the beauty and uniqueness of certain ears of corn. I realized, well, if I shuck them off, put them in a bag, and plant them, it's not the same thing as if I were to lay the kernels from the ear of corn down on the ground in the pattern that came on the ear of corn. So I decided I wanted to do that.

"I used a corn that came from South America called Inca. It makes a big, flat, starchy seed with very big ears. The plants get to be twelve feet tall, and the ears are frequently over your head. I liked that corn. So I planted a row of those seeds in among other corns that were multicolored. The next year I found some multicolored kernels occasionally in an ear of a whole Inca white corn, a pink, blue, or yellow seed.

"So I gathered up the twenty or thirty ears, and I pulled the fifty seeds that were colored out of those ears. The next year, when I planted the same corn patch with another set of a dozen interesting ears, I had saved those individual seeds I had picked out of the Inca corn and I planted those. That year at the end of the harvest, when I looked at those, there were crinkled seeds. I picked the few crinkled seeds, and there was an occasional crinkled seed that was colored in the ears of corn. I picked those out and planted them the third year. I ended up with whole cobs that had crossed to the other corns in the area and made smaller plants, down to nine feet with the ears at eye level. I had a sweet corn that had big flat seeds and was multicolored. We called that Rainbow Inca sweet corn.

"It's something that's open to every gardener, to do genetics and selections, to develop your own corns and develop your own varieties.

"There is a 'gene pool' aspect of maintaining diversity," Alan observes. "My idea of the seed company I was building was to be devoted to the basic diversity inherent in all the varieties of corn and of what's available in the natural world, instead of picking out a very narrow selection that we end up calling a seed line."

So Many Tomatoes, So Little Time

For any backyard gardener, one lament is familiar: "So many tomatoes, so little time." At Seeds of Change, this other prize of the Americas is always a rave. The 1993 catalog offered gardeners sixty-five kinds of tomatoes, and those are just a fraction of the 150 Rich grew in trials at the farm and the many more in the collection.

This staple of Rich's Italian culinary heritage actually originated in the Americas, without which there would be no Italian food as we know it. "Tomatoes, their colors and shapes, I just can't deny what a beauty and joy they are to grow. I was brought up with a lot of pasta, a lot of sauce, and a lot of tomatoes. You take it from seed, you grow it to this luscious summer fruit, and it's salsa and it's celebration. The tomatoes and chiles to me are just good times."

Among the favorites are heirlooms that have survived because of their hardiness, productivity, and flavor, such as the large-fruited Brandywine and the Arkansas Traveler, two truly delicious lineages. For smaller fruits, the Roma Paste and Porter Pink are tops, or for cherry tomatoes, the Fox Cherry and Currants are supreme.

Chile to Repel Sorcery

It's hard to think of tomatoes without chile peppers, and Alan found one of the best from Truckin' Jim Arledge, who earned his moniker as an inveterate hitchhiker who never owned a vehicle, and whose mother gave him the family hot pepper seed heritage on a trip home to Arledge Road in Denton, Louisiana. The Arledge hot pepper turned out to be the most productive even in northern climates, where people need that inner flame to stay warm.

Jimmy Nardello's heirloom frying sweet pepper was a gastronomic calling card at his famous restaurant, a long, red sweet chile that looks hot but is not. For stuffing, the Italian Sweet, the Relleno, and the even larger Corno di Toro are the standards, capacious pods of sweet flesh.

Some like it hot, and there are persistent rumors that Gabriel had a dragon in his family tree. Actually, his mother is descended from Tarahumara Indians from Mexico who eat chiles as a central ingredient of their diet. "Chiles are hereditary in my Tarahumara ancestry," Gabriel says. "Their main diet is corn, beans, and chile, and they don't go a meal without eating a chile. I almost always had a little chile on my plate when I was a kid.

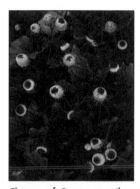

Closeup of Paracress spilanthes growing at the Seeds of Change farm.

"Chile has the highest vitamin C level of anything that you can grow in a garden in a temperate climate, and it's high in iron, calcium, and vitamin A. It's good as an expectorant too, and I eat them for my asthmatic condition. It gets your nose running and pulls a lot of mucus out of your system. Native people always say to eat a chile and it will keep any kind of sorcery away from your life."

Chiles are productive plants in general, and there are varieties for short and long seasons, as well as perennials. There are chiles with vibrant purple flowers, and many other surprising color variations.

"The Purira is one that I discovered more recently in a little town in southern Bolivia," Gabriel says, holding up the vegetable firecracker. "I've always looked for something that would rival the Habanero, said to be the hottest chile. I found this one that's a different species, which we named Purira based on a Quechua word for giving strength. It's also a little village where they grow a lot of chiles in southern Bolivia. It is the only one we've ever seen that rivals the Habanero. I've had a number of friends taste both and say that the Purira is hotter."

Gabriel routinely pulls out a mason jar of homemade chile oil with every meal but breakfast. He has found that the oil preserves the chile extremely well without sacrificing flavor or freshness. He and Emigdio, the resident fire-eaters, are the only ones who dare to share the brew.

The Spice of Life

Tomatoes and chiles regularly combine at Seeds of Change into mouthwatering salsas of unspeakably delicious flavor, and Gabriel adds a special ingredient little known in North America but prevalent in the South.

Quilquina is a unique spicy herb whose seed heads look like dandelions. "I used to taste it in South American cuisine," Gabriel offers, "and I realized it was one reason their salsas tasted so different, even from those in Mexico and Central America. It's used in all their favorite chile sauces, and its flavor is somewhere between arugula, cilantro, and rue. Most people either love it or hate it. I love it, and I believe it will be a new spice here."

While traveling in Ecuador in 1979, Gabriel climbed the back side of a 19,000-foot active volcano into the Amazon basin. He was accompanying a local medicine man collecting plants in the natural unspoiled beauty. At the time, he was suffering painful tooth problems, and hiking in the high elevation didn't help.

The medicine man was encouraging Gabriel to identify and try plants, and indicated that he would let him know if there was something really not to test. "He wanted us to be in tune, to open up to our intuition, and to follow it to see if there's a new plant that we can discover."

Gabriel noticed a cone-shaped flower that resembled another medicinal plant. "I decided to pop a flower in my mouth and try it. It surprised the heck out of me. I felt as if I were going to heave out my whole stomach, not vomit, but more as though all the mucus wanted to come out my nose. I felt like I was going on a ride—literally. I managed to chew down the whole thing, slowly, and I started to feel a tingling, numb sensation. Suddenly I didn't feel my toothache nearly as much. The medicine man saw me put the whole flower in my mouth, but it was too late. He assured me I'd live through it. Then I saw how well it dealt with my tooth."

The potent herb is spilanthes, known in Latin America as the "toothache plant." Gabriel brought it back to the States, grew it out, and made a sample tincture. Herbalists were impressed and now offer it for fungal infections and colds, noting it has a chemical composition similar to that of echinacea, but emphasizing its greater strength. Simultaneously it turned out that Alan had collected another spilanthes species, paracress, whose leaves make a picante salad treat. But the toothache plant is truly a mouthful, a lingual explosion that has levitated more than one guest adventurous enough to bite into the pretty, innocent-looking cone-shaped volcano at the Gila farm.

Stalking the Bean

On the safer side, the tepary is a southwestern Sonoran native bean voted the tastiest by the Gila farm crew. It is small and nutty, with very high protein and very low fat content. It's easy to digest, and most people don't get gassy from it. A favored food among southwestern Indians, it is exceptionally drought-tolerant, and can withstand scalding surface temperatures up to around 180 degrees. Teparies are very prolific and resist bean beetle problems well. If the beetles do go after them, the plants can still make a crop even with their leaves stripped. On a trellis, they will grow six or seven feet up and proliferate inexorably.

Teparies cook in about two hours, and there are a lot of interesting ways to prepare them. The farm likes to make a soup mix, with posole and some chiles. Pâté is the most popular way. Bean chips with tepary flour have a wonderful flavor too.

Alan Kapuler discovered one of his favorite beans because of foul weather. He had been growing the yellow Hutterite heirloom bean for several years, never even considering eating it because he was growing it out as planting stock. Then the elements took a hand in deciding his dinner.

"It's unusual in the Pacific Northwest when you get two feet of snow and it's fifteen degrees out. You can't go anywhere, and you don't even think about it. But you can go to the bean room to get some beans to cook up for dinner. We did this several years ago for six or eight days, and for the first time we got to eat a pound or two of the rare heirloom beans we'd been growing out for sixteen years. When we did that, we were very surprised. One of the beans we soaked overnight and cooked the next day turned very quickly—in a couple of hours—into a deliciously thick, creamy white soup. We'd never seen anything like it. It was the Hutterite bush bean, and we

recognized that it was that characteristic, cooking rapidly and making a very delicious thick, creamy soup, that made this an heirloom, why people have passed it on from generation to generation. A religious sect from Europe, the Hutterites, carried this as one of their heirloom seeds along with a belief in a God that entrusts one to freedom."

The Third Sister

Another favorite staple in the Kapuler household is the third of the "Three Sisters" of the Americas: corn, beans, and squash. "I don't know when we first started baking winter squash in a gas oven," Alan puzzles. "It turns out that when you bake a squash in a gas oven with nothing on it, some of the varieties are so exceedingly delicious you can't believe that nobody ever told you about it. This is extraordinary food. You don't need to put butter on it. You don't need to put brown sugar on it. All you need to do is cut it in half, clean it out, save the seeds, and bake it. Our families love it."

Alan and family have grown and eaten about a hundred varieties of squash in the last twenty years. Their favorites are generally winter squash, either Cucurbita Moschata or Cucurbita Maxima. The Kapulers have settled on the Buttercup and the Hokkaido, whose flesh is dark orange and finely textured and has unsurpassable flavor. They also like the Sibley heirloom, from the Hubbard line, and the Green Hubbard. The Sweetkeeper is a prized heirloom of the Pacific Northwest, with very thick, sweet flesh. Among the Moschatas, their favorites are the Butternuts, from the small Ponca to the Waltham and the largest, the Tahitian.

For the Pecoraros, the squashes of choice are Cucurbita Pepos, summer squashes that are close allies to pumpkins. "Picking favorite squashes," agrees Rich, "has really always been pretty tough. I can sit down at the dinner table and ask my family for their favorites, and one says Crooknecks, the other likes Scallopinis, and the other, Zucchinis. We really love the Cocozelles too. They're all beautiful."

Winner Staples

"It's the staple grains and the staple vegetables that have become our most akin," Rich says gently as white lightning flashes across the nocturnal backdrop of rugged mountains, prophesying early snow. "It means a lot to us that we have our winter food."

"I have a real affinity for carrots and onions because of the sturdiness and the strength they have on our organs, and the steadiness as a mainstay in our diets. The Royal Chantenay carrot has fine-grained sweet flesh, and we voted it in the best-tasting varieties. It's a total winner. The Nantes varieties are also an especially delicate and delicious heirloom carrot with a history from France, where they cultivated them in French-intensive gardens."

This year the farm held a Diversity Festival with a special carrot-juice contest. The local community came to perform a taste test on thirty varieties of carrots, selecting the Chantenay as an unequivocal favorite.

"Onions are so close to life it's not even excitement as much as it is just part of us," Rich continues. "We eat them all the time. They represent the beginning of the season because they're hardy plants that you can begin in the coldest weather, get them started in the greenhouses. It's the first thing that you begin. It stays with you all winter. You're still eating them while you're starting them again."

Alan agrees. "In recent times, my favorite crops increasingly include onions and leeks. I knew I had to start growing my own onion seeds. They're little black seeds. You buy a pack of onion seeds, and you have two hundred seeds in a pack. You scatter it on a flat, and up come these tiny, thin, frail seedlings very easily and rather rapidly. In seven days you get a bunch of nice little sprouts coming up. Then I transplant them into beds, and from one pack you end up with one hundred or two hundred pounds of onions.

"I couldn't believe how much food you got out of a pack of these tiny little onion seeds. Then if you have bright daughters, who like to braid onions, and you hang them in your house, you surround your kitchen with beautiful yellow, round, flat, white, elongated shapes, all these different colors and all these different flavors of onions. It was a discovery to me. Onions turn out to be one of the essential staples for a garden."

Walla Walla sweets are a general favorite, another Pacific Northwest heirloom, but they don't store well. Sweet Spanish onions store very well and are a staple, along with the heirloom Red Wethersfield. The elongated Italina Bottle onion is also excellent for fresh use and short storage.

"But I didn't know about leeks. Leeks are a crop that grow better where you can overwinter them, as in the Pacific Northwest. I found out that the Winter Giant leeks make three-inch stems. You're cooking in the kitchen, you go get a leek, and you chop it up and put it in miso soup and in stir-fries. The Winter Giant is a thick-stemmed, short, hardy leek we use a lot. Most people are familiar only with potato and leek soup."

Alan's perennial leek patch is a backyard gardening staple. "Heirloom leeks are excellent, excellent home gardener's food. If you have a little patch, even just five square feet, you can grow a lot of food when it comes to onions and leeks. Highly nutritious and very empowering."

The Salad Days

A Seeds of Change summer salad can be a mystical experience. The huge salad bowl fills with glistening, vibrant leaves and colored flowers only a botanist can identify. It's definitely the salad edge.

One farm favorite is roquette, also known as arugula, a pungent green that has become a new salad rave across the country. When picked young, the arrow-shaped leaves are tender and mildly peppery, adding great flavor to salads. When larger, they can be steamed or sautéed. This fast-growing leaf is turning the American palate toward strongly flavored greens.

Other farm favorites include Persian Garden cress and Osaka Purple mustard; they add a tangy bite to any salad, which may also contain half a dozen kinds of lettuce. The large-leaf Black Simpson lettuce mingles with the delicate, small-headed Formidana or Sucrine, and the thicker leaf, very sweet, delicious Savoy Romaine. "Little bits of flower petals are nice," adds

Rich, "from nasturtiums to primrose, curled mallow, borage, licorice mint, and calendula. A small garnishing is tasty, unless you want a whole pile of flowers to cheer yourself up."

"What we now have is a gourmet vegetarian diet," Alan Kapuler grins. "It means that you make a salad out of twenty-five different kinds of leaves, six different kinds of lettuce. I've been eating lettuce for thirty-five years, and when I first started growing butterheads, I realized this is a whole different food from the standard crispy, colorless lettuce that I was accustomed to. Lettuces like Deer Tongue and Rouge d'Hiver are incomparable.

"And now you have kale," Alan continues about a favorite vegetable he has been instrumental in reintroducing. This gardener's favorite is a very high nutrition food rich in anticancer beta carotene. "Kale was not in the kitchen. It wasn't even in the market. Kale was something that poor peasants ate in northern climates because they were starving. That's not really true. But kale is a staple. It's nutritious and delicious, and it's beautiful. It's a cruciferous vegetable with the same anticancer properties as broccoli."

Red Russian kale was recently listed as one of the best-tasting popular favorites by *Organic Gardening* magazine. Growers around the country almost unanimously agreed on its favored place in the garden.

"You also have kohlrabies and brassica leaves of other kinds, whether savoy cabbages or sorrels and cresses," Alan continues. "It's incredible the salads you can make, but you don't know that until you start growing a lot of it yourself, because you don't see most of it in markets and stores. There's a very minimal selection of vegetables in stores. You can get cabbage, but savoy cabbage was not something I ever saw, beautiful Savoy Chieftain cabbage. Chinese cabbage was pretty rare. Nobody really used Chinese vegetables. Here, we use bok choy as a staple. You love Chinese food? Why not make it at home?

"We start with bok choy and its close relative lei choy, major ingredients in chow mein, chop suey, and miso soup (cook the stems first, and add the leaf blades later). A dainty and attractive salad plant is tat soi, called rosette green for the spirally arranged small dark green leaves on small petioles.

Also part of the Chinese salad puzzle is mizuna, with feathery leaves and six very tasty, thin, crunchy leaf stalks. Finally you can add hon tai sai, with purplish leaves with dark purple veins and bright yellow flowers. Here's a Chinese salad or soup with greens that you can find only in your backyard."

Group Melon

For Rich, it's hard to think of summer without dreaming of melons. "Watermelon is a remarkable phenomenon of the annual garden. Its ability to fill us up with its sweet sustaining water has carried us through many a sweaty day in the fields. In the hot, dry days of May when we approach planting time, the thought of watermelon feasts to come gives us a tingle of excitement about doing this work on the earth. We have heard of coastal African cultures who survive happily on watermelon and fish. But many home gardeners have had disappointments with growing watermelons. We encourage them to try again. The return is worth its weight in melons. Melons, to us, are the unfolding. How can such a large thing grow from a seed?"

The Gila farm tested around a hundred watermelons last year and is testing a hundred and fifty in 1993. The Early Moonbeam is a ravishing favorite, yellow-fleshed and thin-skinned. Its excellent flavor is a summer romance. "Another prize of the south," says Rich, licking his lips, "is the Black Diamond. These melons can get to be forty-five pounds, and I know that sounds gargantuan and outrageous. How can you eat something that big? But if you had ever sat down on a hot day with ten people around a forty-five-pound Black Diamond whose every bite was delicious right down to the rind, you might want to grow it too. We really hope to reintroduce a lot of the high-quality heirloom melons for their diverse qualities and expand this culture again into people's gardens."

GROWING CIVILIZATIONS

Restoring the fabric of diversity invokes the intertwining lineages of plants and human cultures. "Open-pollinated seeds and the old-time heirloom seeds are incredible," Rich emphasizes. "They have particularities that are diversity in themselves. They lock into small groups of people who carry their own strain. It was diversity in human culture, and diversity in bioregions. The open-pollinated seeds are particular to the places where they came from. When you grow them, you're really tracking down their ancestors. Even if it's flower seeds kept in the family, there's always a connection back to where they came from. Some plants aren't so good in some parts of the world; they were never meant to be. They are just part of the fabric of diversity, and diversity is part of life.

"We're trying to grow civilizations, in a sense," Rich muses. "We're taking crops from civilizations, cultures, and microcultures within cultures. Here we are gifted with the seeds of Bolivia, chiles or different kinds of corn where some of the people of their own nationalities don't even know that they existed. All they know is that their strain existed, and they had the integrity to keep it. They just made sure that they took care of what was the gift to them.

"We're not out there trying to prove that this is better than a hybrid because it's going to outperform it. But if you get the right ones, they sure are going to be as good, and you're also going to be carrying the real heritage of the people."

For Emigdio Ballon, the issue is a very personal one. "I learned a great deal from my mother about seeds and the earth. But when she died in 1985, I lost a lot of knowledge, because I didn't pay attention to the things she knew. I was too influenced by college and education at that time.

"It's one of the hard situations today because so many people don't grow the food, and so they lose the knowledge. Right now in the developing countries, you see a big dependency on fertilizer and hybrid seeds. For thousands of years we didn't depend on these. The people are losing the dedication to Mother Earth. We are losing our identity. We don't want to be Indians anymore. We lose the tradition of the relationship with Mother Earth. For me, this is very sad.

"But I am still doing the work I learned from my ancestors. I believe the future of my people depends on growing these foods. That's why I am involved with agriculture and working with Seeds of Change. Seeds of Change is doing the work of preserving the earth."

Gabriel agrees. "The problem is that the diversity is disappearing, and we can't wait for the experts to take responsibility. That was part of what Seeds of Change was founded on, the principle that all of us have to take responsibility for preserving what diversity we can. We try to create the awareness that people have a real ability to make a difference."

For Alan Kapuler, the mission is very clear. "When I saw that the backyard gardeners were able and willing to maintain diversity where seed companies, universities, and all the government agencies were totally uninterested, I realized that it's in the hands of the backyard gardener that the salvation of diversity is going to remain, because we are destroying all the native habitats. So, rather than having the conservation of genetic materials based on an economic success model, we need to have the conservation of genetic materials based on interest and devotion to life by a large fraction of our population. What we will have left is the few plants that are interesting that devoted people are willing to carry, grow, and pass on to the next generation."

SHREDDING THE FABRIC

The hearty seeds that managed to survive the countless threats and vagaries of wild nature now face extinction by a more sinister force: the hand of man. Probably the greatest danger to genetic diversity today is the multinational seed industry.

"The attempt to monopolize seeds and food is as old as history," according to seed experts Pat Mooney and Cary Fowler, authors of *Shattering*. "Many seeds have long been worth more than their weight in gold."[13] Ironically, the modern commercial seed industry is a stealthy thief in the dark night of the biodiversity crisis.

Food Chain, or Chain of Fools?

We live with a green giant today who has no cause to be jolly, because the loss of biological diversity very immediately endangers our food system. In the disembodied supermarket society of the late twentieth century, it is easy to forget that the essential food that provides human sustenance comes out of the earth under the most capricious conditions by the precarious grace of the right mix of rain, sun, soil, and good seeds.

"The single most serious threat to the global food system is the threat of genetic erosion," observes Vice-President Albert Gore, who has studied the situation closely for well over a decade.[14] Seed specialists Fowler and Mooney are even more adamant. "Perhaps the biggest single environmental catastrophe in human history is unfolding in the garden. The loss of genetic diversity in agriculture—silent, rapid, inexorable—is leading us to a rendezvous with extinction, to the doorstep of hunger on a scale we refuse to imagine."[15]

When the potato traveled from the Americas to Europe circa 1570, its value soon surpassed silver or gold for the poor, for whom it quickly became one of the real treasures of the Americas, a staple food supporting millions. Following a "mini ice age," however, a fungus attacked the "Lumper," the single kind of potato that people grew in 1845. The blight rotted its way across the uniform potato population, destroying half the crop. The following year it wiped out virtually the entire crop in Ireland, and a million people who relied on it died, while another million and a half fled the stricken country.

Plant breeders later identified another strain from the potato's biological center of origin in Peru and bred it to make a new plant resistant to the rot. The event marked the modern beginning of the coevolutionary game of crops and robbers, making the food chain safe from the grim reapers of disease and pestilence.

Echoes of the Irish potato famine resounded across the United States in 1970. The southern leaf corn blight struck the U.S. crop, destroying half the corn from Florida to Texas, a gaping total of 20 percent nationally. It became known as the "genetic shot heard 'round the world," but this time there was a key difference. Plant breeders had not only made the mistake of sowing huge expanses of a very few similar kinds of corn (corn-monocultures), they had actually inserted a single gene, Texas male cytoplasm,

"I recognized every Thanks-
giving that when we've taken
a corn harvest, it was the story
of your life. Every harvest you
make is another harvest in
which you succeeded in growing part of the living legacy
that gives rise to our collective
existence." **Alan Kapuler**

into all of them. The breeders had hoped to gain an industrial advantage by inserting this designer gene intended to eliminate the need for expensive hand-detasseling. However, that single gene proved susceptible to the deadly fungus, which tore through the crops like a prairie fire.

According to the ensuing report issued by the National Academy of Sciences, the highly touted hybrid corn was as "alike as identical twins." The Academy concluded that the crop was "impressively uniform genetically and impressively vulnerable" and referred to the infamous Irish lesson of 125 years before. The plant breeder Garrison Wilkes commented grimly, "Imagine what a burglar could do if he got past the front door of a building and found that all the apartments shared the same key."[16]

The enemy was uniformity. But the potential saving grace of fresh genes from other resistant plants in the wild was itself eroding as aggressive human encroachment continued to shrink native habitats and ecosystems around the world. Genetic erosion has become an avalanche in the late twentieth century. Of the cornucopia of reliable cultivated food plants available to our grandparents in 1900, today 97 percent are gone. Since the arrival of Columbus, 75 percent of native food plants have disappeared in the Americas.

These old varieties are the products of millions of years of evolution and as much as twelve thousand years of human selection and coevolution. They are the plants on which generations of people have survived, the plants that have shown their ability to adapt to all the variability of nature. Called land races or peasant varieties, they are the work of "sophisticated, capable people who walked their fields with a keen eye for the best plants to be saved for seed, the result of intelligent, innovative minds and often the work of geniuses."[17]

"The garden seeds currently being dropped from mail-order catalogs are the best home-garden varieties we will ever see," laments Kent Whealy, co-founder of the Seed Savers Exchange, a leading seed conservation group. "Far from being obsolete or inferior, these are the cream of our vegetable crops. If our vegetable heritage is allowed to die out, home gardeners will become ever more dependent on gigantic seed companies and the generic varieties they choose to offer. That means giving up our right to determine the quality of foods our families consume."[18]

Kent and Diana Whealy founded the Seed Savers Exchange in 1975 after Diane's father gave her a bequest of seeds brought four generations before from Bavaria. The Whealys began to monitor the loss of our "irreplaceable garden heritage." They found that "44.6 percent of all the non-hybrid vegetable varieties available in 1984 had been dropped from mail-order catalogs by 1991, and those losses appear to be escalating."[19]

The Hybrid Double-cross

The Whealys have identified the biggest single trigger of extinctions today as the introduction of new hybrid varieties by multinational seed companies. The major seed companies drop more of the old kinds as they introduce new hybrids, and the reliable heirloom and traditional varieties are then almost certain to disappear.

The multinational seed companies favor hybrids, which are the genetic offspring of two parent crosses, for several reasons. The central commercial appeal is that they can patent hybrids as proprietary, and thereby own, control, and profit from these seed varieties. In addition, because the *first-generation (F1) hybrids* are mainly "mules," which do not reproduce true to form, gardeners and growers are compelled to return each year to the company store. In the infrequent cases where hybrids do reproduce adequately, their productivity is greatly diminished. Further, the companies design the hybrids to grow mainly within the narrow tolerances of petrochemical products in which the companies also often have a financial interest.

These companies breed the hybrid seeds mainly for large farmers and for industrial traits such as uniform ripening, suitability for mechanical harvesting, toughness of skin for shipping, and cosmetic appearance. These are agroindustrial characteristics, not appealing values for a healthy food system or for small farmers or gardeners.

The modern hybrid cross is actually a double-cross. The system creates an unhealthy dependency where once farmers and gardeners had the power to save and trade their own seeds. Above all, the emphasis on hybrids has displaced the vast reservoir of native, regional, and folk seed stocks and caused many of them to disappear altogether.

The ecological impact of hybrids has increasingly come under serious critical scrutiny, however. In an op-ed piece in the *New York Times*, George Ball, Jr., president of W. Atlee Burpee & Company, a large garden seed company, defended hybrids as "plants, not monsters" and complained about "hybrid-bashing," a likely reference to groups like Seeds of Change and the Seed Savers Exchange that have been raising the issue publicly. As the *Times* author identification states, Burpee sells mostly hybrid seeds, which are the foundation of their business. The hundred-year-old Burpee was considered the preeminent garden seed company in the country until 1972, when the formerly family-owned business languished after selling out to the multinational giant General Foods and later to ITT. Burpee was purchased in 1991 by Geo. J. Ball, Inc., a large family-owned business specializing in hybrid flower seeds. Burpee is distinguished by selling to backyard gardeners and does not otherwise represent the agendas of the multinational seed industry.

The arguments that Mr. Ball makes in behalf of hybrids are fairly representative of those of the hybrid seed industry at large and therefore worth examining. The hybrid industry is sincere in its point of view, and it is vitally important to address the issue as public policy relating to biodiversity.

The argument contends that, rather than reducing diversity, "hybrids may represent a dramatic increase in genetic diversity."[20] This point of view appears difficult to defend, because hybrids are "built" from existing genes and plant stock. No breeder has yet created a new gene. For example, according to Fowler and Mooney, "All of Mr. Burpee's hybrid zinnias are descendants of one tiny flower found in row 66 of Burpee's fields at Santa Paula, California, in 1948."[21] Such breeding contributes to more varieties, but not to greater diversity.

Mr. Ball's thinking, which is in line with that of the industry, goes on that "there is no question that old-fashioned heirloom flowers and vegetables have an appealing quaintness that is in sync with the back-to-basics zeitgeist:

'Save the 100-year-old eggplant!' However, an astute gardener will tell you that the benefits of a modern hybrid over an older variety are like those of a new car over a 1918 Model T. It might look nice in your garden, but you wouldn't want to drive it across the country."[22] Actually, it is inappropriate to compare plants to cars in any way at all. Plants are not machines, and they were not built by people in the first place. In fact, plants precede humanity by quite a biological stretch of time and got along quite well without us.

This eggplant-driven logic holds that an "heirloom may be a novelty, such as an unusual shape, color or fragrance, but those qualities are often offset by inferior performance in the areas most important to most home gardeners: yield, resistance to disease and size of fruit or flower."[23] Many gardeners obviously disagree, and they are voting by their increasing purchases of nonhybrid seeds. Gardeners are a singularly practical, no-nonsense breed. Besides the perceived quality of heirloom vegetables in the categories of productivity, health, and size, gardeners often find them to taste better and have more nutritional content.

Hybrid enthusiasts protest that the fanciers of heirlooms are exhibiting nostalgia. It is understandable that people are nostalgic about the plants handed down through generations, plants that supported their ancestors, who thus survived to beget them. The heirlooms are proven survivors. These are plants with true breeding, the "greatest hits of the gene pool," not mere fashion victims of annual seed catalog hype.

Dismissing the problem as mere veggie retro fails to address the core issue, however. The real question is about *hybrid* versus *open-pollinated* seeds. Seeds of Change is not intrinsically opposed to hybrids. In fact, as a plant breeder and geneticist, Alan Kapuler has bred hybrids, which the company offers, such as Rainbow Inca sweet corn. But Alan took the process a step further to continue to breed true hybrids through several generations beyond the first-generation (F1) plants. He bred until the plants stabilized into *open-pollinated hybrids that do reproduce true to form*. This is precisely what sophisticated gardeners have done for thousands of years to create what we today call heirloom and traditional varieties.

"All the genetic information that exists in organisms in the world is its own living history of life. It's expressed in organisms. You may have a thousand varieties of corn. The composite information of all those corn varieties is the gene pool of corn. The gene pool of corn is not expressed completely through any variety of corn. It's the whole set of all the corns that's the gene pool."
Alan Kapuler

As Alan Kapuler notes, "Anyone who has examined natural species in relation to hybrids will see value in both. Uniqueness falls to the species that have millions of years and generations in their development. Our human-derived hybrids generally flower sooner in greater profusion and produce mature crops more rapidly in regulated bursts. Both directions have merit, but the gene pool of the planet needs species to rekindle the fires burned out from our limited needs."

Hybrid supporters contend that the hybrids are more disease-resistant. This assertion may be true in some cases. In most cases, however, disease resistance must be seen in a larger context. As Alan Kapuler notes, "If hybrids are so disease-resistant, why are they packaged and sold with specific fertilizers, herbicides, and fungicides? They require finicky feeding regimes, pampering by killing competing organisms, and extravagant amounts of water and angel-food-cake soil." In fact, the hybrids are specifically designed to grow within the narrow tolerances of petrochemical agriculture and, as such, are more vulnerable and dependent. From an environmental point of view, hybrids are relative evolutionary newcomers with a strong chemical dependency, and they have already shown themselves vulnerable to a host of diseases.

Seeds of Change is interested in the best of all kinds, including hybrids, but only stable, open-pollinated hybrids such as those Alan has bred. We also want a sensible balance between hybrids and the species whose lineages nature has taken millions of years of evolution to create.

But the central issue is that hybrids are at the soft center of a food system that is teetering on a dangerously small platform of plants. The world today relies on just one hundred fifty food plants, and only twenty of those produce 90 percent of our food. Nine are widely used, and account for three-quarters of the human diet. Of these, just three—rice, corn, and wheat—account for half. These are truly slim pickings, considering that there are thirty thousand to eighty thousand edible plants.

Enter the Bean Counters

We live today with an altogether primitive menu derived from just a couple of hundred food plants domesticated by our Neolithic ancestors. Actually

90 percent of the people who have ever lived were hunters and gatherers who spent just about three weeks a year collecting a year's worth of grains. Wild food was abundant, and people were not. The diet was truly diverse. People grazed on three thousand to five thousand plants. The biologist Gary Nabhan estimates that Native Americans in the Southwest regularly sampled eleven hundred plants.[24]

But around twelve thousand years ago, people figured out how to plant seeds, and they then sowed an environmentally dubious but unquestionably radical change in human history. Although agriculture has a wholesome, idyllic, pastoral image, it has probably been one of the most destructive human endeavors. The Bible speaks of a whirlwind of ensuing natural disasters, including floods, droughts, plagues, and infestations resulting from poor land management practices. Agriculture precipitated widespread topsoil erosion, water pollution, deforestation, and the ravaging of the landscape by domesticated animals.

Agriculture also made possible the ascendancy of the original bean counters. By producing a surplus of grains, farming created the social basis of material wealth for a ruling class and bureaucracy.

In a brief flurry of horticulture, people domesticated several hundred food plants, and they proved to be durable and dependable over a lengthy period of time. Survival is its own testament. Not only did these plants show the necessary strength and adaptability in the natural world, but the people and cultures that relied on the plants survived by coevolving with these sturdy allies. People planted multiple mixed crops, and many cultures prized the variability found in any one strain, saving those special seeds that showed unusual traits.

Ecology is a dynamic process, and one of its abiding characteristics is its highly idiosyncratic nature. Organisms adapt with astonishing specificity to niches in place, time, and conditions. Evolution can actually occur very rapidly, even within a generation, in response to environmental conditions. So it is that there are thirty thousand kinds of rice in the world, or eighty thousand varieties of wheat, or ten thousand types of apples, each with distinct and meritorious characteristics.

All these cultivated food plants, or *cultivars*, also have *wild relatives*, un-domesticated ancestors that often grew around the edges of early gardens. They provided fresh rounds of resistance and strength to the new plants, which were wholly dependent on humans for their survival.

Centers of Diversity

A brilliant Russian botanist, Nikolai Vavilov, discovered in the 1920s that there are centers of diversity around the world where these wild plants originated and then evolved into their myriad forms. Vavilov, an ornery genius who scoured the world for seeds, discovered eight centers (later expanded to twelve), mainly around the equator, where the plants had enjoyed the longest coevolution in nature, permitting multiple mutations and permutations. In a luminescent twenty-year burst, Vavilov and his army of twenty-six thousand assistants managed to transport two hundred thousand species from around the world to the first major seed bank in the world in Leningrad.

Tragically, in a conflict of scientific opinion with a Stalinist Russian scientist, Vavilov was banished to a military prison camp, where he died in 1943. Meanwhile, the seed bank he had amassed came under threat during the terrible siege of Leningrad-St. Petersburg, which lasted for nine hundred brutal days during which six hundred thousand people starved to death. His loyal botanists risked bullets and bombs to venture into nearby fields to propagate potatoes for their collection. When they ran out of food to eat, they faced the awful choice of either eating their collection or starving to death. Soldiers entering the facility found their emaciated bodies amid untouched sacks of rice, potatoes, corn, and wheat, a legacy they held more valuable than their own lives.

Fortunately the martyrdom of Vavilov and his band of botanists was not in vain. They knew that the species diversity they were gathering was already seriously on the wane in the twentieth century. They had seen the invaluable role played by these many kinds of plants and their wild relatives as backup genetic resources for failing domesticated crops, beginning with a troubling series of blights in the 1870s.

Years later, Asia's rice crop was threatened with a disease, sending scientists scurrying through forty-seven thousand kinds of rice stashed in seed banks around the world. But they finally found what they needed in the wild, a plant growing in a valley in India, just before that valley was flooded by a dam.[25]

The land races and their wild relatives have held the key to renewed disease resistance; they have helped restore the dynamic equilibrium that is at the core of adaptive evolution. Today's crop species are estimated to have acquired 50 percent of their increased productivity from breeding with old strains.

Hybrids Rattle the Food Chain

When breeders first created hybrid corns in 1926, their appeal was obvious and immediate. The result of the secret crossing of two parent lines, hybrids exhibited higher yields and "hybrid vigor." But even more importantly, they produced a proprietary advantage for their inventors, who were the only ones possessing the trade secret of how they did it. In addition, in the next generation of the hybrid seed, the yields dropped sharply, so that farmers couldn't save the seed as they had done for countless generations. Soon almost all commercially sold corn was hybrid. By 1956 the inventors were obtaining patents on their work, and companies like DeKalb and Pioneer Hi-Bred became wealthy.

Following World War II, two gigantic industries rattled the food chain with hybrids. The decentralized diversity that characterized U.S. vegetable production gave way to the technological imperative of the food processing industry, which sought uniformity for its automated logic. As the biggest industry in the world, food was about to become frozen on the road and denatured on the assembly line.

Simultaneously, manufacturers discovered a use for the massive amounts of nitrogen-based chemicals left over from World War II weaponry. In a literal shift from nitrogen swords to chemical plowshares, they fashioned petrochemicals into fertilizers and a host of toxic applications against insects

A mere 7 percent of farms control over 50 percent of agricultural production. Fifteen agribusiness corporations provide 60 percent of farm supplies. Sixty companies perform 70 percent of food processing. Three cereal companies provide 80 percent of prepared breakfast cereals. Six companies handle 95 percent of wheat and corn exports. (Jack Doyle, *Altered Harvest*.)

and diseases. Since 1945, the increase in overall pesticide use has risen 3,300 percent,[26] while the increase in overall crop loss due to insects *has also risen*—20 percent in the same time period.[27] In 1991, 2.2 billion pounds of pesticides were applied in the United States and sales that year of conventional pesticides alone, which comprise just half the total, equalled $7.78 billion.[28] These chemicals are very, very big business.

The forces of mass food production and chemical farming converged to produce an industrial agriculture more akin to mining than farming. Companies chose crop varieties based on traits attractive for qualities such as uniform ripening, toughness of skin for mechanical harvesting, and tensile strength for shipping. These "genes of commercial importance" took precedence over those for nutrition and even taste.

Food processors began to mandate the varieties that could be grown, even for experimental purposes. There was no room for a bioregional variety of foods in the Westinghouse refrigerator of Doris Day in the fabulous fifties. The issue was tonnage when a mere 1-percent increase in tomato solids could mean an added $100 million a year to producers, ketchup for the American Dream of the "same hamburger all across the country."

But the genetic uniformity of hybrids did not hit its stride until Norman Borlaug made the hybrid wheat that seeded the so-called Green Revolution. Borlaug bred a wheat that produced very high yields when powered by large quantities of nitrogen fertilizer and petrochemical pesticides and herbicides, as well as copious water. He would win a Nobel Prize for feeding the spiraling population of the world's hungry poor. Unfortunately, the gains proved to be short-term.

After first proving the "miracle" strains of wheat in Mexico in the 1950s, Borlaug released them into India, Pakistan, and Turkey with the support of the Rockefeller and Ford foundations. At first, the Green Revolution did achieve miraculous results. It increased Mexican wheat yields sixfold in twenty years and soon accounted for 95 percent of the crop. India's wheat production doubled, and it became food self-sufficient, a momentous achievement.

By 1976, the developing countries planted the new seeds on 44 percent of all land in wheat and 27 percent of all land in rice.[29] But the Green Revolution was affordable only as long as it was massively financially subsidized by governments, and as long as petrochemical prices were low. The miracle hybrids were not cheap—at two to three times the cost of other seed—and they made several seed companies very rich. They also demanded lots of costly equipment, from tractors to the irrigation gear that transported the flood of necessary water. They required ever more chemical inputs, a factor of 600 percent from the 1960s to the 1980s. Because the fertilizer stimulated intensive plant growth, it also encouraged more weeds to grow, requiring more herbicides to kill the unwanted growth. The powerful pesticides also killed off the many beneficial insects, and farmers thereby had to deal with larger numbers of their natural prey.

Closeup of tat soi rosette greens at the Seeds of Change farm.

Modern agribusiness compounded the danger of crop uniformity by planting vast expanses of these few kinds of hybrids. These amber waves of grain are huge monocultural bull's-eyes that pose a virtual invitation to extinction. By creating a single worldwide environment of basic uniformity, the Green Revolution opened the farm gates wide to the prospect of a blight or a pest that could conceivably exterminate, not only whole crops, but the genetic conformity that now stretched across entire regions and continents.

There has been a systematic erosion of genetic diversity by the seed industry. After first reducing the variety of available kinds, the industry introduced one-gene resistance, splicing the same gene into virtually all the crop varieties and planting them in large monocultures. Moreover, breeders have used a very few elite varieties as the main parent strains. In 1981, a survey of a hundred plant-breeding programs found that breeders employed these elite species for 95 percent of wheat, 83 percent of corn, and 79 percent of soybeans for pest-resistance traits in new varieties.

The federal Office of Technology Assessment is adamant about the foolishness of genetic centralization. "Pressures brought about in the evolutionary process have developed such a high degree of complexity in both resistance and virulence mechanisms that breeding approaches, especially those using single-gene resistance, can easily be overcome."

According to the National Academy of Sciences, a given technological advance in crop production often rests on small numbers of genes. If one of these genes is incorporated into many varieties, the crop becomes correspondingly uniform for that gene. If a parasite with a preference for the characteristics controlled by that gene were to come along, the stage would be set for an epidemic.

The promise of the Green Revolution has since faded to a toxic brownout. Four decades of a chemical-dependent hayride have devastated the country's soil. Far worse than the infamous Dust Bowl of the 1930s, U.S. topsoil is being depleted at the terrifying rate of an inch a year, an annual loss of an area the size of Connecticut. Millions of years in the making, an estimated 75 percent of topsoil has vanished since the Europeans set foot, livestock, and plow on the continent. Meanwhile, a third of cropland is exhibiting marked decline in productivity. Historically, topsoil depletion has been a root cause in the demise of several civilizations.

Agricultural chemicals have widely polluted water supplies and aquifers as well. Almost half the waterways in the United States are now classified by the Environmental Protection Agency as damaged or threatened, and agriculture is considered the largest single nonpoint source polluter (wastes that do not emanate from a single point source). Pesticides and nitrates from synthetic fertilizers have shown up in groundwater in twenty-six states.[30] Clean drinking water may soon become the "oil of the '90s," a matter capable of causing wars, certainly never part of the peaceful promise of the Green Revolution.

This boom-and-bust cycle of chemical dependency and short-term-memory hybrid genetics has reduced "the life of a new cultivar to that of a pop record."[31] Crop losses from pests have increased 20 percent since the 1940s.[32] The pesticides don't much bother the bugs, which are more populous than before. Ironically, in the last forty years, the percentage of crops lost to pests has doubled, while losses to disease have also increased. Over a thousand wheat farms in Australia and twelve in England are being overrun with weeds resistant to the herbicides. Over five hundred species of insects are known to have developed resistance to the chemicals that are supposed to control them.

Yields, the main benefit touted for hybrid seeds, began to level off or drop by the mid-1980s. In addition, per capita production fell because of the degradation of the land with severe salinization and related problems created by the heavy inputs of chemicals and the system's thirst for water.

LIFE IS CHEAP—FOOD IS NOT

The Green Revolution's promise of cheap food ended with the Arab oil embargo of 1972. Oil prices skyrocketed and, with them, the costs of the petrochemical-based farming regimen. The formula of expensive seeds, costly chemicals, and high-tech equipment that already favored only the larger, wealthy farmers drove the centralization of agriculture into even fewer, bigger hands. As a consequence, more people left family farms and crowded into hungry, unemployed urban areas.

But the most destructive impact of the Green Revolution was the hybrid double-cross, which brought the world to the brink of the mass extinction of ancient crop varieties. The introduction of hybrids caused the systematic elimination of the many local endemic seed varieties that had served people reliably for countless centuries and millennia. Many of them disappeared permanently in favor of the "progress" of the "miracle" seeds.

Several countries subsequently tried to depart this treadmill of hybrid dependency by returning to their proven native species. Nevertheless, countless strains of ancient native crops bit the dust. "Since the domestication of agriculture," writes the investigative journalist Mark Schapiro, "perhaps 90 percent of all plant varieties have developed through the forces of nature; 9.9 percent by the efforts of humanity up to the present century; and 0.1 percent by modern breeding methods. Yet today's modern corporate breeders, in barely a wink on the evolutionary time scale, have turned that one-tenth of one percent into a living threat to the rest of our genetic base."[33]

"The seeds came with the genetic code of the society that produced them," lament seed specialists Fowler and Mooney. "They produced not just crops, but replicas of the agricultural systems that produced them."[34] With the extinction of the seeds also went the loss of the traditional cultures that coevolved with them.

Ironically, however, the materially rich countries of the north are botanically poor. Most of the invaluable germ plasm that Nikolai Vavilov identified and collected originates in the biologically rich countries of the South. The South, which holds the living treasure, is increasingly disinclined to share its genetic resource so freely with the North. It has certainly not gotten a fair deal in the past. Several countries have closed their doors entirely to stem the gene drain to the North. Others are demanding intellectual property rights and royalties, a proposal received by large business interests in the North with all the enthusiasm reserved for open-heart surgery.

After all, one potentially useful gene from the South can contribute a farmgate value of $1 billion a year in the North. Germ plasm from the South is estimated to contribute around $66 billion of value annually to the U.S. economy. With genes now being patented by large multinational corporations in anticipation of the "Gene Revolution," access to the gene pool is a high-stakes game whose outcome will determine the complete control of the world food supply. It is not going to be a free lunch.

VERTICAL DISINTEGRATION

The cumulative peril from this concentration of genes and lineage is not merely biological. It is also wrapped in corporate monopoly and bar-coded with patents.

At the same time that the National Academy of Sciences identified dangerous uniformity in the biology of crop production, this dispassionate body also found that this "uniformity derives from powerful economic and legislative forces."[35] A peculiar convergence of corporate forces has aligned to create an inbred monopoly seeking to corner the agricultural market literally from the ground up.

The seeds of Job's Tears.

The U.S. food system is the largest industry in the world at over a trillion dollars a year. It contributes over one-quarter of the U.S. gross national product and supplies one of five jobs. Since its incipient automation after World War II, it has become increasingly centralized, marching to the orders of the huge food processors controlling massive markets.

By the 1960s, the Great American Dream of the same hamburger all across the country was becoming a reality. The Green Revolution united the food production apparatus with the giant chemical and pharmaceutical industries, generating enormous profits from the sales of chemicals in agriculture. With the introduction of hybrid seeds into the equation, it was only a small step up the ladder of vertical integration to the golden rung of the seed industry.

Estimated at $45 billion a year, the seed business was especially attractive for its very high profits and profit margins. Analysts viewed it as safely harnessed to a rising population with a constant appetite. But controlling seed also represented a virtual monopoly over this absolute necessity of food and agriculture, the first link in the food chain. As one Upjohn corporate official revealed, "Farmers plant seeds every year. It's a meat and potatoes business."[36]

In the last twenty years, over a thousand independent seed houses have been acquired by multinational corporations and Fortune 500 players, mainly from the chemical and pharmaceutical industries. Many of these companies manufacture the synthetic fertilizers and pesticides onto which they are yoking the seed trade. Gardeners would be puzzled to find their seed catalog orders going to the parent companies of Monsanto, Royal Dutch Shell, Upjohn, Sandoz, Imperial Chemical Industries (ICI), and Ciba-Geigy, entities more likely to be associated in the public mind with antibiotics and gas pumps than gardening.

Patenting Life

The multinational seed companies are now furtively pursuing what may be the most sinister final act of the millennium: the gene rush. The scramble is on to control life's very genetic information, or "genfo," as Alan Kapuler terms it. The caper is taking place increasingly under frozen lock and key in unsafe deposit boxes containing fleeting, incomplete samples of the world gene pool. The "common heritage" of the gene pool is becoming concentrated in the few hands of the most powerful interests that control the world food supply. They are working to patent seeds and the genetic alphabet at the core of life.

The genfo race is speeding toward its destination of uniformity on the wheels of patents. The Plant Variety Patent Act (PVPA) of 1970 forever changed the world of seeds by granting certificates of protection to hybrid varieties. According to the official story from the U.S. Department of Agriculture, the act was to assist global trade and spur scientific innovation. The consequences have been the opposite, serving instead to restrict the flow of germ plasm and increasingly privatize and concentrate its control. The very large seed companies hold the vast majority of plant and vegetable seed patents. Seed patents have created monopolistic pricing, and because they are expensive to obtain, patents exclude all but the largest players, thereby limiting competition.

Ironically, the seed industry objected to plant patenting in the 1950s on the grounds that one cannot patent living things. It changed its position radically by 1970, and access to seed is among the most highly controlled functions in agriculture today. Farmers and scientists are now unable to exchange germ plasm freely as has been customary throughout human history. With the addition of a seed certification law, farmers are now commonly prevented even from saving their own seed or selling modest quantities to a neighbor, an ancient tradition of self-reliance. One seed company has mounted and won twenty lawsuits against farmers and other seed handlers for unauthorized sales of the company's soybeans.[37]

Because traditional open-pollinated seed varieties and land races cannot be patented, they have been devalued and largely retired from the playing field. In Europe, for example, the major seed companies have banded together to form the Common Catalog, an officially sanctioned listing in which only patented varieties may be sold legally. In reality, this means solely the patented corporate hybrids. Commercial trade in the traditional seeds that grandmother got from her grandmother is becoming illegal. Over two thousand open-pollinated old varieties have already been removed from the European market. In Britain, three firms now control almost 90 percent of the garden seed market. In Europe, three-quarters of traditional vegetable seeds are at risk of extinction because of the hybrid monopoly.

Meanwhile the seed industry denies the statistical reality that the introduction of hybrids is a primary cause of the extinction of old varieties. "The seed industry is whistling a merry tune as they pass the graveyard at night," comment Fowler and Mooney grimly.[38]

Patent protection was of profound importance to the large multinational companies accustomed to dealing in such currency for pharmaceutical drugs and petrochemical products, where a single proprietary product patent can be worth serious money. Monsanto, for instance, rakes in $1 billion a year from Roundup, its most popular pesticide. "To be enforceable, laws require that new patented varieties be internally consistent and uniform," observe Fowler and Mooney. "This quest for uniformity pleases both lawyers and pests."[39]

The Gene Rush

The issue of patenting reached another historic threshold in 1980 when the Supreme Court ruled that a genetically engineered bacterium could be patented as a proprietary life form. The ruling opened the door on owning life, including specific genes. Merely changing a gene or two in an otherwise ancient organism could now secure it in a Wall Street portfolio. Fewer than a dozen companies own most of the plant patents, and more and more seed companies are owned by or linked with biotechnology entities.

The first biotechnology patent out of the gate from the "gene-jockeys" was issued to DuPont Agricultural Products in 1992 for a soybean gene with tolerance for a class of herbicides. Other companies are also patenting specific genes and technological processes. Among them is the ability to place genetic identifiers, marker molecules that are the owner's cellular signature to prevent unauthorized use. "It's like being married to the only redhead in the world—if you see a redheaded kid, you know where it came from," says a cheerful representative of Pioneer Hi-Bred.[40] This kind of cellular surveillance is bound to limit the flow of genetic diversity.

Generally the hybrid industry has oriented its work almost exclusively to mass crop varieties for farmers. Its primary criteria for desirable attributes have been yield, speed, and uniformity, industrial values with little interest for backyard gardeners. But a few of the larger home gardening seed companies had breeding programs of interest to multinational corporations, and they were acquired, including Northrup King (by Sandoz Ltd., the gigantic chemical-pharmaceutical multinational) and Ferry-Morse (by Groupe Limagrain, the huge French agroindustrial multinational). Only five major companies today dominate the U.S. home gardening seed market, and three in Europe control 80 percent. The companies sell mainly the same seeds to gardeners as to farmers, but farmers are their primary market. Farmers get the top-grade product because of serious liability issues to do with crop failure.[41]

Seed Banks or Seed Morgues?

Ethiopia, where coffee originated, had lost almost 90 percent of its tropical forests by 1965. Meanwhile new diseases are attacking coffee today, and Ethiopia has closed its doors on the transfer of germ plasm. The situation underscores the importance of seed collections. The seed industry and the federal government for years have assured the world that they maintain deep seed banks for just such an eventuality. The state of the world collection system is not reassuring, however.

Storing the world's largest and most valuable seed collection on an earthquake fault midway between a nuclear plant and a nuclear weapons facility is the sort of thing governments seem to have a knack for doing. Apart from its geomantic bad fortune, the primary U.S. Department of Agriculture National Seed Storage Laboratory at Fort Collins, Colorado, which contains around two hundred fifty thousand samples, has also suffered multiple difficulties, including power failures, broken refrigeration equipment, and understaffing that has left enormous, chaotic piles of seeds uncatalogued.

"Seeds of Change ended up having to do something that was somewhat unnatural. But to get the seeds out to people is to get them back into the natural state again. What we're doing now is an amazing harnessing of civilizations. We're holding the seed as guardians, and trying to get it out again so that it can actually return back to its natural state." **Rich Pecoraro**

Coffee rust virtually destroyed the coffee industry in Ceylon, Asia, and East Africa. An epidemic of stem wheat rust in 1904 caused the United States Department of Agriculture to begin a disease-resistance program, and in 1917 the epidemic struck again, causing Calvin Coolidge to declare two "wheatless days" a week. Two more epidemics occurred, which wiped out 65 percent of the U.S. durum wheat in 1953 and 75 percent in 1954. The National Academy of Sciences report on the subject in 1972 found that "wheat rust epidemics of modern times are clearly genetically based." (Fowler and Mooney, *Shattering*.)

It is actually possible that more genetic diversity is becoming extinct in the seed banks than in the wild. Seeds are alive and cannot be treated like library books. Samples must generally be grown out within five years to retain their viability. According to a plant physiologist at Fort Collins, "Within five or ten years, you may have lost half of the genetic material you started with."[42] Investigators in 1989 found that less than a third of its samples even germinated, making it not a seed bank but a "seed morgue."[43] Seventy-two percent had not been tested in five years.[44]

Public attention on this scandalous situation, including a high-profile lawsuit brought by the activist Jeremy Rifkin, caused an uproar that led to improvement of the facilities, completed in December 1992. Officials at the lab contend that they now have "the most modern and efficient seed storage facility in the world."[45] The system includes liquid nitrogen cryotanks for "state-of-the-art storage media for long-term seed storage." Director Steve A. Eberhart also contends that the lab's germination rates are higher than reported in many samples, and that many of those with low germination rates came to the facility in that condition.

Nevertheless, the goal of maintaining viable seed stocks is best served by frequently growing them out. There are many subtleties to grow-outs. Seeds are highly responsive to local conditions and adapt accordingly, as is the genetic nature of life. This phenomenon creates "genetic drift," producing a somewhat different strain that may no longer hold the original characteristics. Scientists from the Fort Collins facility grew out a native southwestern corn in a plot in Iowa. The primary attribute of the corn is its tolerance of less than ten inches of rain a year. In Iowa it rains enough that the seed is almost sure to drift (perhaps even float).

The world's seed collections do not really reflect diversity at all; they mainly represent moderate collections of the world's main food crops. After the early formation of Leningrad's Vavilov Collection Center and the National Seed Storage Lab at Fort Collins in 1958, a loose network of underfunded, uncoordinated gene banks formed globally to collect about half a million varieties, predominantly cereal crops, along with some legumes (beans) and potatoes. One disturbing study found a direct correlation between seeds collected and the geography of road systems, in other words, drive-by diversity.

The conditions and budgets abroad and in the developing countries are far worse than in the United States. In the former East Germany, where a world-class collection contains sixty-eight thousand accessions, including perhaps the world's best tomato and barley collections, one observer characterized the conditions as appalling.[46] In India, four important species an hour are being lost in a country with forty-five thousand plant species, a third of which exist nowhere else. The country has set up 419 "gene sanctuaries" because "biodiversity is the long-term security for the poor."[47]

The biologist Garrison Wilkes asserts that only fifteen of the world's seed banks are viable. There is a lack of funding to grow out collections on any regular basis, and inventories are usually incomplete and inaccurate. In addition, a common problem is that seeds are often dried improperly at high temperatures, which kills them. Many seeds exist in samples too small to regenerate, as well. Collections such as the Seed Savers Exchange contain numerous varieties not held by the seed banks. Of the 1,799 varieties of beans grown by the Seed Savers Exchange network, only 147 were listed in the U.S. National Plant Germplasm system.

The Richest Storehouse

No coherent worldwide collection system exists today even to begin to address the problem of the loss of plant genetic diversity. Even if it did, human systems inevitably break down, and nature is a far surer repository for the living treasure. Though the world's one hundred seed banks and thirteen hundred botanical gardens can provide some measure of backup, natural ecosystems are the true and lasting homes for species.

Experts agree that the destruction of the tropical forests is the most menacing habitat loss, because these forests hold as much as two-thirds of the biodiversity on the planet. The tropics have never been covered by glaciers during an Ice Age, as the northern temperate forests have. Consequently life has evolved uninterrupted, spawning an extraordinary variety of life forms in continuous coevolution.

According to Vice-President Gore, "Most biologists agree that the rapid destruction of the tropical forests, and the irretrievable loss of the living species dying with them, represents the single most serious damage to nature now occurring. The wholesale annihilation of so many living species in such a breathless moment of geologic time represents a deadly wound to the integrity of the earth's painstakingly intricate web of life. . . . The world will lose the richest storehouse of genetic information on the planet."[48]

Substantial damage was done early on with the European arrival in the Americas of the plantation economies of sugar, rubber, cocoa, coffee, and bananas. But just in the last twenty years, cattle have ravaged a quarter of all the forests in Central America. Already 65 percent of the forests of western Amazonia have been cleared or converted into palm-oil plantations. The tropical rain forests around the world now amount to less than half their original prehistoric cover.

According to Edward O. Wilson, "If destruction of the rain forest continues at the present rate to the year 2022, half of the remaining forest will be gone. The total extinction of species this will cause will lie somewhere between 10 percent and 22 percent. The real figure might reach as high as 50 percent or more thereafter."[49]

These forests also serve as the lungs of the earth. There is a direct correlation between tropical deforestation and global warming. Climate change is certainly no ally of inflexible hybrid monocultures, plants whose adaptable wild relatives have already succumbed to extinction by lumber mill, banana plantation, or cattle ranch.

It seems foolish to believe that humankind can build vaults to capture and contain the complexity of living biology that nature has taken billions of years to evolve in the living laboratory of the earth. Though preservation by seed banks is one valuable and necessary strategy, it is unstable and very limited in scope and capability. The preservation of wild ecosystems must be

Three-fourths of the soybeans grown today originated from six plants from China. All the sorghum in the United States contains cytoplasm from one original plant. The Latin American coffee industry's botanical lineage returns to one tree in the Amsterdam Botanical Garden. (Fowler and Mooney, *Shattering*.)

The seeds of Simmons Red
Streak Lima Beans

the centerpiece of conserving biodiversity, along with the creation of living gardens where life may continue its evolution.

The New Pharmers

Control of the world's seeds casts a lengthening shadow in the artificial light of the impending biotechnology revolution. Biotech pivots on the manipulation of genes. Access to the gene pool is the ticket for entry into the game. Increasingly, control of the germ plasm is falling into the private hands of companies whose interests are proprietary and profit-driven. At the same time that First World governments and corporations bemoan the imminent global danger of extinction of humanity's "common heritage" of the gene pool, they are organizing the most centralized system of privatized control ever conceived, one that fits other commercial agendas, not the interests of the public or the environment.

Jack Doyle, director of the Agricultural and Biotechnology Project of Friends of the Earth, sees a dangerous conflict of interest at hand. "On balance, biotechnology will help major chemical and pharmaceutical corporations maintain their pesticide position in agriculture, while giving them the means to gradually develop and sell a range of genetically altered crop, microbial, and biological products."[50]

The original promise of biotechnology was that genetic engineering would help eliminate the use of chemicals and pesticides by splicing in traits such as pest and disease resistance. To the contrary, it turns out that the companies are engineering plants with increased tolerance for the pesticides, herbicides, and chemicals produced by their parent chemical and pharmaceutical companies. Twenty-seven chemical-pharmaceutical companies today are actively working to make major crops resistant to chemicals, including Royal Dutch Shell, the largest pesticide manufacturer, which now owns one of the largest seed companies.[51]

The chemical giant Monsanto has perfected a Roundup-tolerant gene made from a bacterium that it is using in soy and canola breeding programs. Roundup is the company's herbicide flagship, a $1-billion-a-year cash cow to which the company is understandably attached. Biotech leader Calgene is developing cotton varieties resistant to bronoxynil, which is a reproductive toxin in humans and thus considered hazardous to farm workers. According to Vice-President Gore, "The Department of Agriculture has declared herbicide-resistant plants a research priority and is actively supporting the field test of bronoxynil- and 2-4-D-resistant potatoes, and the Forest Service is encouraging the use of herbicide resistance in forestry, greatly expanding the market for toxic chemicals."[52]

Some seeds are now routinely coated with chemicals prior to sale. These agrigenetic packages are specified by the producer, a vertically integrated package deal of hybrid seed, chemical fertilizer, and toxic pesticide or fungicide. By controlling the first link—seeds—these companies are assuring the use of their chemical product lines.

Ciba-Geigy, the Swiss chemical-pharmaceutical giant, sells herbicides for weeds that compete with sorghum. Because the chemicals also harm the sorghum, the company provides another chemical to treat the sorghum seeds to protect them. Ciba-Geigy sells this chemical directly to the seed companies, which treat the seeds prior to sale to farmers.[53] Little if any data is available on the chemicals' effects on the seeds and emerging plants.

Just as seeds have been an essential product for large companies to control the world's most basic industry of food, genes now represent the final frontier. A second Green Revolution is at hand, but this time it is a Green Gene Revolution, a bioengineered food system based on the ingredients of privatized germ plasm and the menu of monopoly.

Biotech: The Green Gene Revolution

Poised on the two-headed cusp of the biotechnology revolution, the seed genetics industry comprehends the depth of public controversy it could provoke. Scientists are reporting to work today at the gene bank and the cell library. Using tissue culture technology, they take cellular samples of a plant and grow it out in the laboratory. They cook up large batches of plant embryos and bathe them in liquid fertilizers and pesticides. Then they ready them for sale to farmers and gardeners, eliminating all the chancy, costly, time-consuming vagaries of agriculture and seed production. How will the

Four kinds of potatoes that are very closely related genetically make up almost three-quarters of U.S. acreage. Only ten varieties of wheat dominate, although there are 250 available varieties. Four kinds of rice account for 65 percent of the crop, two peas for 96 percent, and three snap beans for 76 percent.

twenty-first-century Norman Rockwell picture eager gardeners poring over their spring seed catalogs in gleeful anticipation of embryo-planting season?

The Green Gene Revolution is mutating from monocultures to clonal-cultures. Entire fields will be planted in monocultures of identical clones derived from the cell tissue of a single plant, chemical-fed and lab-bred.

Using such methods, the genetics industry contends that it can produce even greater genetic variability in the lab than is found in nature, since genes are the source of biological diversity. Given the immense variability found within nature and its incomprehensible complexity, this assertion is hard to take seriously. In light of the failures of the Green Revolution, the similarly extravagant promises of the Green Gene Revolution do not inspire confidence.

The scenario of bioengineering food takes on added significance in considering the prospective larger yields that can be produced. The human population is continuing to expand exponentially. Today's population of 5.5 billion people is expected to double or triple by the middle of the next century. The world will need to produce as much food from 2000 through 2020 as people have collectively consumed in the last ten thousand years. But since 1984, world grain production per capita has fallen 1 percent a year. In 1990, eighty-six nations grew less food per head than they had a decade before.

With a lot of mouths to feed, the commodity futures on food are looking bankable. Several of the major companies have already experimented with single-cell proteins (SCP) manufactured by microorganisms. According to the Office of Technology Assessment, "With the advent of new biotechnology, and the threat of potential world food shortages, interest in single-cell protein may once again return."[54]

Above all, a bioengineered food system is programmed for cellular centralization beyond biological precedent. Nature does not favor centralization. To the contrary, nature appears to rely on diversity precisely as a hedge against all the evolutionary permutations that threaten the life of an organism and its prospective lineage.

Rescuing the Living Treasure

Modern social ecology seems to support the mistaken belief that humans can exist separately from nature and natural law. The culture of corporate centralization exemplified by plant patenting is as dangerous a strategic threat to the gene pool as the actual physical loss of organisms and genes. The acquisitive corporate vector to own life is now pitted against the gene-rich Third World nations, which possess key germ plasm, and against a loose confederation of passionate seed collectors.

Spreading diversity into many hands and lands is merely biological prudence. If diversity is to be saved, it may well be by the direct individual actions of visionary botanists and biologists and committed backyard gardeners creating a green necklace of living gardens in newly grown centers of diversity around the world.

Traditionally, gardening has been regarded in Western culture as the province of the dumbest sons. Ironically, gardeners are emerging as principal biological heroes in the struggle of the era to maintain the biological diversity that sustains life on the planet. Backyard biodiversity is becoming prime territory for the conservation of life.

DEEP DIVERSITY

Alan Kapuler is exalted in the sanctuary of his seed room in his Oregon home, surrounded by the thousands of varieties he has amassed over a twenty-year cycle. He knows every seed here in this one-person center of diversity. All the batches are meticulously cleaned, winnowed of off-kinds, and germination-tested. He prowls about the room like some kind of amazing two-legged pack rat muttering in Latin. He is cataloguing two large collections he just inherited, a rare grouping of beautifully speckled Castor beans and a heritage of poppies from the seed collector Frances Hoffman. On the walls are maps of the world flora that he contemplates frequently, looking for the gaps in his collection, scouting the structure of diversity. He often travels the short route to the Oregon State University library to study the botanical literature.

In the early part of this century, blights took Bartlett pears. Blights took sorghum in 1924, and 86 percent of the oat crop in 1946, when thirty oat varieties succumbed to the blight of a common genetic parent. (Fowler and Mooney, *Shattering.*)

Nature is active today, however, and with his wife and three daughters, Alan walks a quick distance through driving snow to a funky greenhouse under the seasoned stature of an old native sequoia. To the trained eye, the emerald enclave is a virtual treasure house of rare plant species. Plants are growing everywhere, as his family takes broom handles to the interior of the plastic roof to shake off the weight of the unusual snow. His three daughters giggle and run about like a pack of enchanted animals, thrilled at the exotic snow and its countless possibilities for mischief.

Each girl has a special plant collection in the greenhouse. Dylana, the fair-haired, round-faced, six-year-old youngest, is partial to esoteric cacti, which her father helps her collect, she explains bashfully. Eliyrea especially likes the mint family (at the moment she also favors theatrical hats for her wide-eyed eight-year-old fantasies).

Kusra, the eldest at thirteen, is gentle and friendly. When I ask her about her favorite plants, the orchids, she matter-of-factly reels off a list of Latin names, stopping when it becomes obvious I have no idea what she's talking about. She is a serious plant person who can hold her own with any Ph.D. botanist from the Ivy League. Even the mention of ivy is certain to provoke a spontaneous Latin commentary.

Kusra and Alan invariably wander off to the corner of the greenhouse where a small, misted room is sealed off. The warm, moist cubicle is a mini–rain forest of rare orchids, more than two-thirds of the species of the entire Asian Lady Slipper genus. Alan and his father have nurtured several of them for thirty years, and Kusra for virtually her entire short life. She has taken striking photographs of these otherworldly beauties and sends them to friends as cards.

"In terms of diversity, the only plants I knew something about were orchids," Alan notes. "I liked species, meaning the ones that grew wild. They weren't hybridized. They just grew here on the world." The greenhouse orchids look like flowers from outer space, parading wild bursts of color in perfectly shaped feminine forms. "They call them Lady Slippers because the goddess of wisdom walks around on the earth in the flowers of these plants," Alan reveals.

"I've looked at orchids for four decades now. I feel very grateful to have discovered that, on your windowsill or in your small little greenhouse, you can grow some true treasures of the earth. They grow for your whole life, and if you take care of them, they propagate and make more, and you can pass them on to your kids. If you grew them from seed, these are plants that may take five to ten or twenty years to flower.

"There are times when you'll look at a flower or take a breath of something fragrant, and it will rejuvenate your own sense of wonder at being alive. You'll lose some of the ingrained cynicism that comes from living in a world where everything has to have a use. You'll have a plant with a beautiful tiny little flower. Someone will say, 'What good is it?' When people say that, I wonder, 'What good are you?'

"Here's the gift that we were born into. It's marvelous, it's interesting, and a lot of it doesn't have any use that we know about. Yet it gives us a thrill about why we're alive and why it's worth being alive. The dominant view of diversity is always based around use value. It's a very narrow view."

Indeed, the standard dialogue on diversity revolves around a shallow ecology of food plants and a few big-ticket species with basic use values mainly as clothing, medicine, and shelter. Yet most of the biological realm remains unexplored, and we don't know even within the nearest order of magnitude the number of species in the world. Even what we do know, we don't know much about. "Over 99 percent of species are known only by a scientific name, a handful of specimens in a museum, and a few scraps of anatomical description in scientific journals," says Edward Wilson. "It is a myth that scientists break out a bottle of champagne when a new species is discovered. Our museums are glutted with new species. We don't have time to describe more than a small fraction of those pouring in each year."[55]

Teosinte, one of the oldest wild relatives of modern corn.

Biologically speaking, we are not playing with a full deck. Diversity is deep, and virtually all of it is unexplored. The subtle, hidden biological connections among life forms in the kindom remain an invisible world to us. Yet clearly evolution has struck a fantastically complex balance of forces, veils within veils of mysterious relationship of which we remain numbly ignorant.

Tragically, these life forms are rapidly becoming "history, not biology," as Alan observes. Strange extinctions are occurring around the world today in which entire populations, seemingly whole and healthy, fall off the face of the earth in a matter of months. Several species of frogs have vanished in such mass extinctions, and their disappearance is a biological warning, a canary in the ecological coal mine signaling that something is very wrong.

One of the senseless ironies of chemical farming is that it kills the microbial life of the soil. Microorganisms actually manufacture the soil, among other tasks. They are among the least understood and most important organisms on earth. A mere teaspoonful of soil from central Norway contains five thousand kinds of bacteria, Wilson points out. A few hundred miles away in flats off the coast, another teaspoonful contains five thousand more, all different and most unknown.[56] Still, microbial diversity is virtually unexamined, a neglected frontier of profound importance.

If lethal agricultural pesticides were really effective in killing all the insects and microbes, the land would become sterile, and nothing would decay and rot away. The human population would be dead in about six months, the rest of the creatures soon after, and finally the plants. Without fungi, plants could not have colonized the land, and vice versa. Predators that do not enhance their prey eliminate their food supply. The real law of the jungle is a partnership founded on diversity and mutual interests.

The Community of Life

Nature seeks dynamic equilibrium, and planet earth is a literal theater-in-the-round with a diverse cast of characters on a living set dressed by ecosystems. Biologists have identified total ecosystems as the key element in preserving diversity. Although there are biological keystone species upon whose existence entire communities depend, the extinction of single organisms is less the issue than the conservation of habitats that support the totality of community life. Biologists have learned that ecosystems must maintain a certain critical size, or they decay rapidly beyond repair.

"Lewis and Clark came here to the Pacific Northwest around 1805," Alan points out. "There were half a dozen botanists who explored the region, and then in the 1820s they released pigs into the Willamette Valley. What they ate, we have no idea. Prior to Caucasians being here, the Indians managed the valley by setting controlled fires. In recent epochs, we have had to deal with the growing of large monocultural fields of grains and with intensive grazing by animals. What do we call a native flora anyway?"

Observers point out that we are burning books we haven't even read yet. How do we save what we don't even know? This urgent question has haunted Alan Kapuler the biologist for many years. The anguishing prospect of flying blind in a blizzard of extinctions is torturous.

The Beginning of Wisdom

By the mid-1980s Alan's mounting interest in gardening with an expanded palette of vegetable species was not quelling his deeper alarm at the shrinking deck of biodiversity. "After growing hundreds and hundreds of batches of seeds several times, and ending up growing 120 tomatoes, it got me to wondering whether I wasn't wasting my life by not growing the kinds that really needed to be grown. The question is, What really needs to be grown? What can anybody do toward figuring out what needs to be grown?

"I'm gardening in the backyard and looking around and realizing there's a weed over there. I don't know what it is. You're sitting on a piece of earth, and right outside there's an interesting plant, but you don't know what it is. When you can identify it nine times out of ten, you're beginning to find out about diversity. Go into anybody's backyard; can you tell every tree, every family? You begin to recognize the degree of ignorance that we all have about the local biosphere.

"When I started to make the seed list to sell seeds, it made a lot of sense that five or six families are what grow in the Pacific Northwest in the autumn. That led me to put the seed list in biological groups. By the time you're done with all the food crops, you say, 'Well OK, but what about all the other plants that there are?'

"So I began to want to know about how the ones that we were growing fit into the rest of the plants, and that got me on the journey of looking for a way to formulate the world flora. I need to know what the fabric of the world flora is to know what to grow and save. That's what I can be doing as I run a seed company."

Poring over botanical volumes and science journals in the Oregon State University library, Alan came across the taxonomic work of Rolf Dahlgren, an innovative Danish botanist who died in 1988. Taxonomy is essentially plant genealogy, a literal "roots" of plants that shows their kinship relations. "In all cultures, taxonomic classification means survival," remarks Wilson. "The beginning of wisdom, as the Chinese say, is calling things by their right names."[57]

In the work of Rolf Dahlgren, Alan found a key to understanding the structure of plant diversity. "What Dahlgren did is a continuation and development of what people interested in plants have been doing for as long as people have been walking on the earth," Alan explains. "See the plant with the red flowers? It has good fruit. You tell your kid, 'I want you to go get some berries from the tree that has the good-tasting fruit.' She says, 'Which one?' You say, 'The one with the red flowers.' As our minds work, we associate in patterns of relationship. When you look at similarities it's called cladistics, looking at relationships coming from common ancestors having characteristics in common. There are old plants that gave rise to other plants that gave rise to other plants. We're looking at lineages, histories written in the genetic material that have to do with the fabric of life."

In the nineteenth century, Linnaeus was considered the father of modern taxonomy because he systematized the plants and used the Latin two-name system, a genus name and a species name. Alan found that Dahlgren was one of the first to use extensive modern chemical and biochemical information, molecular information on who's related to whom, and how. Dahlgren also provided a two-dimensional, bubble-shaped mapping system, innovative because it moved away from linear, alphabetical lists to a more open framework of holographic knowledge.

A Genetic Road Map

For Alan, the Dahlgren system provided the missing link by showing the natural structure of plant kinship, a genetic road map that permits the systematic conservation of biodiversity. By knowing the relationships, he suddenly saw the possibility of figuring out how to collect a representative sample of the full deck of the world flora.

"I'm a seedsman and I'm growing seeds and I want to know, What should I grow? What's really rare? The first thing you find out is that there are 540 flowering plant families. How many have I ever seen seeds offered for? Temperate zone, tropical zone, all the vegetables and the flowers we grow—what part of the basic framework of the whole thing am I looking at? I haven't seen half of them.

"For example, the Umbels are nine tribes, six subtribes, 385 genera, and 2,853 species. Which ones are available as seeds? When I went through and finally laid out in depth how a tribe is built and what's available, I saw that there are no seed supplies at all in the United States for five out of the nine tribes."

The system opened up Alan's concept of a seed company as a broader vehicle, beyond food plants or plants with known use values. Along with offering large "gene-pool" sets of particular plants such as corns or tomatoes, he would offer many rare seeds of plants without any immediately known virtue except significance to genetic diversity.

The Dahlgren system revealed to Alan hidden relationships among plants. He found that the carrot is first cousin to ginseng, for example. The implications of this kind of discovery are profound. If you are looking for medicinal plants, why not start with their known relatives?

Kingram Gardening

The Dahlgren taxonomy also suggested to Alan a revolutionary approach, not only to seed collecting, but to gardening. He invented the idea of "kingrams," garden layouts based on kinship relationships that can actually demonstrate evolution in your backyard. "It's a new paradigm in gardening," he says exuberantly. "Every one of us as individuals can be curious about some groups, which we can collect and grow to begin to see what nature has wrought. You can see it in a tree; you can see it in a grain of sand. I see it well in the distribution of species in a genus. When we take those species and genera—there are thirteen thousand genera and some three hundred thousand species—and we continue to lay out those fabrics in kinship gardens, we will make new discoveries about how life is built."

In early research tests at the Seeds of Change farm, Rich Pecoraro has found that the kinship relationships among seeds directly correlate with their affinities to growing conditions. Creating the kinship gardens will open up a living laboratory of evolutionary biology. Only two other Dahlgren gardens exist today, in Hungary and China. The sole U.S. professional institution that has shown interest in the area is the Missouri Botanical Garden under the direction of Dr. Peter Raven, a brilliant botanist who collaborated with Dahlgren.

Until the recent discoveries of molecular biology, taxonomy was a musty nineteenth-century antiquarian subject, a faded flower pressed between the dusty pages of botany. But according to Dr. Michael Novacek, dean of science at the American Museum of Natural History, "Systematics is no longer old-fashioned stuff. It's a whole new realm that gives you a way to look at all the genetic relationships between organisms."[58] The inner molecular journey is already revealing many puzzles of evolution and of life itself.

The Dahlgren system was also made possible by computers, which can compile large bodies of information and relate them on many different levels. Alan and his collaborators have entered about three-quarters of the known world flora onto a Dahlgren database, and the taxonomic database is likely to yield many insights into the plant kindom. He likes to call his kingrams "molecular phylogenies of biohistory," a catchy gardening idiom if ever there was one.

Backyard Evolution

"As I've been looking at orchids for years," Alan ponders amid the heavy scent of his greenhouse sanctuary, "I've wondered, How does evolution occur? It happens when individuals become successful and propagate and turn into large numbers in a certain area. Then when the climate changes and the boundaries are different, some of them are able to succeed and grow in new conditions, and they turn into clusters of related species."

Leaning intently forward, Alan's eldest daughter Kusra points me to one particularly radiant orchid. She tells me that she and Alan suspect that we are witnessing evolution in action, the development of a new genus right before our eyes.

"As Kusra and I study the Chinese Lady Slipper *Paphiopedilum micranthum*, we find indications that it may represent a new genus, the next higher level of grouping, which is considerably more unusual than finding a new species. With three hundred thousand species of plants, there are about thirteen thousand genera. Since discovery of the emergence of a new genus happens only rarely, understanding how to see it allows us to understand what is happening.

"There are many kinds of interesting plants that people can grow in small groups and collections. Although we need to conserve habitats, we need to have the living plant, so when we want to rebuild the habitats we have the stuff to start with. Nothing is more important than conserving our diversity."

The seeds of Mandan Red corn.

1. Edward O. Wilson, *The Diversity of Life* (Cambridge, MA: Harvard Univ. Press, 1992), p. 15.
2. Wilson, *Diversity of Life*, p. 74.
3. Joseph Campbell, *Historical Atlas of World Mythology*, vol. 2, *The Way of the Seeded Earth* (New York: Harper & Row, 1988).
4. Kathleen Harrison, speech given at the Seeds of Change Conference, September 1991.
5. David Suzuki, *Metamorphosis: Stages in a Life* (Toronto: Stoddart, 1987), p. 228.
6. *American Orchid Society Bulletin* 31, no. 9 (September 1962).
7. *American Orchid Society Bulletin* 35, no. 7 (July 1966): 544.
8. National Academy of Sciences, *Lost Crops of the Incas: Little-Known Plants of the Andes with Promise for Worldwide Cultivation*, report of an ad hoc panel of the Advisory Committee on Technical Innovation (Washington, DC: National Academy Press, 1989), p. 18.
9. National Academy of Sciences, *Underexploited Tropical Plants with Promising Economic Value*, report of an ad hoc panel (Washington, DC: National Academy Press, 1975).
10. National Academy of Sciences, *Amaranth: Modern Prospects for an Ancient Crop*, report of an ad hoc panel of the Advisory Committee on Technology (Washington, DC: National Academy Press, 1984).
11. *Lost Crops of the Incas.*
12. *Lost Crops of the Incas*, pp. 1–13.
13. Cary Fowler and Patrick R. Mooney, *Shattering: Food, Politics, and the Loss of Genetic Diversity* (Tucson: Univ. of Arizona Press, 1990), p. 176.
14. Albert Gore, *Earth in the Balance: Ecology and the Human Spirit* (Boston: Houghton Mifflin, 1992), p. 144.
15. Fowler and Mooney, *Shattering*, p. ix.
16. "Will We Run Low on Food?" *Time*, October 19, 1991.
17. Fowler and Mooney, *Shattering*, p. 139.
18. *Garden Seed Inventory: An Inventory of Seed Catalogs Listing All Non-hybrid Vegetable Seeds Still Available in the United States and Canada*, compiled by Kent Whealy, 3d ed. (Decorah, IA: Seed Saver Publications, 1992).
19. Whealy, *Garden Seed Inventory.*
20. George Ball, Jr., "Stand Up for Hybrids," *New York Times*, Op-Ed Week in Review, March 21, 1993.
21. Fowler and Mooney, *Shattering*, p. 84.
22. Ball, "Stand Up for Hybrids."
23. Ball, "Stand Up for Hybrids."
24. Gary Nabhan, Native Seeds/SEARCH.
25. Gore, *Earth in the Balance*, p. 136.
26. David Timentel et al., "Handbook of Pesticide Management in Agriculture," 2nd edition (Boca Raton, FL: CRC Press, 1990).
27. Timentel, Cornell University, as quoted by Lisa Y. Lefferts and Roger Blobaum in "Eating as if the Earth Mattered," *E Magazine*, January/February 1992.

28. U.S. Environmental Protection Agency, "Pesticides Industry Sales and Usage, 1990-1991 Marketing Estimates," Washington, DC, Fall 1992.

29. Fowler and Mooney, *Shattering*, p. 60.

30. Lisa Y. Lefferts and Roger Blobaum, "Eating as If the Earth Mattered," *E Magazine*, January/February 1992, p. 32.

31. Lawrence Hills, unpublished transcript of the Seeds Conference, held in Rome in 1981 by the International Coalition for Development Action (headquartered in Barcelona, Spain).

32. Lefferts and Blobaum, "Eating as If the Earth Mattered," p. 33.

33. Mark Schapiro, "Seeds of Disaster," *Mother Jones*, December 1982.

34. Fowler and Mooney, *Shattering*, p. 76.

35. National Academy of Sciences, *Genetic Vulnerability of Major Crops*, 1972.

36. Schapiro, "Seeds of Disaster."

37. Rollie Henkes, "Tomorrow's Seeds: Patent Pending," *The Furrow*, September 1992.

38. Fowler and Mooney, *Shattering*, p. 87.

39. Fowler and Mooney, *Shattering*.

40. Ronald E. Butler, "Patents: A Gradual Learning Process," *Seed World*, September 1992.

41. Jack Doyle, *Altered Harvest: Agriculture, Genetics, and the Fate of the World's Food Supply* (New York: Viking, 1985), pp. 191–192.

42. *New York Times*, September 21, 1981.

43. Associated Press, *Chicago Tribune*, March 27, 1989.

44. Associated Press, *Chicago Tribune*, March 27, 1989.

45. Personal letter from Steve A. Eberhart, Director, National Seed Storage Laboratory, USDA, Fort Collins, Colorado, April 9, 1993.

46. *Los Angeles Times*, September 24, 1991.

47. Reuters, August 16, 1992.

48. Gore, *Earth in the Balance*, p. 116.

49. Wilson, *Diversity of Life*, pp. 276–77.

50. Doyle, *Altered Harvest*, 229.

51. Doyle, *Coop America Quarterly*, Spring 1992, p. 16.

52. Gore, *Earth in the Balance*, p. 140.

53. Schapiro, "Seeds of Disaster."

54. U.S. Congress, Office of Technology Assessment, *Commercial Biotechnology: An International Analysis*, Washington, DC, January 1984.

55. Wilson, *Diversity of Life*, p. 132.

56. Wilson, *Diversity of Life*, p. 141.

57. Wilson, *Diversity of Life*, p. 44.

58. Jon R. Luoma, "Sophisticated Tools Are Giving Taxonomy a New Lease on Life," *New York Times*, February 18, 1992.

NUTRITION
PER ACRE AND THE NEW
CUISINE

Farmers are the health-care
practitioners of tomorrow.

Robert Rodale
chairman of the board,
Rodale Press, Inc.

nlike the seed industry at large," says Alan Kapuler passionately, "Seeds of Change is not interested so much in yield per acre as in *nutrition per acre*. We eat food for nutritional value. Seeds of Change is unique in the seed industry for making nutrition a primary criterion for seed and variety selection."

Alan has identified tomatoes with very high vitamin content that the company promotes. The Double Rich contains as much vitamin C as an orange; the Caro Rich has as much vitamin A as a carrot. Seeds of Change is establishing a new set of nutritional markers that will result in crop improvement across a much wider diversity of foods, many of which have been displaced by commercial agribusiness food production or have never before been widely available. Backyard biodiversity provides a great opportunity for nutritional gardening.

Today there is a great deal of evidence linking diet to health. Though it may be hard to change the world, we can change our diet. Moreover, changing our diet is also proving to be one of the most influential actions we can take to benefit the environment.

Substantial data indicates that a plant-based diet promotes good health, and that certain foods have specific therapeutic effects. Some of these healthful foods are so potent as to be considered "nutriceuticals," foods that can actually act as medicines.

The kinds of seeds used to grow these foods can also make an important nutritional difference. But there is also a body of evidence indicating that the way foods are raised, harvested, stored, and shipped exerts major influence on their nutritional content. Identical seeds may produce plants with substantially different nutritional values depending on whether they are cultivated organically or chemically. The way plants are processed into food products also affects nutritional values quite dramatically.

Diet and Health

According to the surgeon general, 68 percent of U.S. disease today is diet-related. Thirty percent of cancer is diet-related, according to the National Academy of Sciences. The cost of health care consumes 12 percent of the gross national product, sickening the economy. Federal health agencies and many medical experts now recommend a diet based mainly on vegetables, grains, and fruits, with much less meat and fat.

Today's dominant mode of animal-based agriculture has had severe environmental consequences, but personal health issues are an even greater concern to most people. High amounts of animal fat and protein are harmful to health. Poisons from pesticides also collect in the fatty tissues of the bigger animals higher on the food chain; 55 percent of pesticide residues in the U.S. diet come from meat, but only 11 percent from fruits, vegetables, and grains. For instance, even though DDT was banned in 1978, 99 percent of nonvegetarian mothers' milk contains the deadly chemical, as compared with only 8 percent of vegetarian mothers' milk.[1] Recent studies showed that women with the highest exposure to DDT had four times the breast cancer risk of those with the least exposure.[2]

The overall message is pretty straightforward: Don't have a cow. An impressive consortium of forces, including the National Cancer Institute, the National Research Council, and the Senate Select Committee on Nutrition and Human Needs, is advocating a plant-based diet to improve the national health. In its watershed 1982 study "Diet, Nutrition and Cancer," the National Academy of Sciences emphasized the importance of fruits and vegetables high in vitamins C and A. The Academy found that vitamin C foods can inhibit the formation of cancer-causing substances and lower the risk of stomach and esophageal cancers. It documented the fact that vitamin A

In 1985, North Americans consumed only half the grains and potatoes they did at the turn of the century. Today, according to a USDA survey, only 10 percent of Americans consume the recommended three or more servings of vegetables and two or more servings of fruit or juice daily. Twenty-three percent don't eat any vegetables, and 43 percent don't have fruit or juice. Meanwhile, however, Americans are consuming a third more dairy products, half again as much beef, and almost triple the poultry. This diet results in more fat by one-third and excessive protein levels. (EarthSave, "Our Food, Our World: Realities of an Animal-based Diet.")

•Sixty-four percent of U.S. cropland is used to produce grain to feed livestock, and only 2 percent for fruits and vegetables for human consumption. Livestock production sucks up half of all the water used in the United States and requires a hefty half the total energy expended in American agriculture. Livestock are also directly responsible for 85 percent of the topsoil loss from cropland, pasture, rangeland, and forest.
•Water pollution from livestock is greater than that from all municipal and industrial sources combined.
•According to the Worldwatch Institute, "Oil is used in the livestock industry for fuel, for transport and tractors, chemical fertilizers, and pesticides; so much, in fact, that the animal products could be considered a petroleum byproduct." (EarthSave, "Our Food, Our World.")

foods containing beta carotene, as well as foods in the cabbage family, reduced the risk of lung, breast, bladder, and skin cancer.[3] Fruits and vegetables provide the vast majority of vitamins A and C in the U.S. diet.[4]

A very unusual scientific study recently added to the convincing evidence in favor of a plant-based diet. The study tracked 6,500 Chinese in sixty-five counties across rural China and found that a balanced, primarily vegetarian diet drastically reduces the risk of contracting the diseases that are the main killers in Western society. Rates of cancer and heart disease were dramatically lower, as was osteoporosis. A primary diet of rice and a variety of vegetables engendered an extremely healthy life. Among the most common vegetables eaten in China are cabbages, mustards, onions, garlic, celery, spinach, turnips, radishes, cucumbers, gourds, eggplants, watercress, carrots, yams, potatoes, lettuce, and wild greens, as well as soybean products, including miso and tofu, and beans such as fava, kidney, mung, and aduki. Only 10 percent of the Chinese diet comprises meat and fish, and it is consequently very low in fat.

Within Seeds of Change, many people are vegetarians. Several others, myself included, are not. There are varying belief systems within the group, ranging from strict vegan and macrobiotic to omnivorous. Diet is always an extremely complex and emotional issue, and we do not have a unified group ideology about it. A diversity of diets is a realistic and acceptable condition of life. Seeds of Change supports the very real health and environmental benefits of a primarily plant-driven menu and supports vigorous social change in that direction.

Hippocrates' first law of medicine is to "do no harm," and there is little question that nutrition is largely a safe course of action, unlikely to endanger people. Changing the food system to one that is more plant-based is likely to go a long way toward improving the national health, reducing the national medical bill, and restoring the environment.

Food: The Primary Medicine

The concept of "food pharmacy" is emerging as an advanced way to use diet to achieve optimum health. Increasing numbers of studies have documented the anticancer properties of vegetables, whole grains, and fruits, as well as their benefits for a healthy heart and for prevention of many other illnesses.

A mix of beets, including Detroit Dark Red, Yellow Mangel, and Lutz Salad Leaf beets, freshly picked at the Seeds of Change farm.

Foods with documented anticancer properties include broccoli, cauliflower, green cabbage, Chinese cabbage (bok choy), kale, radishes, turnips, carrots, and green onions. Vegetables and fruits high in beta carotene have shown strong effects against lung and other cancers. These include such foods as carrots, spinach, broccoli, kale, squash, and apricots. Foods high in vitamin C that reduce the risk of stomach and esophageal cancers as well as heart disease include tomatoes, broccoli, and brussels sprouts. The cruciferous vegetables, broccoli, cabbage, cauliflower, turnips, and brussels sprouts, are linked with reduced risk of cancers of the gastrointestinal and respiratory tracts. Fiber, from such sources as beans, broccoli, brussels sprouts, and whole grains, protects against colon cancer. Selenium and vitamin E, found in whole grains, are anticancer agents. Research by the National Academy of Sciences on foods that prevent cancer found broccoli and brussels sprouts were generally the most potent.[5]

According to the nutritionist Jean Carper, evidence suggests that eating cabbage raw or cooked as seldom as once a week may cut your chances of colon cancer by 66 percent. Eating a carrot or half a cup of spinach a day reduces the risk of lung cancer by half, even for former smokers. A tablespoon of olive oil can counteract the cholesterol of two eggs. A hot chile meal three times a week clears the respiratory system and helps prevent colds and bronchitis, or can actually treat emphysema. Two teaspoons of jalapeño pepper can protect against heart disease.[6]

A full cup serving of kale daily contains enough beta carotene to prevent cancer and heart disease, according to James Duke, Ph.D., a food pharmacy

Although only about 3 percent of people in the United States are vegetarians, fully 20 percent deliberately eat a diet high in vegetables today. Of the increasing numbers of people eating more fresh vegetables, grains, and fruits, 80 percent cited health concerns, and 40 percent ethical reasons.

expert at the U.S. Department of Agriculture. Dr. Duke points out that tomatoes can lower hypertension, soybeans can prevent cancer, fava beans help prevent or alleviate Parkinson's and Alzheimer's diseases, raw onions can help treat diabetes, and heroic garlic prevents hypertension, heart disease, and cholesterol.[7]

Nutriceuticals

Intriguing scientific studies now show a direct link between nutrition and the body's immunity. According to Jane E. Brody in the *New York Times*, "Researchers studying the often-surprising effects of nutrition on immunity report that dietary manipulation can become a promising new tool to foster recovery or prevent disease in millions of people. 'We are discovering that some nutrients can be used, not so much as foods, but as modulators, manipulators, or stimulators of the immune system,' said Dr. Robert A. Good, a pediatrician and immunologist at All Children's Hospital in St. Petersburg, Florida. 'This could turn out to be pretty powerful medicine if we understand it better.

"'In recent years,' Dr. Good elaborated, 'scientists have been teasing out the immunological effects of nutrients like dietary fats, amino acids, vitamins A, E and B-6, and the minerals zinc, iron, copper and selenium.'"[8] They are finding, for example, that the amino acid arginine can help prevent postoperative infections and that common polyunsaturated fats can impair immune responses that protect against cancer.

Even large companies are embracing nutriceutical foods. Ocean Spray is interested in the "cranberry factor" for treating cystitis, an infection of the urinary tract. Lipton is working with a brain researcher to design a soup that could boost memory in the elderly, including those with Alzheimer's disease. Campbell Soup is researching "good mood" foods.[9]

"We can isolate and extract and regulate the beneficial compounds and formulate 'designer food' products that could fight disease," according to Dr. Herbert Pierson, a toxicologist who directed the National Cancer Institute program to study *phyto-chemicals*, micronutrients that have disease-prevention properties. Among Dr. Pierson's findings are that onions lower cholesterol, and chiles are pulmonary strengtheners. "The future is prevention," continues Dr. Pierson, who believes that food products have a starring role. "It's more cost-effective than looking for new drugs." Dr. Pierson added that delays in the approval of new drugs and the high number of drugs that fail the screening process have forced science and the government to "look at food as preventive medicine of the future."[10]

"Aminostrone"

"The correlation between folk medicine and phyto-chemicals is astounding. It convinces me that people's tastes are shaped at least in part by a subliminal knowledge of what keeps them alive," says Dr. Chris Beecher, an assistant professor of medicinal chemistry at the University of Illinois at Chicago who has catalogued over nine hundred phyto-chemicals (plant medicines) common in nature that studies have found could prevent certain diseases.[11]

One of the oldest folk food remedies is minestrone. Minestrone is probably a universal concoction, a generous blend of fresh vegetables in a rich soup that has traveled the world's folkways for centuries. While contemplating the role of food in nutrition, Alan Kapuler speculated that a principal source of nutrition in minestrone might have been overlooked.

"Several years into gardening, I was growing 120 varieties of tomatoes because I was curious about heirlooms," Alan recalls. "I know I'm not going to be growing 120 kinds of tomatoes for the rest of my life. All I knew was that I wanted the most nutritious tomatoes out of the lot. I wondered how to find that out—do something that's nutritional. It occurred to me to test for free amino acids."

As a molecular geneticist, Alan knew that free amino acids are at the core of the genetic code. Nucleotides and amino acids are the cellular chemical units that combine to form DNA, RNA, and proteins. Twenty amino acids specified by the genetic code build protein. One of the great discoveries of molecular biology was that the genetic code is built from twenty amino acids and nucleotides, specified by triplets of nucleotides. This is the core of life. Alan wondered whether free amino acids might be a

In animal studies, adding the "nonessential" amino acid arginine to the diet enhanced immune responses and preserved immune function in the face of malnutrition and advancing cancers. (Jane E. Brody, "Intriguing Studies Link Nutrition to Immunity," *New York Times*, March 21, 1989.)

more direct route to nourishing the body, rather than proteins, which must then be broken down into amino acids for digestion.

Alan also knew that doing tests for free amino acids is one of the easiest biochemical determinations. "If you spray amino acids with ninhydrin, they turn purple. One of the basic and first things they teach you in elementary biochemistry is how to do liquid chromatography. The people at Rockefeller had figured out how to separate peptide and amino acid mixtures so that, if you broke a protein into peptide fragments, you had all the twenty amino acids of a protein. Then you could analyze the amino acids and figure out the composition. You could actually look at how the proteins made from twenty amino acids are built differently, distinguishing a blood protein from a skin protein by the exact definition of its composition."

Alan got a sheet of window glass, poured cellulose powder on it, and then put one drop of tomato juice on the bottom. He took rubbing alcohol diluted with a little water and created liquid chromatography of amino acids. "I took 120 varieties of tomatoes, and spotted their juice on the bottom of plates. The results amazed me. There were these big purple spots all over them. Nobody ever told us that tomato juice was loaded with free amino acids."[12]

As a student of molecular biology looking at the food system, Alan gained new insight. "You could see that different tomato varieties have different patterns. Proline stains yellow rather than purple, so you could see that salad greens had a lot of proline in them. I started squeezing the juice of everything that I had in the garden, and there were amino acids in everything. I had grown up in biochemistry, where the notion was that free amino acids were basically found in the seeds of legumes. Early in the history of biochemistry, before the discovery of the genetic code, researchers found toxic amino acids in the legumes, creating a negative bias against their investigation. But here was a clear spread of the twenty essential amino acids across a wide diversity of the common vegetables."

Alan began a systematic investigation of the common vegetables for their content of free amino acids. "A good example was the Burbank tomato. Luther Burbank, who is a legendary name, spent his whole life crossing, selecting, and deriving plants, and was interested in the flavors of fruits and the fragrances of flowers. Burbank was a hero of mine, and when the Seed Savers Exchange offered an heirloom tomato that Burbank selected, I got some seeds and grew out this tomato. It turned out to be an early, productive small-bush tomato with medium-sized red fruits.

"When I squeezed the juice and got an amino acid analysis, Burbank's tomato came out with the most free amino acids of eight varieties. I was truly flabbergasted. Here was a man who did no chemistry and no analysis but selected a very highly nutritious variety of tomato.

"Then we started to juice potatoes. Potatoes were a staple in our diet, and I didn't think there'd be many free amino acids in potatoes. My notion of a potato is a bag of starch, which is all sugar, but I knew there was a little protein in potatoes. We squeezed the juice of potatoes and found they're loaded with free amino acids. There are more amino acids that make proteins in a potato than there is protein in a potato. What that does theoretically is to double or triple the known nutritional value of a potato.

"In collaboration with the head of the bioanalytical laboratory at Washington State University, Dr. Sarangamat Gurusiddiah, I ran tests on thirty-nine different kinds of vegetables. I never expected to find all twenty amino acids that make proteins free in the juices of common vegetables. This important discovery immediately made it evident to me that one could differentiate nutritional cultivars based on this data. I realized that perhaps minestrone is really 'aminostrone.'"[13]

The various amino acids have distinct characteristics and therefore potential applications to health or medical conditions. The Peacevine cherry tomato, for instance, is remarkably higher in the calming amino acid gamma-amino butyric acid; Seeds of Change likes to call it the mellow tomato. One of the primary energy sources for the brain is glutamine. Alan found that okra, onions, snap beans, asparagus, black salsify, Chinese artichokes, potatoes, and Bolivian yacon have high glutamine levels. Among the vegetables the very highest in free glutamine are peas, which challenges the notion of calling someone a "pea-brain."

In theory, Alan speculates, "One could design certain salads for demanding mental work, and others for difficult physical labor. Instead of eating pills, we could eat fruits and vegetables, growing them as we learn to heal ourselves."

Eating food in combination, such as corn and beans, has served to provide us all twenty amino acids because each food complements reciprocal deficiencies. Another way to achieve the same end is by supplementing food with amino acids. For example, rice and millet, whose proteins are low in methionine, threonine, and lysine, have been successfully supplemented with free amino acids in Japan, Brazil, and India, among other countries. In Japan it is common to add lysine to amino-acid-deficient grain flours and breads. In the United States, it is illegal, but one could legally achieve the same results by supplementing wheat with the juice from potatoes.

The area of free amino acids clearly requires more research to substantiate this work. The widespread use of amino acids in other countries and other positive experiments indicate that more research is appropriate and that its results potentially have broad relevance.

The scientific understanding of nutriceuticals and medicinal meals is very young, and it is clear that this field holds great promise for the future of health and medicine. The heritage of diversity of agricultural crop cultivars provides a living resource of healthy foods with tremendous value. These seeds of diversity hold new keys to molecular nutrition.

Nutritional Erosion

Hippocrates, the ancient Greek medical mentor who said, "Let your food be your medicine," mercifully did not live to see the invention of iceberg lettuce. Like this half-witted lettuce, most modern hybrid food plants have not been selected for their nutritional value.

The nutritional quality of foods is determined by two main factors, which raise a classical philosophical question: Is the outcome determined by the original genetic composition, or by the environment? Is it nature or nurture?

According to the National Academy of Sciences, "Nearly all plant breeding programs in the U.S. emphasize yield, uniformity, market acceptability, and pest resistance. Plant breeders have lacked resources to extend their evaluation to factors of nutritional importance for reasons of time, effort, cost, technology, and lack of defined goals. Nutritional quality has not been recognized as a distinct dimension in plant breeding programs."[14]

To add deficiency to injury, however, breeding F1 hybrid plants for the typical industrial traits—tensile strength for shipping, uniform ripening, and cosmetic appearance—generally *lowers* the plants' nutritional values. Along with soil erosion and genetic erosion, nutrition is eroding at its base.

Researcher Jack Doyle interviewed a tomato breeder at the University of California, M. Allen Stevens, who stated that "some of the characteristics considered desirable for mechanical harvest are in opposition to those needed for vitamin C." Doyle goes on to point out that breeding to maintain the crimson gene in certain tomato varieties for cosmetic reasons can lead to a decrease in beta carotene.[15]

"The genes for yield and those for protein content were connected to one another, but not in a complementary way," Doyle describes. "In fact, the more breeders selected and cross-bred for increased protein content, the lower the yields of a cereal variety would be. Conversely, breeding for yield often lowered the protein levels of a crop." He records that an official of the Northrup King seed company stated, "In wheat generally, protein and yield are inversely correlated."[16]

Doyle reports that Alan T. Spiher, who headed a food review process for the Food and Drug Administration, said that "data show that a recently developed new variety intended for mechanical harvesting and the concomitant marketing techniques developed for this variety, deliver to the consumer a tomato having about 15 percent less vitamin C content."

Tinkering with the infamous Lenape potato, which was relentlessly bred for improved "chipping" quality, actually turned it into a "poison potato" that had to be quickly and quietly removed from the market. Despite such events, the FDA decided against monitoring or regulating the potential adverse effects of plant breeding.

"Plant breeders and seed companies say consumers are more interested in shape, color and consistency than nutrition," Doyle continues. "They wouldn't buy a yellow tomato in 1956 with more carotene. The juice was more toward orange juice in color and consumers wouldn't buy it. Asgrow [a large seed company] invested a lot of money and was left holding a big bag of seed" of the yellow tomato. The companies have since continued to maintain that consumers are more interested in cheap and abundant food than nutrition.[17]

Despite the unfortunate fact that generally there is an inverse correlation between yield and nutrition, the prevailing philosophy of these large food producers remains that nutrition is a much less important consideration than yield and tonnage, and even taste. The prevailing attitude is that consumers do not care about nutrition. "Even the poorest of the poor do not eat for the sake of nutrition," says one typical scientific textbook on crops and nutrition. "Food in all societies is considered one of the pleasures of life, and the decision what to eat is guided by the money available, tradition, and the taste of food, but usually not on the nutritional quality of food."[18]

High-Nutrition Hybrid: Defeating Success

In conventional food farming, nutritional enhancements are generally designed to feed livestock rather than humans anyway, a fact illuminated by the following story, in which breeders successfully created a hybrid corn with improved nutritional content, only to drop the corn like a hot potato.

Researchers at Purdue University discovered a corn with a high content of lysine, an essential amino acid that people, pigs, and chickens must get from food sources because they cannot synthesize enough of it themselves. Through breeding, they doubled the corn's lysine content and found that it dramatically improved nutrition for children, hogs, and poultry. "Hogs fed

Closeup of a squash blossom, early summer at the Seeds of Change farm.

the new corn gained five times more weight in a forty-five-day period than did others from the same litter fed regular corn."[19]

In many impoverished countries where corn is a primary staple, there is a prevalent disease of malnourishment called *kwashiorkor*, which causes an enlarged liver, bloated stomach, and sometimes death among children. "High-lysine corn can have miraculous effects on these malnourished children," *Saturday Evening Post* science writer Dr. Cory SerVaas told Doyle. Dr. SerVaas found that an emaciated child (whose usual diet was corn gruel and corn soup) given the new high-lysine corn showed immediate signs of improvement. "Not only did he gain weight," Dr. SerVaas reported, "but his bones began growing again as well. In three months, he had recovered completely."

But the high-lysine corn had a liability from the producers' point of view: it yielded 10 percent less than other hybrid corns. It also had other problems initially, suffering more insect damage and containing less starch, unacceptable to an industry dedicated to tonnage. Although several companies experimented briefly trying to resolve the problems, most dropped the work, with the exception of one company, which persisted and finally succeeded. Crow's Hybrid Corn Company matched conventional yields and overcame the insect and rot problems, but sadly the corn today is used only for animals, where it improves milk production in dairy cows.

The experiments with high-lysine corn, whose consumption appeared to improve human health, did lead to further tests. "In a study in a Guatemalan village on the fortification of maize with soybean flour and lysine, a significant reduction in morbidity and pre-school mortality was shown in children consuming fortified maize products in contrast to a control group consuming normal maize."[20] According to the authors, the discoveries of nutritionally superior maize stimulated intensive searches for similar genetic variants for amino acid composition in other cereals. One result was the first high-lysine barley, Hiproly, from Sweden. Pigs fed Hiproly showed "optimal growth without the addition of protein or amino acid supplements."[21]

A similar process occurred with a hybrid high-lysine sorghum that showed improved nutritional qualities in feeding trials compared with normal sorghum. "However," the authors concluded, "invariably the yield of these high-lysine genotypes in maize, barley, and sorghum is lower than the parental types from which they derive."[22] In addition, there were other drawbacks, including "seed appearance, size, reduced weight, slow drying and greater susceptibility to pest damage."[23]

In general, any breeding improvement in grain protein has been stymied by a "negative correlation between protein and yield."[24] As a consequence, there has been little work to improve the protein content of grains, including rice, corn, and barley.

It seems unfortunate that these successful examples of breeding hybrids for nutrition have not been taken further by the industry. That they haven't underscores the essential role of intention when creating hybrid seeds.

Open-Pollinated or Hybrids?

Food plants from open-pollinated seeds have shown superior nutrition over modern F1 (first-generation) hybrids, although there has been only minimal research on the subject. Because most F1 hybrids have been bred for industrial traits, the inverse correlation between breeding for industrial traits seems to favor higher nutrition from the open-pollinate plants.

Iceberg, a modern hybrid lettuce bred for industrial traits, has much less vitamin A than standard loose-leaf varieties such as romaine. European and North American varieties of potatoes have, in many cases, much lower protein and vitamin C content than the traditional varieties they are replacing in areas of South America. Delicious, Jonathan, McIntosh, and Spartan apple varieties are measurably lower in vitamin C than many older apple varieties.[25]

More research is vitally necessary to understand the effects of breeding plants for nutrition. A different set of agroindustrial priorities on the part of food producers and seed companies can be encouraged. Market demand resulting from consumer awareness may be the strongest force in changing their agendas.

Organic: The Birth of a Notion

Introductions of organic food products have increased by 400 percent since 1986, and organic beverages by an astonishing 1,450 percent. Two percent of farmers now grow organically, and by 1994, about 3 percent of the total U.S. food business is projected to be organic, reflecting a jump to $10 billion a year from the present $2 billion level. At that point, 8 percent to 9 percent of produce in America will be organically grown.

"If the nation's health depends on the way its food is grown, then agriculture must be looked upon as one of the health services, in fact the primary health service," wrote Lady Eve Balfour, who was among the first proponents of organic agriculture in this century.[26] Like her successors, J. I. and Robert Rodale, Lady Balfour recognized that there was a meaningful nutritional discrepancy between organic foods and foods raised chemically.

Lady Eve Balfour, niece of the British prime minister Sir Arthur Balfour, decided at the age of twelve to become a farmer. She and her sister later bought New Bells Farm in Suffolk and learned about agriculture during the depression in the 1920s and 1930s. Around 1938 she met the century's seminal organic proponent, Sir Albert Howard, and began to expound on her life's work on the relationship between organic agriculture and health. Her classic book *The Living Soil* (1943) stimulated an entire organic movement and led to the formation of the British Soil Association in 1946.

Lady Balfour's belief was that the primary factor in health is nutrition, and that the nutritional value of food is largely determined by the conditions under which it is grown. She undertook many experiments to document her theories and concluded, "The tests which have been made demonstrate that food grown from fertile soil rich in humus means good health and happiness, while the same food produced from soil impregnated with chemical artificial fertilizers causes bad health and sterility."[27]

During the period of the 1920s and 1930s, several U.S. scientists noted that food quality, along with animal and human health, declined when the synthetic NPK trinity of nitrogen/phosphorus/potassium was substituted for organic manures and compost. So striking were their findings that the scientists and over four hundred medical doctors in England published a statement in the esteemed British medical journal *The Lancet* calling for a revolution within medicine. They argued for a greater emphasis on preventive medicine with a balanced fertile soil as the foundation of a healthy diet.

These early proponents of organic farming advocated biological means of production over chemicals and poisons. They preferred the use of methods such as crop rotation and the use of beneficial insects and compost and manure. They espoused a model of cooperation with nature rather than domination.

The philosophic basis for organic agriculture is the health of the soil, yet even today scientists have barely scratched the surface of this revolutionary notion. The Soil Biotron in Michigan is the only laboratory in the United States that exclusively studies soil. It is an underground facility with a literal window on the mysterious interactions among plants, nutrients, animals, and microorganisms living underground. "Scientists have a very poor understanding of how energy and nutrients are transferred among organisms in the soil," admits Dr. James A. Teeri, a professor of biology and director of the station. "We know that there are lots of decomposers in the soil, and lots of small animals," says another Biotron scientist, "but we don't know much more."[28]

The Rodale Institute, which has been the central institution in the United States studying sustainable organic agriculture, recently altered its mission statement to reflect a new emphasis on the study of the soil, saying that heretofore "the soil has been treated like dirt." The Rodale Center plans to elevate the study of soil to its rightful place in the cycle of the biology of food production.

"Agriculture is a production-consumption-recycling system," observes Dr. Stuart B. Hill of McGill University. "By focusing on production and neglecting to recycle, soils have become depleted, imbalanced and even toxic. One of the aims of ecological or organic farming is to correct and avoid this situation."[29]

The Organic Prince

Like Snow White after biting the poison apple, the American public has been awakened by an organic prince at the dinner table. After the 1989

Closeup of a green hubbard squash.

national scare over Alar, the toxic chemical used to redden apples, people responded quickly in the marketplace by buying organic. Nearly a quarter of U.S. food shoppers now purchase organic foods at least once a week. The growth in sales of organic products doubled in the 1980s and is projected to double again in the 1990s.

Organic food is a movement turning into an industry, and it is consumer-driven. Consumers report three clear motivations for their organic choice: food safety, environmental health, and nutrition. Where once organic food was considered the province of tree-hugging, gap-toothed hippies, it has now entered the mainstream as a statement of quality and taste. Nutrition is playing an increasingly prominent role in the choices people make concerning their food, and, unfortunately, there is good reason to re-examine what we eat. The methods by which fresh vegetables, grains, and fruits are raised seriously affect their nutritional quality and safety.

Nutritional Farming: Organic Versus Chemical

Despite the enormous potential benefit that good nutrition holds for our nation's health, there has been only minimal government-sponsored study into the question of nutritional differences between foods raised organically and chemically. Many scientists have denied that environmental or cultural practices used to raise plants have any measurable effect. They maintain instead that the plant's original genetics are the sole determinant.

Although there is insufficient data to make broad generalizations, the few existing studies do indicate a clear pattern of evidence differentiating organic from chemically grown foods.

- Chemically grown foods exhibit a variety of toxicities and nutritional deficiencies.
- Organically grown foods show minimal toxicity and superior nutrition.

The Downside: Chemical Fertilizers

Nitrogen fertilizers are the basis of conventional chemical agriculture, and they exhibit several negative effects on crop nutrition and safety. They produce nitrates, chemicals that can be toxic. They also negatively affect other nutritional factors.

- According to Sharon B. Hornick, a soil scientist with the U.S. Department of Agriculture, "High nitrogen fertilization can increase yields and, in some cases, protein levels of certain grains, but in many cases the amino acid content of that protein is actually adversely affected. For instance, wheat and barley grown with high levels of chemical fertilizers are less nutritious with respect to protein quality than organically grown grains, despite their being higher in basic protein."[30] According to several experiments, true protein content was lower after application of NPK fertilizer, compared with organic fertilizer application.[31]

- Nitrogen fertilizers increase the amounts of toxic nitrates in dietary intake. Studies show that between 25 and 85 percent of the nitrogen in plants is derived from added nitrogen fertilizers. According to the National Research Council, six of the top seven, and nine of the top fifteen, foods with oncogenic (cancer-causing) risk are produce items, with high nitrate content from pesticides or nitrogen fertilizers.[32] According to a twelve-year comparison study, nitrate-nitrogen of vegetables from organically treated soil was sixteen times less than that of conventionally grown products.[33]

- Leeks and carrots grown in France were found to have significantly higher nitrate content when grown with conventional NPK inputs. In general, the authors of a study found, "the present practice of biological [organic] farming can significantly reduce the nitrate in vegetables in spring and summer, as was previously shown with lettuces in Switzerland."[34] Organically grown lettuces and potatoes were substantially lower in nitrates. The use of organic fertilizers can greatly reduce the nitrate content of vegetables. Organic agriculture could cut

At the same time that the nation's top scientists and health officials advocate a diet high in fruits and vegetables to improve the national health, these same products are subjected to immense amounts of nitrate-laden poisons. In the United States, ten pounds of pesticides are applied each year for every man, woman, and child, although, ironically, only 2 percent actually hit the bugs.

Closeup of Hopi early white sweet corn leaf and male flower growing at the Seeds of Change farm.

roughly by half the ingestion of nitrates from vegetable sources, this study concluded.

- Hornick also found that vitamin C content decreases in crops as available fertilizer nitrogen increases. "In controlled hydroponic experiments with available nitrogen as the only variable, ascorbic acid (vitamin C) in kale decreased by more than 50 percent when the nitrogen rate increased."[35]

- Excess nitrogen can also reduce carbohydrate synthesis, which can result in a lower content of glucose, a sugar that affects taste.[36]

- Excess nitrogen fertilization generally is found to diminish insect and disease resistance, deplete the storing ability, decrease the taste and flavor of fruits and vegetables, and decrease the protein value of processed foods made from those crops, according to Dr. Hornick's research.[37]

The Upside: Organic Nutrition

Organically grown produce has been found to contain higher nutritional content in several other studies. Doctor's Data, a private analytical laboratory conducting human nutrition research for medical doctors and patients, compared the levels of twenty-six important minerals as found in organically and conventionally grown foodstuffs.[38] The group took eight representative samples of organically grown and chemically grown foods purchased off the shelf in various stores in the Chicago area and used a state-of-the-art analytical device to measure the concentration of twenty-six minerals known to be vital in human nutrition. They compared nutritive values of organically and conventionally grown sweet corn, wheat, fresh pears, potatoes, fresh apples, rice, zucchini, and other crops.

- The organically grown foods were generally much higher in mineral content than their conventionally grown counterparts. This trend was evident throughout the testing procedures for all items tested.

- Four minerals that are considered harmful to humans—

Eighty percent of the known health risks come from thirteen pesticides on fifteen crops and products. Of greatest concern are tomatoes, beef, potatoes, oranges, lettuce, apples, peaches, pork, wheat, soybeans, beans, carrots, chicken, corn, and grapes. Broccoli, whose crucial health benefits are well documented, is treated with fifteen separate chemicals, and it can't be peeled. Apples can have up to a hundred different pesticides on them, seventy on bell peppers, and a hundred on tomatoes.

Carrots.

aluminum, cadmium, lead, and mercury—were generally lower in the organic foods than in the chemically grown foods.

Although the initial study has yielded some very important data, it does not contain a broad enough sample base in scientific methodology to draw definitive conclusions as to the superiority of one growing method versus another. Still, these results indicate that further study could have profound implications.

In a different comparison, which evaluated carrots and celeriac (celery root), the authors found the nutritional differences in these two vegetables resulting from the use of organic fertilizer to be significant.[39] This study showed that

- Organically grown carrots were 12 percent higher in beta carotene and significantly higher in vitamin B-1 than those grown with synthetic fertilizers. The authors concluded that cultural techniques appear to be the principal cause of the variation in beta carotene content.
- Organically grown celery roots generally weighed less and had lower total nitrogen-nitrate (–56 percent) and zinc (–19 percent), but were higher in dry matter, phosphorus, and vitamin C (+11 percent) than chemically grown celery roots.

The Schuphan Study

Probably the best long-term analysis of the nutritional superiority of organically grown foods is the comparative study by Dr. Werner Schuphan, for many years director of Germany's Federal Institute for Research of Quality in Plant Production. Dr. Schuphan spent thirty-six years researching soils and plants fertilized with compost and then, in 1974, undertook a twelve-year comprehensive study to further compare organic fertilizers, such as biodynamic compost and stable manure, with conventional fertilizers such as NPK or NPK-amended barnyard manure.[40]

Dr. Schuphan's conclusive study favored organic foods with findings that include the following:

- Organic foods have far higher mineral and trace mineral contents, except for sodium. The greatest increases found in organic produce were in iron and potassium. Magnesium and calcium were also substantially higher.
- Organic spinach contained 64–78 percent more vitamin C (ascorbic acid).
- Organic savoy cabbage contained 76–91 percent more vitamin C.
- Organic lettuce contained 59 percent more vitamin C.
- Organic crops have increased relative protein.
- Organic spinach and potatoes contained 11–47 percent more methionine. Heavy nitrogen fertilization results in a decrease in crops of the sulfur-containing amino acid methionine. According to Schuphan, diminished methionine content of crops due to heavy nitrogen fertilization results in decreased biological value of plant proteins.
- Organic manure application results in extremely low contents of nitrate-nitrogen. No hazards to health could be expected when such a "low-nitrate spinach" was fed to infants.
- Using chemically fertilized crops as the standard, Schuphan also demonstrated increases in dry matter in organically fertilized plants. In some organic crops, the gain in dry weight (after dehydration) was as high as 69–96 percent above the conventional norm. "The measure of a plant's food value is not in its size and weight at harvest, but rather in its dry weight, which more accurately reflects its actual contents," adds the researcher Gar Hildenbrand of the Gerson Institute. "Large, beautiful vegetables can be waterlogged and low in nutritional values. As one might suspect from the increased nutrient levels in organically fertilized crops, their dry weight is above that of their chemically fertilized counterparts."[41]

Fresh-picked scallopini squash awaiting processing at the Seeds of Change farm.

Animal Feeding Studies

No research has been conducted on human beings on the nutritional differences between organic and nonorganic foods. While field statistics from studies like Dr. Schuphan's measuring vegetables are impressive, some of the most revealing results have been derived from actual biological tests from feeding animals. "These feeding studies relate more directly to health than do chemical analyses, and can reflect factors that may not be detectable by chemical means," says a study from McGill University on the food quality of organic versus conventionally grown plant foods.[42]

A 1991 article prepared by Tina Finesilver of McGill University reviewed the literature on organically versus conventionally grown food, citing the following studies:[43]

- The original agricultural experiments begun by Lady Eve Balfour in the late 1940s at her farms at Suffolk, England, and conducted over a thirty-four year period found that cows on the organic section produced significantly more milk on 10–15 percent less feed than those on the "mixed section," where nitrogen fertilizers were employed as needed. The cows also had a better breeding record.[44]

- The sperm quality of bulls from a breeding station using organic compost applications was superior to that of bulls from a comparable station where pasture land had been treated with NPK.[45]

- The mortality rate at nine weeks of age for three generations of mice fed organically raised grain was 9 percent compared to 17 percent on chemically fertilized grain.[46]

- Hens given organically grown grain began laying at an earlier age, 166 days versus 181 days. The hens produced more eggs over nine months, 192 per hen versus 150 per hen, with a better keeping quality of 27 percent versus 60 percent spoilage after six months at room temperature.[47]

- Rabbits raised on organic hay showed superior fertility characteristics, including ovary weight, number of ovulations, number of egg cells found, percent fertilized egg cells, and number of uterine glands, compared to two groups of rabbits fed intensively fertilized hay.[48]

Other experiments supported the same conclusion: that organic diets provide health benefits to animals.

- A 1975 report comparing a common diet, which was a commercial preparation, with one of similar components that were organically grown over three years of experiments showed a significantly higher number of rabbits born alive in the organic diet group. The percentage of animals alive after ninety days in the organic diet group also was highest.[49]

- Organically grown produce fed to animals resulted in better egg production in chickens and increased disease resistance in other animals fed on the produce.[50]

- Organic dairy herds were shown to produce a higher milk yield on a lower ration of concentrates. Both the fertility of animals and their overall state of health were significantly better when they were organically raised.[51]

Animal feeding trials by the respected British nutritionist Sir Robert McCarrison early in the century found impressive results. In 1926, Sir Robert tested millet raised organically for its capacity to maintain the weight of pigeons and to promote the growth of rats. "Millet and wheat grown on fields treated with organic manure were found to be superior to the samples receiving no manure or chemical manure."[52]

Fair or Foul?

"Mirror, Mirror, on the wall—who's the fairest of them all?" asked Snow White's wicked stepmother. Large percentages of the foods that are treated with toxic pesticides are treated just to enhance their visual appeal and price. Today, our obsession with vegetable vanity, the superficial cosmetic appearance of our foods, has become a disguised threat to consumers' health and safety.

According to the California Action Network, "Experts estimate that 60–80 percent of pesticide applications for oranges, and 40–60 percent of

These nitrogen-based chemicals have since been documented to contribute directly to global warming, heightening the greenhouse effect and the climatic change that scientists believe to be the other single greatest threat to life on the planet besides the loss of biodiversity. Scientists estimate that we are increasing global temperatures dramatically, causing changes in climatic patterns whose impact is liable to be devastating.

Young crookneck squash growing in the field at the Seeds of Change farm.

pesticide applications for processing tomatoes are related to reducing cosmetic damage. High cosmetic standards require excessive use of dangerous pesticides and postharvest chemicals. As a result, consumers, farmers and farmworkers are exposed to more risks than are warranted by the 'cosmetic' benefit gained. Farmers must bear the cost of applying these extra pesticides. Cosmetic standards are used not, as consumers believe, to ensure the availability of 'quality produce,' but rather to ensure a limited supply of year-round produce at higher prices."[53]

The chemicals in question are all possible human carcinogens, and several are mutagenic, capable of causing birth defects. The fairest foods of them all are definitely not the safest.

How You Pick It

The postharvest handling of fruits and vegetables also affects their nutrient content dramatically. Apples and apricots picked green contained no vitamin C (ascorbic acid). However, if picked either half-ripe or fully ripe, the amount of ascorbic acid increased to approximately 18–60mg per 100g fresh weight, respectively.[54]

During postharvest handling of crops, temperature and humidity can have major negative effects. Therefore, it is important that crops are either consumed or processed immediately upon harvest to preserve their nutritional content.[55]

Yet most often the automated regimen of agribusiness systematically reduces the nutritional content of food plants by its very logic of hybrid seeds, chemical production, industrialized harvesting, protracted storage, and lengthy transport. The clear differences between foods raised organically and foods raised with synthetic methods shows the need for serious scientific investigation.

Organic Seeds: The Missing Link

In the 1920s, the nutritionist Sir Robert McCarrison experimented with cultivating seeds organically and chemically. His tests showed that the seed from a manure-grown crop was superior in its germination rate to other seeds. The longer the manure had been composted, the more impressive was this biological effect.[56]

This experiment is one of the only ones ever conducted on organic seeds. This oversight is more surprising considering the primary importance of this "first link in the food chain." In light of significant data showing the superiority of organically grown foods, testing the differences between organic and chemically grown seeds is crucial.

Seeds of Change was the first company to bring organic seeds to the national market. The company has deliberately worked to place the issue of organic seeds on the agricultural agenda, an action that has caused rumblings of consternation and controversy in the seed industry. Seeds of Change seeds are legally certified as organic, forcing disclosures from a number of other seed companies that had been implying that their seeds were organic when in fact they were not. One seed company responded to the challenge by saying that it "used as little chemicals as possible," which is comparable to being "a little bit pregnant." (Third-party certification is the only legitimate way to justify the claim that the seeds are organically raised. The appropriate agency, in our case Oregon Tilth, applies rigorous standards, physically verifies the growing conditions, and tests soil and water.)

Growing seeds organically is more difficult and requires more skill and care. It is more costly because it demands extra attention and hand labor. But for any committed organic gardener or farmer, it is obvious that the only authentic organic foods must be those grown from organic seeds. The seed industry and the organic community must make an unequivocal commitment to a standard for organic seeds, even if it means transitional hardship.

The seed industry and even the organic movement, however, are showing little sign of a transition toward organic seed production. Growers today do not use organic seeds because sufficient quantities are not widely available and they are more expensive. Proprietary hybrid seeds and patented seed lines that most growers buy are simply not available from seed companies in organic form.

▼▼▼▼▼▼▼▼▼▼▼▼▼▼▼▼▼▼▼▼▼▼▼▼▼▼

In 1988, the Environmental Protection Agency reported that seventy-four pesticides had been detected in the groundwater of thirty-eight states. Of this total, normal agricultural use accounted for leaching of forty-six different pesticides into the groundwater of twenty-six states. ("Biotechnology's Bitter Harvest.")

Closeup of a Black Imperial eggplant growing in the field at the Seeds of Change farm.

Seeds actually face a future filled with more synthetic chemicals than ever before. Aside from being raised chemically, many seeds are also then treated with insecticides or fungicides prior to sale to farmers and gardeners. "I suspect that all seed companies treat most of their seed, except the very few whose specific mission is to sell organic seed," comments François Korn, founder of SeedQuest, a world database on the seed industry. "You will find it most difficult, if not almost impossible, to get essential information in the area of seed treatments," laments Korn, who spent ten years in the fertilizer business prior to working for fifteen years as head of international sales for Harris Moran Seed, a large seed company.[57]

"Companies tend to wholesale-treat seed immediately after milling in order to protect their inventory. Certain companies choose not to treat certain species where treatment may damage the seed. Treated seed is sold both in bulk and in packets. Clearly, however, many seed houses make a special effort to put untreated seed in small packets destined for backyard gardeners. When they do put treated seed in packets (which are appropriately labeled), it is more because of their inability to obtain an untreated seed lot than because they consciously choose to treat a specific species."[58] Seed companies are concerned about liability issues of gardeners handling treated seed and suffering adverse effects.

The main chemicals used to treat seeds are fungicides to help prevent seeds in moist soil from rotting. They include Vitavax 200, Captan, Thiram, Apron/Ridomil, and Baytan, whose manufacturers include Ciba-Geigy, Uniroyal, and a U.S. division of ICI, International Chemical Industries.[59] According to the Environmental Protection Agency, all but Apron/Ridomil are suspected carcinogens, and Captan and Vitavax 200 are believed to cause birth defects.[60]

It is interesting to note that in the legal documents that define the federal laws governing pesticide use, these substances are known as *economic poisons*. You might think the term indicates a negative effect on the economy. Rather, it means that the EPA has to weigh their economic benefits against their toxic effects on health.

▼▼▼▼▼▼▼▼▼▼▼▼ ▼▼ ▼▼▼▼▼▼▼▼▼

Many pesticides pose invisible health hazards as well, whose consequences we have yet to recognize. As Vice-President Gore states, in his book *Earth in the Balance*, "Powerful pesticides can cause behavioral changes in animals in extremely low concentrations. A pesticide called Sevin even in an infinitesimal concentration of one billionth can change the behavior of large schools of fish: their movement becomes uncoordinated." Yet we are pouring 1.8 billion pounds of pesticides into the environment each year.

Treated seeds pose a special problem for certified organic farmers because the chemicals used on them are often not permitted. According to recommendations of the Crop Standards Committee of the National Organic Standards Board (NOSB), seeds treated with "prohibited insecticides" cannot be used, but seeds treated with "prohibited fungicides" are allowed, as long as the growers document efforts to try to obtain untreated seeds. "If you're using a treated seed, you're pretty much applying a fungicide in the spring, which growers of perennial crops such as fruit trees aren't allowed to do," according to Mike McEvoy of the Washington State Department of Agriculture.[61]

The NOSB Committee proposes that growers be required to adopt "effective alternative seed treatments" if and when they become available. But such biological treatments are not coming to market in the foreseeable future. Although farmers can make an effort to obtain untreated seeds by placing orders long in advance, they are still likely to face inertia and lack of interest from the seed industry at large. Organic growers in California are attempting to eliminate a state requirement that would mandate the use of untreated seed in 1994.[62]

The situation is actually getting worse, according to SeedQuest. "Growing environmental awareness causes the trend to be toward less treatment of the crops in the field and more treatment of the seed. We are learning how to apply a wide range of products at the seed level: insecticides, herbicides, algicides, acaricides, and plant growth regulators."[63]

In fact, today at least twenty-seven corporations have launched research programs directed toward the development of herbicide-tolerant crops. These companies, many of which are the world's largest pesticide, chemical, and pharmaceutical firms that have acquired seed companies, are engineering plants to absorb *more* of the chemicals that they also produce. These include virtually all major foods, including at least thirty crop and forest tree species being "purposefully modified to withstand otherwise lethal or damaging doses of herbicides." Biotechnology analysts project that herbicide-tolerant seeds will garner annual sales of $75 million to $320 million in the mid-1990s.[64]

The actual practice of current biotechnology research is not living up to its promise of reducing or eliminating chemicals. It is disturbing to note that of the bioengineered plants under review for government approval, 24 percent were bred for herbicide-resistance, 49 percent for viral- and insect-resistance, and only 2 percent for improved nutrition or taste.[65]

The flower of a broccoli plant after the heads are formed at the Seeds of Change farm.

Taxpayers' money is paying for the development of these herbicide-tolerant plants. State and federal agricultural institutions have spent $10.5 million for genetics research in the last several years. The U.S. Forest Service budgeted $2.8 million to develop herbicide-tolerant forest trees between 1985 and 1990.

Inevitably, the weeds that these chemicals target will develop resistance. Since 1980, the number of resistant weed species has grown from twelve to fifty. Consequently, the cycle of poison will only continue to escalate as "weeds" develop immunity against which chemists must design new, more powerful chemicals.

The creation of these plants means that more chemicals will be entering into the environment and the food system. "According to industry reports, the development of atrazine-resistant soybeans could allow for three times as much atrazine to be applied to corn without damage to the subsequent soybean crop."[66]

Because the linkage between seeds and chemicals is now being spliced into the very genetics themselves, the food system is likely to accumulate further unsafe levels of pesticides. The U.S. Department of Agriculture admits that herbicide-tolerant crop varieties "might carry more herbicide residues." The EPA classifies several herbicides as probable human carcinogens. This unknown realm of genetic engineering may bring new risks as well. "Some genetically engineered plants might be less nutritious or even produce higher levels of natural plant toxins than non-engineered plants."[67]

As agricultural science is penetrating the very genetic core of life, it holds the balance of life and death in its grasp. Designing plants to absorb more chemical poisons is a dangerous and retrograde strategy.

But in the meantime, it is incumbent upon people and companies like Seeds of Change to supply the seeds for a healthy agriculture. Organic seeds are the nexus where genetics and environmental conditioning meet. Organic seeds represent a vitally important keystone of a future agriculture based on the finest genetics enhanced by state-of-the-art organic growing techniques. They are the seeds of a healthy food system, a safe environment, and a diverse gene pool.

Government: Watering Weeds and Pulling Flowers

Even the federal government's own advisers have recommended a national policy shift to sustainable organic farming methods. In 1989 the respected National Academy of Sciences published "Alternative Agriculture," a comprehensive study that found sustainable organic methods superior for reasons of both profit and environmental safety. The Academy committee arrived at four major findings:[68]

1. Farmers successfully adopting these alternative systems generally derive significant sustained economic and environmental benefits. Wider adoption of proven alternative systems would result in even greater economic benefits to farmers and environmental gains for the nation.

2. As a whole, federal policies work against environmentally benign practices and the adoption of alternative agricultural systems, particularly those involving crop rotations, certain soil conservation practices, reductions in pesticide use, and increased use of biological and cultural means of pest control.

3. A systems approach to research is essential to the progress of alternative agriculture. Little recent research, however, has been directed toward many on-farm interactions integral to alternative agriculture. As a result, the scientific knowledge, technology, and management skills necessary for widespread adoption of alternative agriculture are not widely available or well defined.

4. To make wider adoption possible, farmers need to receive

information and technical assistance in developing new management skills.

The Academy found, "Farmers who adopt alternative farming systems often have productive and profitable operations, even though these farms usually function with relatively little help from commodity income and price support programs or extension [agencies]. A wide range of alternative systems and techniques deserves further support and investigation by agricultural and economic researchers. With modest adjustments in a number of federal agricultural policies, many of these systems could become more widely adopted and successful."[69]

Mayo Arrote squash harvested from the fields at the Seeds of Change farm.

The Academy identified multiple benefits to a transition to organic farming. Well-managed alternative farming systems nearly always use less synthetic chemical pesticides, fertilizers, and antibiotics per unit of production than comparable conventional farms. Reduced use of these inputs lowers production costs and lessens agriculture's potential for adverse environmental and health effects without necessarily decreasing—and in some cases actually increasing—per-acre crop yields and the productivity of livestock management systems.[70]

The Academy suggested that government itself was acting as a prime culprit in preventing farmers from adopting more favorable practices. "Many federal policies discourage adoption of alternative practices and systems by economically penalizing those who adopt rotations, apply certain soil conservation systems, or attempt to reduce pesticide applications."[71]

The Academy recommended a shift of funding to assist a policy change. "Substantial annual funding—at least $40 million—should be allocated for alternative farming research. The USDA should distribute the money through its competitive grants program to scientists from universities, private research institutions, foundations, and industry."[72]

"The success of some of these farmers indicates that these alternative farming practices hold promise for many other farmers and potentially significant benefits for the nation. . . . Government policies that discourage

The Advantages of Organic farming:

- Protect the public from toxic residues in foods
- Prevent soil erosion
- Protect water quality
- Save energy
- Protect the health of farm workers
- Promote biodiversity
- Provide superior taste
- Help small farmers

the adoption of alternative practices must be reformed. If these conditions are met, today's alternative farming practices could become tomorrow's conventional practices, with significant benefits for farmers, the economy, and the environment."[73]

Jim Hightower, the former Texas commissioner of agriculture, who is ever practical, took the farmer's point of view at the remarkable moment when the National Academy of Sciences report hit the headlines. "What we've found here, and elsewhere, is that farmers doing this kind of agriculture make money. They pay off their notes, they pay for tractors, and they do it without crop subsidies. There is a conversion coming."[74]

Unfortunately, the huge agribusiness farms that receive about $14 billion a year in subsidies disagreed, as did the $8 billion fertilizer industry and the companies benefiting from producing 430 million pounds of pesticides used yearly on corn, wheat, and soybeans in the Midwest. Although the 5 percent of farmers growing organically achieved yields as much as 40 percent higher without using synthetic fertilizers or pesticides, the nation did not see the "wider adoption of proven alternative systems" called for by the country's top scientists. Unlike Europe, the United States did not start subsidizing farmers to make the transition to organic methods. In fact, today at the U.S. Department of Agriculture, only two of the 129,249 employees are assigned to work on the development of organic agriculture.[75] There is also one full-time employee who studies the flowability of ketchup, just to put government priorities in perspective.

"Our government has been a very poor gardener," said Jim Hightower. "It tends to water the weeds and pull the flowers in our society." As Commissioner of Agriculture in Texas in the 1980s, Hightower promoted organic agriculture, which he calls the "art and science of cooperating with nature," while he advanced the interests of small farmers. He sought subsidies and incentives for organic growers and helped open up larger markets for their products.

Ironically, trying to use government to advance organic agriculture got Jim Hightower weeded out by the large vested agribusiness interests, which plucked him neatly from the garden of state. No significant shift has yet occurred in federal agricultural policy.

Changing the National Diet

Certainly there are no simple panaceas for achieving good health, and nothing works for everyone. They say there are many paths to God. As Norman Cousins observed, we know only a little bit about disease and almost nothing about healing. But the connection between diet and health is well documented, and improving our diet is one direct action people can take in behalf of their own health. The further connection between diet, health, and environment is coming under increasing study, and organically raised foods appear to benefit both health and the environment.

Cocozelle bush squash growing in the field at the Seeds of Change farm.

The government itself has conducted several excellent studies documenting the link between diet and health. Changing the national diet and making it organic are sure to go a long way toward improving the national health, reducing the crippling national health-care bill, and restoring the environment.

THE NEW CUISINE

The menus of many five-star restaurants today reflect deep changes in the new American diet. According to the National Restaurant Association, "The trend toward vegetarian dishes is overwhelmingly driven by health concerns and the taste for natural vegetables and fruit." Twenty percent of diners in the United States now favor restaurants with vegetarian options. Salads and vegetable dishes are the only items that have steadily risen in price over the last five years, as their quality has also improved.[76]

Many chefs today are leading the cultural trend toward healthy foods. They are directing the creation of gourmet dishes in which the vegetable is the star and the local organic farmer is the producer. The combination is looking like a hit.

Alice's Restaurant

The bright California light streaming through a filigree of ferns casts shimmering green patterns over enticing plates of fresh food at famed Chez Panisse. Alice Waters wanted to cook for her restaurant the same personal way she cooked for her friends, and the setting evokes a warm sense of community. She created an atmosphere that nourishes both body and soul, with a hearty connection to the land and the cycles of life.

Backyard biodiversity and organic foods are what the "bioneering" chef Alice Waters first put on the American dining table in 1971. In so doing, Chez Panisse permanently altered culinary consciousness by introducing fresh healthful food based on a diet of diversity. At that early juncture, you could not get anything you wanted at Alice's restaurant. Very often, even the good stuff Alice herself wanted was only found growing in someone's backyard.

Alice and her team of chefs quickly enacted what she calls a "hunter-gatherer culture," tracking only the freshest and purest of ingredients, mainly in season, through the live-food markets of the Bay Area. They also wildcrafted watercress from streams, and edible flowers and berries from remote roadsides. Their search led them to friends' gardens, often the only place to find fresh, unique vegetables.

Bolivian red corn growing in a test plot at the Seeds of Change farm.

One friend had returned from Italy with salad seeds and planted novel tastes such as rocket greens. "I was looking for ingredients such as I'd tasted in Europe," Alice recalls, "little beans and delicious young carrots. I couldn't find them, or the ones we did find didn't taste very good. We often went through several cases of beans, sorting through them to find a handful good enough to use. People heard that I was interested in these things and started to bring them from their backyards."[77] Soon, beautiful bunches of sorrel and radishes started to appear from backyard gardens around Berkeley.

Alice Waters's interest in freshness coincided with the organic gardening movement that was blossoming at the time in California. "It wasn't a conscious, political choice at that time for me. But I certainly was interested in the purity of food. Things from people's backyards were generally just grown in an organic way. Commercially, organic had a bad name in the 1970s in Berkeley. It looked pretty bad. The produce looked kind of beat up. It had a purity about it, but certainly not a consciousness about flavor. I didn't want to have the restaurant associated in that particular way. I just felt that people had to come to food in another way, and they'd wend their way back."

As the restaurant's popularity grew, the emphasis on organic helped spawn a network of urban organic gardeners, including Sibella Kraus. An original "forager," Kraus initiated relationships with small-farm suppliers in outlying areas and in 1983 started the Farm-Restaurant Project. The connection between the farms and a consortium of Bay Area restaurants led to the Tasting of Summer Produce, a gathering like a farmers' market for both the public and the restaurant community where growers display their wares. More suppliers emerged, including the Green Gulch farm of the San Francisco Zen Center. A centripetal network radiated from organic gardens and farms back to the center of the food community at Chez Panisse.

With the growth of the community and the passage of time came a progression in the flavor and appearance of organic produce. "The organic growers today in the restaurant community," says Alice approvingly, "are very, very conscious of flavor and brightness, the size of the pickings and all of the variety."

Diversity of foods has been a hallmark of Chez Panisse. "Once you're on this mission, you just can't stop. There's a whole world of foods out there. We have been propelled more quickly because we have just one menu a day in the downstairs of the restaurant. So every day for twenty-one years, we have tried to come up with something that's interesting to cook and interesting for the customers to have. So we moved perhaps more quickly in discovering different ingredients and ways of cooking them. Varieties have been very, very inspiring to us."

The flower of borage growing at the Seeds of Change farm.

Chez Panisse also pioneered a vision of the interconnectedness among food, environment, and community. "The connection between food and the environment can be pretty profound, and it should be. Most people don't know where their food comes from. Once you see that your fish actually comes out of that water over there, you understand that if you're dumping things in that water, you're not going to have a pure source of food. Those connections have to be made. That's what we're trying to do, to get people to get their hands back in the dirt and make that a really healthy relationship. It's really a two-way thing. We can't live without these farmers, and vice versa. It's the best way to have people understand what they're doing to their natural resources and pay attention to that, to see the relationship of what they're eating to what they're doing out there in the world.

"Definitely present is something aesthetic for me," Alice reveals gently. "I am thrilled to pick and serve those beautiful young leaves of lettuce and colors of dried beans and beautiful tomatoes. It's irresistible. It has a life to it that's terribly pleasing on a lot of levels, aesthetically and physically. It feels so nourishing—I do have an obsession about this.

"Of course, I also care very much about this next generation, what our kids are eating and how to pass this message on to them. I believe you have to come to it in terms of a certain kind of beauty of diversity. Just to pick those little tangerines off the tree, with all the leaves, and all different colors of orange, from very pale to very intense. You come to know all the different kinds of flavors that come with them. It's really a thrill."

RECIPES FROM ALICE WATERS, CHEF, CHEZ PANISSE

CARROT AND RED PEPPER SOUP

Serves 8

Our first double soup: The carrot soup acts as a backdrop for the more pungent red pepper flavor. Pour the carrot soup first into the bowl, then add a smaller proportion of the red pepper soup; the red pepper taste will remain distinct and provide a spicy accent to the deeper flavor.

For the carrot soup:

4 tablespoons unsalted butter

6 cups water

6 large carrots (1 pound, 4 ounces), cut into 1/2-inch dice

1/2 yellow onion (4 ounces), cut into 1/4-inch dice

1 teaspoon salt

1/8 teaspoon freshly ground black pepper

1 1/2 teaspoons lemon juice

Prepare the carrot soup: Melt the butter in a 6-quart stainless steel soup pot. Add 1 cup of the water, the carrots, and the onion. Bring to a low simmer, cover, and stew for 30 minutes.

Remove the cover from the pot. The vegetables should be very soft and the water almost entirely evaporated. If not, continue cooking the vegetables until they are. Add the remaining 5 cups water and bring to a boil. In the blender, puree the soup in batches, for 3 minutes each, and season it with salt, pepper, and the lemon juice. The soup should have a velvety consistency and be slightly thicker than heavy cream.

For the red pepper soup:

2 tablespoons unsalted butter

3 medium red bell peppers (14 ounces), halved, seeded, and diced

2/3 cup water

1/4 teaspoon salt

1/8 teaspoon freshly ground pepper

Prepare the red pepper soup: Melt the butter in a 3-quart saucepan. Add the peppers and the water, bring to a simmer, and cook, uncovered, for 20 minutes, or until the peppers are very soft. Most of the water will have evaporated during this time.

In the blender, puree the peppers with 1/2 cup of water and pass the puree through a medium-fine sieve to catch any bits of skin. Add salt and pepper. If the soup lacks depth, correct it with a few drops of red wine vinegar. If necessary, thin the red pepper soup with a little water so that its consistency is similar to that of the carrot soup.

Serve the soups in warm bowls, pouring 6 ounces of the carrot into each bowl, then stirring 2 tablespoons of the red pepper soup into the center. Optional additions are chopped chervil leaves and crème fraîche thinned with a little warm water to approximate heavy cream. Draw the cream over the surface with the tines of a fork.

GRILLED TOMATO CROUTONS WITH RED ONION VINAIGRETTE, ANCHOVIES, AND FRESH BASIL

Yields 4 Large Croutons

This dish is a celebration of the tomato and should be attempted only at the peak of the season in the summer, when tomatoes are sweet, full of flavor, and not at all watery.

An extravagant variation of this simple dish eliminates the anchovies but adds sliced lobster, first tossed in a little of the vinaigrette, then piled on top of the tomatoes.

For the vinaigrette:

1/2 small sweet red onion (2 1/2 ounces), minced

2 small cloves garlic, minced

Large pinch salt

Pinch pepper

2 tablespoons fruity red wine vinegar

3 tablespoons extra virgin olive oil

For the croutons:

16 fresh basil leaves

8 medium tomatoes

Salt and pepper

4 large slices of sourdough bread,

each 1/3 inch thick

Olive oil

1 large clove garlic, peeled

12 salt-packed anchovy filets, soaked in several

changes of cold water for 15 minutes, drained,

patted dry, drizzled with olive oil

Prepare a charcoal or wood fire.

Prepare the vinaigrette: Combine the onion, garlic, salt, pepper, and vinegar. Let stand for 10 minutes. Stir in the olive oil. Mince half the basil coarse, and add it to the vinaigrette.

Core the tomatoes and cut them crosswise into slices 1 inch thick. Lightly salt and pepper both sides. Brush the sourdough slices with olive oil.

When the fire has burned down to moderately hot, grill the tomatoes on one side only. Do not turn them: they will be soft and difficult to handle. Allow them to cook until they begin to bubble slightly and are soft to the touch throughout. While the tomatoes are cooking, grill the bread to a golden brown on both sides.

Rub the bread with the peeled garlic and arrange two grilled tomatoes on each slice. With a knife, break up the tomatoes on the bread and spread them out to cover the crouton. Arrange the anchovies, three per crouton, over the tomatoes and spoon the vinaigrette on top. Mince the remaining basil. Sprinkle it liberally over the croutons and serve immediately while the croutons are still warm.

LINGUINE WITH CHERRY TOMATO VINAIGRETTE
Serves 4

The quality of this simple pasta depends on the excellence of the tomatoes.

5 cups cherry tomatoes

1 cup virgin olive oil

Red wine vinegar

Salt and pepper

1 1/2 cups fresh bread crumbs

A handful of fresh basil leaves

Linguine for 4

Cut the tomatoes in half and marinate them in the olive oil, red wine vinegar to taste, and salt and pepper. Toast the fresh bread crumbs in the oven until dry and lightly browned. Take them from the oven and toss with some olive oil while still warm. Cut the basil leaves into thin slices (known as *chiffonade*). Cook the pasta, and while it is boiling, put the tomatoes and their marinade in a pan and warm them briefly. Add

the pasta to the pan, toss together with the tomatoes, and serve. Garnish the dish with the bread crumbs and basil chiffonade.

VARIATIONS

Peel large ripe tomatoes and quarter them. Dress them with virgin olive oil, red wine vinegar, salt and pepper, minced garlic, and lots of dwarf basil leaves. Cook fresh noodles and toss the hot pasta with the cold tomatoes.

Finely dice peeled and seeded tomatoes, a mixture of multicolored sweet peppers, and red onion. Season with salt, pepper, vinegar, chopped parsley, basil, and coriander. Boil linguine, drain, toss in olive oil, then mix with the relish and chill.

GRILLED SUMMER VEGETABLE PASTA

Serves 2

2 salt-packed anchovies
Virgin olive oil
3 peppers: yellow, green, red
6 to 8 small Japanese eggplants
Salt and pepper
8 plum tomatoes
1 young red onion
1 or 2 cloves garlic
A few fresh basil leaves
Tagliatelle for 2

Fillet and rinse the anchovies. Pound them in a mortar with a little olive oil to make a smooth paste. Make a charcoal fire. While the charcoal is still flaming, grill the whole peppers so that the skin is black and blistered all around. Let them cool, and peel away the charred skin.

Cut peppers in half lengthwise and remove the seeds and stem. Use a paring knife or a towel to remove any little bits of black on the exterior, then cut the peppers into wide strips. Cut the unpeeled eggplants in lengthwise slices about 1/4 inch thick. Brush the slices with olive oil, and season with salt and pepper. Grill them over the hot fire a few minutes on each side so that they are lightly browned.

Cut the plum tomatoes in half and season with salt and pepper. Grill them skin side down until they get a little color and begin to soften. Slice the onion in rings. Brush with olive oil, season, and grill them until browned and tender. Finely chop the garlic. Cut the basil leaves into chiffonade.

Combine the anchovy paste, tomato halves, garlic, and a tablespoon of oil in a sauté pan. Cook gently a few minutes until the tomatoes release their juices and form a sauce. Add the grilled vegetables and continue to simmer a few minutes more. Set aside some of the vegetables for garnish. Cook the pasta and add to the vegetables in the pan. Season with black pepper and toss the noodles well in the juices. Serve garnished with vegetables and the chiffonade of basil.

Birth, Death, Sex, and Food

At a distance of twenty yards from the Coyote Cafe in Santa Fe, you can smell the unmistakable dark, earthy aroma of roasting chiles. So far from any visible physical source, the scent rises as a smoky puzzle. One wonders whether perhaps trickster chef and restaurateur Mark Miller has alchemically released an etheric chile loop, an Akashic relleno stuffed with the eternal pleasure and nourishment of some of the most cherished foods in history, and the hottest.

"Food should be a catalyst for creating meaning in our lives," Miller says passionately, "and part of that meaning is a sense of place. Cuisine belongs in a certain place, culturally, historically, and geographically. Our food should connect us to our cultural path. We used to have a food legacy when religions were full of food prescriptions."

It comes as no surprise that Miller completed graduate anthropology work at Berkeley in cross-cultural aesthetics before signing on as a chef with Alice Waters. During his tenure at Chez Panisse, he frequented the Oakland produce market, perfecting the selection of fresh and unusual varieties of vegetables and foods for the restaurant. Having grown up in New England, he was already connected to "old farm agriculture," and during his gathering he became "aware that the commercial hybrids were not of the same intensity of flavor as some of the older heirloom varieties."[78]

Three years later he launched, in succession, still in Berkeley, the Fourth Street Grill and the Santa Fe Bar and Grill, firing up the mesquite grill and hot haute cuisine that became widely popular. The fuse of chile peppers was lit, and it burned a trail to Santa Fe, New Mexico, where Miller's Coyote Cafe exploded through the capsicum envelope in 1987.

Though Miller remains an admirer of Chez Panisse for its "honesty, integrity, and spirit of place," his personal destiny lay in a pod. "I just became more expert in the spicier things," the food philosopher declares existentially. "I was concerned with the Mediterranean, but with the Spanish, the Moorish, the Sardinian, the Greek, the North African. I was more interested in those cultures that were more expressive. Certain vegetables are

Closeup of Yellow Ruffled, Orange Queen, and Red House free-standing tomatoes freshly picked from the fields of the Seeds of Change farm.

more expressive than others. Expressiveness can sometimes be subtle, but it has a complexity and a layering. Chiles, for instance, have a multi-dimension of flavors."

It seldom takes Miller long to get around to chile. He points out that chile is not a fad food like the baby vegetables, but an ancient staple. "I've been fighting for chile. Chile is a great food source. It's heavily nutritious. It's been used for eight thousand years in the Americas, and we just relegated it to the backstage because of the status system, because it's not European. We have to lose our Euro-bias. The older foods are usually the ones tied to the older cultures that need to be understood as we become more multicultural and multi-ethnic. We can create a food culture."

The Coyote is suffused with food culture, richly deserving of its world-wide reputation. Surrounded by Mexican and New Mexican folk art, Miller is a true genius of the cuisine of the Americas, and eating at the Coyote or its newer Washington, D.C., counterpart, Red Sage, is an archetypal food experience.

"Nature has a way of taking care of itself," Miller says confidently. "Somehow these vegetables and seeds and cultivars that have survived over time have more to do with an ecological balance that we don't even today understand exactly. Some of the Native American cultures did. When I make wild mushroom tamales, people say, 'Well that's incredible, and it's so different from the greasy tamales that I get at the marketplace.' Wild mushroom tamales are one of the oldest Mexican or Native American foods. They knew very well every single food source that was available that was nutritional and not poisonous.

"Why did the Hohokam Indians have two hundred domesticated plants in the fourth century? Europe in the fifteenth century had only seventeen. Why is it that in Machu Picchu they had agricultural stations testing every particular cultivar of potato and plant, in different soils and geographic orientations? They knew specifically in what soil and at what altitude and what orientation to plant. Why is it that the Incans had enough grain for seven years for all 15 million people of the empire? They understood these processes. It's not coincidence that somebody comes up with thirty or forty different culti-vars of corn. Native Americans in the Southwest had 279 wild plants and 200 plants that they cultivated. They understood perfectly what we call genetic engineering. They didn't come up with these diets randomly. They knew their own bodies. They knew their own taste. They learned foods, and they learned growing seasons culturally. They had a respect for these things.

"They also knew the seasonality of all the food. The best restaurants in America today are using foods from South America, Chile, or New Zealand way out of season. The importance of the seasonality is that it is tied to a cultural mainstream of people who understood their place in nature. The corn poems that were created by the Hopi and the Zuni, the rituals, the colors, were a proto-scientific way of making this knowledge more meaningful in everyday life and giving it respect.

"To me as an anthropologist who spent most of his life studying art, the great thing about art is that it is an affirmation of life. And what does this have to do with vegetables? Our food supply has to be something that is real within our own life experience. As long as we talk about taste and the earth and trees, we get closer to the acceptance of the natural cycle. It has to do with feeding ourselves. It has to do with a generation of ourselves over time, our own death and the death of others around us. It's a mirror. I think that nature becomes a mirror, an education for ourselves."

Miller is a forceful proponent of organic food, and during the summer, when the restaurant's menu is almost entirely organic, the Coyote Cafe supports three organic farms outside Santa Fe. He is building solar greenhouses for year-round growing, buys organic whenever possible, including organic coffee from a Guatemalan cooperative, and proposes that fresh foods should not have to be trucked more than a hundred miles from where they are grown to where they are consumed. He is committed to food with taste, nu-trition, and health benefits.

But above all, Mark Miller's food is organic to culture. "My message is a cultural one. We should not have foods that set one group in society against another. We should not have foods that have hierarchies. We shouldn't have

French food on the top, Italian next, or Chinese food third. We should learn to taste food, and we should learn to respect the culinary and cultural traditions of all countries. All great civilizations have had great food. Lewis and Clark went across America for three years. Their geology, their engineering, and their maps are fairly accurate even by today's methods, and yet we have no recipes and no mention of food.

"I'm trying to get people to respect cultures through the foods that I introduce. If I can get someone to have a molé from Oaxaca, maybe they'll change their mind a little bit about what Mexican food is about and what Mexico and Mexicans are about. We can create in our food supply a social bridge to acting as a cooperative culture, as a multi-ethnic, multicultural society.

"We don't have poems on animals, we don't have rituals of corn dances or reindeer dances. I'm working with the cultures in the Southwest that are the last vestiges of really understanding what food and nature mean. Continually we talk about species that are disappearing—what about endangered cultures? What about endangered philosophies?

"There are only four things that happen internally to people," Mark Miller concludes decisively. "There are birth and death, and sex and food. Everything else is outside of us. Cultures in the past have seen food in this way. Religions have seen food in this way. They have used food as a connection to teach about life."

RECIPES FROM MARK MILLER,
CHEF, COYOTE CAFE AND RED
SAGE, AND *THE COYOTE CAFE
COOKBOOK*

YELLOW SQUASH SOUP WITH RED CHILE CREMA
Yields 6 servings

Here is a simple soup to make late in summer. Ideally, squash should come from your own garden: the homegrown variety tends to be tastier and less starchy. I prefer yellow crookneck squash, which is sweeter than yellow zucchini. When sweating the vegetables, ensure that the heat is low and the pan covered; this way, none of the sweet perfume flavors escape. This soup can also be served cold.

YELLOW SQUASH SOUP

*3 pounds yellow crookneck (or summer squash
or yellow zucchini), cut into large dice
1 1/2 cups finely chopped white onion
2 tablespoons butter
2 sprigs marjoram, finely chopped
2 cups water
1 cup heavy cream
1/2 teaspoon salt, or to taste*

RED CHILE CREMA

*4 whole red dried chiles
1 cup water
pinch of salt*

Put the squash, onion, butter, marjoram, and 2 cups of water in a saucepan. Cover and cook over low heat for about 25 minutes. Allow to cool, remove marjoram, and puree in a blender. Heat the puree with the cream and season with salt, adding a little water if necessary to prevent the mixture from becoming too thick.

To make the Red Chile Crema, place the dried chiles on a baking sheet and roast in the oven at 325 degrees for 5 minutes. Remove seeds, and boil the chiles in 1 cup of water until soft. Puree in the blender, and season with a pinch of salt.

Ladle soup into bowls and decorate with Red Chile Crema on top in a Southwestern zigzag design.

ROASTED CORN SOUP WITH
SMOKED CHILES AND CHEESE
Yields 6 servings

The roasted corn in this soup complements the smoky flavor of the chipotle chiles and the feta cheese particularly well.

*10 ears corn in the husk
5 cups water
4 dry (or canned) chipotle chiles, deveined,
seeded, and julienned
Salt to taste
4 ounces feta cheese (or queso fresco)*

Roast the corn on a cookie sheet in a 400-degree oven for 45 to 60 minutes; the outside of the husks should be dry and brown. Cool the husks, shuck the corn, and cut the kernels from the ears. Puree 3 cups of the corn with 3 cups of water in a blender (reserving the remainder of the corn). Cook the puree in a pan together with the chipotle chiles and remaining water for 10 to 15 minutes over low heat. Add the reserved whole corn and salt. Pour the soup into bowls and crumble the cheese over the top.

Santa Fe Grande, jalepeño, serrano, purira, guajillo costeno, Bolivian rainbow, chilcote, and ajo colorado chiles with red velvet okra harvested at the Seeds of Change farm.

SPICY GREEN RICE

Yields 4 to 6 servings

This dish is a great vehicle for expressing strong herbal flavors, and it always comes as a surprise because of its unusual appearance. The important thing is to be sure there are enough chiles to make it hot and spicy and sufficient green ingredients for color and taste. In addition to the herbs and chiles given in the recipe, you can put in orange zest, avocado leaves, epazote, yerba santa, fresh basil, or marjoram. The rice goes well with grilled fish dishes. It can also be served cold; mixed with chilled shrimp, it makes a great lunch or picnic dish.

> 4 leaves romaine lettuce
> 6 roasted poblano chiles
> 2 roasted serrano chiles
> 1 large clove garlic
> 2 tablespoons minced onion
> 1 cup loosely packed cilantro leaves
> (about 1 small bunch)
> 1/2 bunch parsley
> 3 1/2 cups water
> 4 1/2 tablespoons butter
> 2 cups long-grain rice
> 2 teaspoons salt

In a blender, puree all ingredients except butter, rice, and salt. Melt 2 1/2 tablespoons butter in a large saucepan and add rice. Cook 3 to 4 minutes over medium heat until translucent, taking care not to scorch the butter. Add water, salt, and the pureed ingredients, bring to a boil, and cook for 2 minutes. Reduce heat to lowest setting, cover, and simmer for 20 to 25 minutes, until water just evaporates. Add remaining 2 tablespoons butter, and fluff up with a wooden spoon. Garnish with fresh chopped cilantro or basil, if desired.

MARK'S RED CHILE SAUCE

Yields 4 cups

I like this variation of Red Chile Sauce because the combination of different types of red chile gives it dimension. It goes better with more complex, heartier dishes.

> 4 ounces whole dried New Mexico red chiles
> 2 ounces whole dried ancho chiles
> 2 ounces whole dried cascabel chiles
> 2 whole canned chipotle chiles picked
> from adobo sauce, or
> 2 dried chipotle chiles rehydrated
> 1 teaspoon adobo sauce from can of chipotle
> chiles, or 1 teaspoon of water used to
> rehydrate dried chiles
> 2 quarts water
> 1 pound roma tomatoes
> 1/2 cup chopped white onion
> 1 tablespoon olive oil
> 5 large cloves garlic, roasted, peeled, and
> finely chopped
> 1 teaspoon roasted ground cumin
> 1 1/2 teaspoons roasted ground
> Mexican oregano
> 1 teaspoon salt
> 2 tablespoons peanut oil
> (Chicken stock, if necessary)

Remove stems and seeds from chiles. With a comal or black iron skillet, or in an oven at 250 degrees, dry-roast all the chiles except the chipotles for 3 to 4 minutes. Shake once or twice, and do not allow to blacken. Add the roasted chiles to the water in a covered pan and simmer very low for 20 minutes to rehydrate. Allow to cool. Blacken tomatoes in a skillet or under a broiler (about 5 minutes). Sauté onion in the oil over low heat until browned.

Drain the chiles, then put them and the chipotles in a blender with 1 teaspoon of adobo sauce or 1 teaspoon of the water used to rehydrate them. Add blackened tomatoes, onion, garlic, cumin, oregano, and salt. Add 1 cup liquid. (Taste the chile water first. If it is not bitter, use chile water; otherwise use chicken stock.) Puree to a fine paste, adding more chile water or chicken stock if necessary.

Add oil or lard to a high-sided pan, and heat until almost smoking. Refry the sauce at a sizzle for 3 to 5 minutes, stirring continuously. Do not allow sauce to get too thick; add water if necessary.

TARASCAN BEAN SOUP
Yields 4 servings

This soup's hearty nature is appropriate, given the legendary fierceness of the Tarascan Indians of Michoacán, with whom the dish originated. The Tarascan civilization of the fourteenth and fifteenth centuries was one of the few that was never conquered by the Aztecs and was one of the last in Mexico to fall to the Spanish conquistadores. This version is one of the most popular soups we have ever served at Coyote Cafe.

1/2 pound dried red kidney beans (1 1/4 cups)
2 sprigs epazote, finely chopped (optional)
1 teaspoon salt
2 teaspoons toasted dried oregano
Water
1/2 large white onion, sliced
1 tablespoon olive oil
1 pound roma tomatoes
2 cloves roasted garlic
2 tablespoons pureed chipotle chiles in adobo
2 pasilla de Oaxaca chiles (or anchos
or mulatos), stemmed
1/2 cup peanut oil
8 ounces Monterey jack cheese, cut into 4 slices

Place the beans in a saucepan with the epazote, salt, and oregano, and enough water to cover the beans. Cover pan, and bring to a boil. Reduce to a simmer, and cook for about 90 minutes until the beans are soft. Stir occasionally, and add more water as necessary.

Preheat oven to 350 degrees. Sauté the onion slices briefly in olive oil. Cut the tomatoes in half and remove the seeds. Place tomatoes on a baking sheet and roast at 350 degrees for 45 minutes. Transfer tomatoes to a blender, add the cooked beans, garlic, onion, and chipotle puree, and blend. Add a little water if it seems too thick. Put puree through a medium-to-fine-meshed sieve or pass through a food mill, removing seeds and skins. Heat soup over low heat in a saucepan.

Meanwhile, lightly fry the chiles in the peanut oil for a few seconds, just until softened, and then cut into strips. Lay slices of cheese and chile strips on the surface of the soup after seasoning with salt to taste. When cheese has melted, ladle soup into heated bowl.

Vegetable-Driven Trotter

Meanwhile, two thousand miles away in Chicago, another restaurant, called Charlie Trotter's, is elevating food to a peak experience.

Charlie Trotter and his "degustation" may sound like a racehorse in a weather event, but Charlie actually is a virtuoso chef, and his degustation is a culinary cloudburst. Among his most popular creations is the vegetable degustation, for which Trotter has become deservedly famous.

"A degustation is a tasting menu," Trotter explains enthusiastically, "not just an appetizer or an entree, but a series of courses that make up a whole meal with no one course being more important than any other courses. It's not like having everything lead up to an entree or key on a main appetizer. It means a progression of four, five, six, or seven savory courses and two, three, or four delicate little fruit-oriented dessert courses. We've been doing the vegetable degustation for five years now."[79] The meritorious meals leave his guests in a state of succulent surrender, anguished at choosing between yet another irresistible serving of some exquisite morsel and recognition of the inevitably finite nature of the physical body.

A quarter of the customers, who have often waited on a six-month reservations list to eat at the discreet brownstone, order the vegetable degustation. "It's what I like to refer to as vegetable-driven cuisine," Trotter observes of what he calls his Americanized French cuisine. "Right now we're doing an all-potato menu. A study in potato. We're kind of famous for our tomato menu that we do every August and September until the first freeze of tomatoes, and that's been really unbelievable. We enjoy the possibility of working with thirty different varieties of heirloom tomatoes and doing different things with them—very different things. Playing on the different acidity levels of the tomatoes and different meaty levels, and roasting them whole and making a terrine out of them, and making a risotto out of them, or mixing them with quinoa, or making a little broth or flavored water out of them.

"Sometimes we'll focus a whole menu right around one foodstuff, or other times, different times of the year, we'll incorporate mushrooms, root vegetables, squash and asparagus and artichokes." Trotter's asparagus degustation is a consummate performance, with roasted asparagus and beet terrine, asparagus soup with morel flan, and grain pilaf with crispy asparagus and water chestnuts.

"We have vegetarians who come, but we have a lot of people who are not vegetarians who may eat out several nights a week and find it a great refreshing change. I don't like to call it a vegetarian menu. I like to call it a vegetable menu. I'm trying to make the point that you can enjoy vegetables without necessarily being caught up in vegetarianism, just enjoying vegetables because they're wonderful foodstuffs. You can have a meal that's all vegetables. You don't have to focus it around a fish course or a meat course or something like that."

Foxtail millet after harvesting from the fields at the Seeds of Change farm.

Trotter's success is a clear marker of the trend toward a healthy menu. Although he denies any association with the past stigma of health food, his meals are virtually devoid of butter and dairy products, and he offers a tantalizing assortment of vinaigrettes and infusion oils, which he says simply taste much better. "They have a fraction of the calories of conventional sauces, are easier to digest, and taste better. They do not mute or block the basic flavors as does a sauce with a lot of butter or cream."

He too serves an impressive 75 percent organic foods. "We use as much organic produce as possible for flavor reasons. I find that you can't beat the taste of things that are picked in the height of their freshness and ripeness. It's hard to fudge the rules if you're getting something that is really the way it should be at the height of its season at its ripest moment. It's good to know that you are eating unadulterated food. It makes for a truer, more natural cuisine. That's been part of the driving philosophy of why we use organic food at this restaurant.

"But we don't hit our customers over the head with it," he continues. "If they're inquisitive, if they're interested, we'll tell them specifically about our use of organic and natural product, but otherwise we don't make that big an issue of it. We're not a 'health food restaurant.' We're not a restaurant that seeks to put forth any sort of political philosophy. We're a restaurant that's trying to serve the finest possible food. In that pursuit we end up using a lot of natural product."

Like the other top restaurateurs, Trotter contracts directly with organic farms in the region. "The quality just seems to get better and better. I await each summer with the greatest anticipation because several new farmers are going to pop up, and people that were growing things for me last year are growing them even better this year. And they're growing more things, so it just gets more exciting every year. We get some of what I think are the best tomatoes in the country from farms in the northern part of the state."

The crops of the Incas have not been lost on Charlie Trotter. "I'm sure we use more quinoa than any restaurant in America. We've been using it for about five years. I just ate it one day. I bought some in a health food store, and I liked it. I found it was sort of like the best of couscous and barley. It had this chewy al dente texture that barley had, yet it was more interesting than barley. It almost had a couscous characteristic to it. So we began to use it a lot. In fact, we just did a photo shoot today, and we served organic oxtail-studded quinoa with several little vegetable juices on the plate. We've done quinoa desserts. We've made a quinoa pudding like a rice pudding. It is extremely popular, and we cater to a very sophisticated clientele here.

"We're happy to turn people on to what we think are pretty exciting new foods," Trotter says modestly. But whatever his protestations, Charlie Trotter is purposefully promoting a relatively healthy table, artfully populated by diverse vegetables and grains, lifted one spoonful at a time into the food system.

RECIPES FROM CHARLIE TROTTER, CHEF, CHARLIE TROTTER'S

GRILLED MARINATED TOFU WITH SPICY SOBA NOODLES AND SPICY PICKLED VEGETABLES

Serves 6

GRILLED MARINATED TOFU

1 pound tofu, drained and cut into
2-by-1-inch rectangles
Marinade:
1 cup water
1 cup dried shiitake mushrooms
1/2 cup soy sauce
1/2 cup red wine vinegar
1/2 cup sherry
1/2 cup olive oil
1 tablespoon fresh oregano, chopped
1/2 tablespoon black peppercorns
1/2 teaspoon kosher salt

Method: Simmer dried shiitake mushrooms in water for 20 minutes. Add remaining marinade ingredients, and simmer for 5 more minutes.

Lay the tofu in 1 layer in a shallow pan. Pour marinade over tofu and marinate a minimum of 8 hours and up to 24 hours. Strain marinade and reserve. Remove the shiitakes, thinly slice, and reserve for garnish.

Grill the marinated tofu over medium high heat till it is dark brown and crunchy on all sides. Garnish with the shiitakes, and pour the marinade on top of the tofu. Serve with Spicy Cold Soba Noodles and Spicy Pickled Vegetables.

SPICY COLD SOBA NOODLES

1/3 cup soy sauce
1 tablespoon molasses
1/4 cup sesame oil
1/4 cup tahini
1/4 cup brown sugar
1/4 cup chili oil
3 tablespoons balsamic or red wine vinegar
1/2 bunch of scallions, white and green parts,
thinly sliced
Salt to taste
1/2 pound soba or Japanese buckwheat noodles
Bowl of iced water

Method: Place the soy sauce in a pan over high heat, and reduce by half. Turn heat to low, stir in molasses, and warm briefly. Transfer to a mixing bowl. Add sesame oil, tahini, brown sugar, chili oil, vinegar, and scallions, and whisk to combine. Season to taste with salt if desired.

Bring a large pot of salted water to a rapid boil. Add noodles, and bring back to a boil, stirring occasionally, until they just begin to soften, about three minutes. (Soba noodles can overcook very quickly, so stay nearby.)

Have a large bowl of iced water ready. Drain the noodles, plunge in iced water, and drain again. Place in a colander and rinse well under running water. Combine noodles and sauce, toss well, and chill.

SPICY PICKLED VEGETABLES

1 quart white wine vinegar
1 quart plus 1 cup water
1 teaspoon crushed red chili pepper
1 tablespoon black peppercorns
1 cup salt
1/2 cup sugar
Carrots

Jalapeño peppers

Napa cabbage

Daikon radish

Sweet red pepper

Cucumber

Method: Slice vegetables into 1-by-2-inch pieces, 1/8 inch thick, and set aside. Combine all other ingredients, and bring to a boil. Remove from heat and pour over vegetables. Chill, marinating vegetables in liquid. Drain and serve with Spicy Cold Soba Noodles and Grilled Marinated Tofu.

WARM ASPARAGUS SALAD WITH BLACK WALNUTS AND CREAMY CHÈVRE VINAIGRETTE

Serves 6
SALAD

48 spears asparagus, trimmed of tough
green ends and blanched
1 teaspoon walnut oil
1/4 cup Missouri black walnuts, roasted
12 shallots, sliced into rings and sautéed in
walnut oil until just browned, then cooled
to room temperature
2 organic tomatoes, peeled, seeded,
and julienned

Method: In a warm nonstick sauté pan, toss the asparagus in the walnut oil until warmed through. Add the walnuts, shallot rings, and tomato pieces and warm them through. Divide this mixture evenly on the plates, and drizzle some of the vinaigrette on top. Serve.

VINAIGRETTE

4 ounces chèvre (e.g., Laura Chenel's log chèvre)
8 ounces walnut or hazelnut oil
3 ounces rice wine vinegar
Salt and pepper to taste

Method: Blend all the ingredients until thoroughly mixed, thinning with water until the consistency of heavy cream is reached.

TRIO OF GRAINS WITH ORGANIC SWEET CORN COULIS

Serves 6

I love grain. It is so versatile and so healthy that it is almost hard not to incorporate somehow. This particular grain dish is one of my favorites and has been well received by my patrons.

COUSCOUS

1 cup cooked couscous
1 1/2 tablespoons cucumber, finely diced
1 1/2 tablespoons roasted pine nuts
1 1/2 teaspoons mint, chiffonade (sliced
paper-thin)
1 1/2 teaspoons lemon juice
2 tablespoons tomato concasse (tomato pulp
without seeds)
1 tablespoon herb-infused olive oil
Salt and pepper to taste
Fried sage leaves for garnish

Method: Heat the above ingredients in a double boiler, and form the desired shapes, such as timbale (shape of a large sewing thimble) or quenelle (using two spoons, pack mixture in top of one spoon and toss it back and forth with the other spoon to achieve a triangular shape). Place shapes on a plate. Garnish with fried sage leaves.

BASMATI RICE

1 cup cooked basmati rice
2 tablespoons spinach, sautéed and chopped
2 tablespoons homemade organic tomato paste
1 1/2 tablespoons zucchini, finely diced and

blanched (must be diced <u>first</u>)

Salt and pepper to taste

Finely julienned, lightly fried zucchini

Method: Use the same method as above. Garnish with finely julienned, lightly fried zucchini.

QUINOA

1 cup cooked organic quinoa

2 tablespoons shiitake mushrooms, finely sliced and sautéed

2 tablespoons shiitake mushrooms duxelles (puree with chunks in it)

1 tablespoon roasted bell peppers, finely chopped

1 1/2 teaspoons tarragon, finely chopped

1 1/2 teaspoons hazelnut oil

Salt and pepper to taste

Method: Use the same method as above with no garnish.

SWEET CORN COULIS (PUREE)

18 ears organic sweet corn

Method: Grill the corn with the husks on over a live fire for 10 to 12 minutes until corn is cooked inside. Remove the corn from the cob and blend in a blender or food processor with enough water to get the desired consistency. Pass through a fine strainer. Season and serve with grains.

PAVÉ (BRICK) OF TOMATO AND NAPA CABBAGE WITH BASIL WATER
Serves 8

20 napa cabbage leaves

16 large vine-ripened red tomatoes

3/4 pound aged goat cheese, finely ground

Salt and pepper

Method: The green outer leaves of cabbage are best for this purpose. Remove the stems, blanch the leaves and shock them in cold water, then dry them with paper towel. Core the tomatoes, and slice them 1/4 inch thick. Slightly dry these slices on a nonstick baking pan in a 300-degree oven for 35 minutes.

Using grapeseed oil, lightly oil an 8-by-12-by-2.5-inch baking pan, then line it with foil. Assemble, seasoning lightly between the layers. Line the bottom of the foil-lined pan with napa cabbage leaves. Sprinkle some of the goat cheese on top of this layer. Place a layer of tomatoes on the cheese. Sprinkle this layer with goat cheese. Continue this process until you use all the ingredients, then cover the terrine with foil, and bake at 350 degrees for forty minutes.

Remove the terrine from the oven and weight it with another pan of equal size. (A couple of bricks in the pan work well to weight it.) Allow the terrine to cool completely, then refrigerate for a couple of hours. After the terrine has cooled, remove the top layer of foil and turn the terrine onto a cutting board. Carefully remove the remaining foil. Slice the terrine into diamond shapes. Roast the pavés in a 400-degree oven for 8 to 10 minutes or until hot in the center. Serve in a bowl with basil water.

BASIL WATER

1 pound organic celery root, peeled, chopped

1 pound organic leeks, cleaned, chopped

1 pound organic onions, chopped

1 pound celery, chopped

1/4 pound organic parsnip, chopped

2 gallons of water

1 pound organic basil

Method: Simmer all the ingredients (except the basil) for 90 minutes. Strain, reduce to 4 cups. Steep basil in the liquid for 1 minute, and strain again.

POTATO, LEEK, AND WATER CHESTNUT RISOTTO WITH RED-WINE-INFUSED SUN-DRIED TOMATO COULIS (PUREE)

Serves 6

1 Spanish onion, finely chopped
8 cloves garlic, peeled and chopped finely
2 tablespoons olive oil
1 cup arborio rice
4 cups water (or vegetable stock)
2 potatoes, peeled, cubed, and poached al dente
4 leeks, cleaned, cut into rings, and poached al dente
2/3 cup fresh water chestnuts, cooked, peeled, and chopped
1/2 pound spinach cleaned, blanched, and chopped
Salt and pepper to taste
6 ounces red-wine-infused sun-dried tomato coulis

Method: Over a medium heat, sweat the onions and the garlic in olive oil until translucent. Add the arborio rice, and sauté with the onion and garlic for 2 minutes or so, stirring constantly. Little by little add the water or stock, stirring constantly, waiting until the liquid is thoroughly absorbed before adding more. This process will take approximately 30 minutes. When the rice is done, that is, barely cooked through, but not mushy, stir in the potatoes, then the leeks, then the water chestnuts and spinach. Season to taste.

RED-WINE-INFUSED SUN-DRIED TOMATO COULIS

Makes 2/3 cup

1 medium onion, chopped
1 medium carrot, chopped
2 tablespoons butter
4 cups red wine
1/2 pound sun-dried tomatoes, softened in water

Method: Over a medium heat, cook the onion and the carrot in the butter until caramelized. Add the wine, and slowly reduce to 2/3 cup. Place the tomato pieces and the wine in a blender, and blend until smooth. Pass through a fine strainer. Season to taste.

Assembly: Ladle a 1-ounce pool of the warm sauce on each of 6 plates, and scoop a mound of the risotto onto the sauce.

QUINOA AND WILD MUSHROOM MAKI ROLLS

Serves 6

1 cup cooked quinoa
1/2 cup shiitake mushrooms, sautéed in a small amount of olive oil, finely cubed, and seasoned
1 tablespoon basil leaves, chiffonade (sliced paper-thin)
1 teaspoon wasabe
2 teaspoons hoisin sauce
1 teaspoon soy sauce
1 8-by-8-inch piece nori seaweed

Method: Mix the first seven ingredients thoroughly, adding a little salt and pepper if necessary. Lay the piece of nori out and lightly mist it with water. Lay the quinoa mixture in a cylindrical mound along one side of the nori and roll it up tightly like a cigar. Cut into six pieces.

Frankenfood: The Ultimate Food Fight

These and fifteen hundred other chefs from across the country couldn't stomach the idea of the new cuisine Campbell Soup company had in mind. The angry chefs came together around the Pure Food Campaign to protest the imminent release of the Flavr Savr Tomato, co-produced by Campbell and Calgene, a biotechnology company heavily involved in genetically engineered agricultural products. Nor did Campbell expect the public outcry that ensued over the prospect of "Frankenfood" when people displayed a vehement resistance to eating a plant genetically altered with a gene from another pool.

The Pure Food Campaign, founded by the activist Jeremy Rifkin, was objecting to the unregulated, uninvestigated release into the U.S. food system of a gene-altered food, and highlighted two problematical elements in the replicant tomato. Calgene had inserted an anti-sense gene to prevent the tomato from ripening too quickly during shipping, enabling it to be picked at a later stage of ripeness. The second gene was more controversial, a molecular marker gene derived from a bacterium that is antibiotic-resistant. Critics were concerned that the presence of the antibiotic kanamycin could eventually render antibiotics useless through extensive exposure in food. In other words, some people prefer to get their antibiotics on the side, and others simply don't want to participate in a mass medical experiment.

The companies downplayed the controversy by pointing out that breeding of crops has been going on for a long time with no ill effects. Then Vice-President Dan Quayle agreed, and said that after eight years of study, the Food and Drug Administration was going to forgo further investigation and permit the engineered products into the market without even label identification. Wolfgang Puck, the famed chef of Spago's, was outraged. Because his line of gourmet frozen pizza doesn't contain ordinary tomato, the government had forbidden him from marketing it without onerous labeling.

Puck threw his celebrity voice into the growing protest with another fifteen hundred professionals from the food industry who share all restaurateurs' horror of patrons getting ill from their foods. Campbell quickly withdrew the tomato, which was dubbed the "Edsel of the 1990s."[80] Wall Street biotech mavens quivered at the prospect of the tens of billions of dollars already invested in the once limitless future of this controversial venture. Getting "the bugs out" took on an added dimension for the biotechnology industry.

The event was a tomato in the face for the financial and biotech communities. Calgene, which has lost $83 million since its founding by a University of California tomato scientist and others in the early 1980s, has spent about $25 million on tomato research and marketing alone.[81] Sales of such products were once expected to generate $10 billion by the year 2000, however, and investors have forked over at least $500 million for ag startups, not including what was invested by the major players like Monsanto, DuPont, Ciba-Geigy, and Imperial Chemical Industries, which have each spent comparable huge sums. Monsanto, which suffered an earlier defeat on BGH (bovine growth hormone), a gene-spliced hormone intended to increase cows' milk production, took a write-down of an undisclosed value on its loss in 1992. But Monsanto's vice-president for plant science declared, "We're prepared for war."[82] This is one food fight that is shaping up to become very serious.

To make their unpopular case for bioengineered food, the large agrigenetic corporations are recycling a familiar scenario from the Green Revolution, updating it with a transgenic carrot and the stick of Third World hunger. Because the developing countries comprise 70 percent of the world's population, a figure slated to rise to 90 percent within a generation, Third World food production must double in twenty-five years to accommodate the growth. The World Bank and other agencies have already invested $180 million in agricultural biotechnology toward this goal.[83] However, given the essential failure of the Green Revolution, which promoted a similar "pump up the yields" model, there is little cause to place any greater faith in the "Green Gene Revolution." If anything, it is likely to continue to further supplant native seeds, native peoples, and local farmers in favor of high-cost, high-tech displacements.

The issue of bioengineered foods raises many questions. A mundane though lethal danger is the vagary of biomanufacturing. The thirty-one deaths and the one thousand people injured from genetically engineered tryptophan in 1991 do not make for an encouraging picture of the safety of biological production or the efficacy of government regulators, who were not even aware of the source of the problem.[84]

Nevertheless, the USDA announced in 1992 that it will no longer even require permits for field-testing of genetically altered foods, because it had not found any problems—yet. The FDA then announced that it will not regulate bioengineered foods, a paradoxical decision for an area of such great unknown consequences with the capacity to affect human health so profoundly. Simultaneously the FDA has been busily working to ban non-toxic herbs with a five-thousand-year empirical history of safe human use. The FDA position may not reflect a scientific standard as much as a double standard.

In 1984 then Representative Albert Gore's Science and Technology sub-committee's report "Environmental Implications of Genetic Engineering" discussed the likelihood of "low probability, high consequence" events that could cause genuine peril to health and the environment. "While there is only a small probability that damage could occur, the damage that could occur is great. Assessing the risks presented by deliberate releases should not be simply a game of environmental roulette. If it is, many benefits of this new technology will be lost, and disastrous environmental conse-quences could well be permitted to occur."[85]

To cross species boundaries that nature does not is to enter unknown terrain. If the bio-trekkies wish to do so, perhaps, like other heroes of medi-cine, they should do it on themselves first. Interspecies communication is certainly a worthy pursuit. Whether to subject a society to it involuntarily, however, is a horse of another color.

Native Nutrition

At a time when government agencies are muddling through just trying to define what "organically grown" means, it's puzzling to contemplate their readiness to release genetically altered foods into the human and natural environment without even a serious look-see. Strong evidence exists that diet is not tamper-proof, and it should be carefully studied before fundamental changes on the scale of "genfood" are permitted. The human diet has remained relatively stable for thousands of years, at least until the advent of synthetics in the mid-twentieth century. One disturbing lesson comes from observations of the changes in the diet of Native Americans, whose health has suffered greatly since changing from traditional foods to modern ones.

In the southwestern United States, the Pima and Papago tribes, who now call themselves O'odham, the People, lived for many centuries on a traditional diet that was partly farmed and partly gathered from native wild food plants. Known as the Bean People, the Tohono O'odham relied heavily upon farming the native tepary bean, as well as amaranth and sixty-day corn. They also wildcrafted a diet of mesquite pods, tree cholla, prickly pear cactus, chia seeds, and acorns from live oaks. They were an extremely healthy people. Today they have the highest incidence of diabetes in the world, after changing to the Standard American Diet of fat, sugar, and processed foods after World War II.[86]

Gary Nabhan of Native Seeds/SEARCH (Southwestern Endangered Aridlands Resource Clearing House) initially came upon this medical detective story as an ethnobotanist studying traditional native food plants. He began to unbundle an impacted pattern of primal diets, human evolution, and personal health. Nabhan saw how the genetic makeup of a people was adapted over thousands of years of a familiar diet. Garrison Wilkes, a biology professor and specialist on food crops, suggests, "Ethnic nutrition has gone on for generations and generations. Certain mothers cooked a certain way, their children were stronger and better because of it, so they lived longer and produced more children. It doesn't make sense to ignore this."[87]

It is not enough, in other words, to identify nutrition in terms of abstract, disembodied nutrient quality or quantity and ignore the genetic familiarity and whole composition from which it originates. "The tight, individual fit between health, genetics and ancestral ethnic diet is widespread. For example, Japanese tend to suffer strokes even with relatively low cholesterol levels, which may show a genetic susceptibility held in check by their traditional diet. A Norwegian team has recently discovered a hidden health factor in the diet of Eskimos: whale and seal blubbers, the supposedly unhealthy fats that dominate Arctic diets, have been found to contain high amounts of the mono-unsaturated fats linked to lower cholesterol levels."[88]

The O'odham peoples discovered that reverting to their traditional diet reversed their health problems. They also found that several of their traditional foods have very important medical benefits for controlling diabetes. In a medical study in Australia, southwestern native foods like the tepary bean were found to have a significant effect on controlling blood-glucose responses while flattening blood-sugar levels, both important factors in controlling adult-onset diabetes. In contrast, the study found that Western foods caused rapid, high blood-sugar responses.[89]

The native foods also had an immediate and dramatic effect on weight loss among the O'odham; people dropped a hundred pounds with the change of diet. "These findings may also prove valuable to non-Indians," wrote Jane E. Brody, dietary columnist for the *New York Times*, "who are susceptible to overweight and diabetes, and perhaps also those prone to high blood pressure and heart disease. The benefits stem primarily from two characteristics of the native foods: their high content of soluble fibers that form edible gels, gums and mucilages, and a type of starch called amylose that is digested very slowly. The combined effect is to prevent wide swings in blood sugar, slow down the digestive process and delay the return of hunger."[90] Yet the study found that even those Indians still eating lots of corn and beans are consuming varieties with little or none of the nutritive advantages of the old strains.

The connections among diet, environment, genetics, and cultural tradition appear to be far more profound than has been previously recognized. They illustrate the gravity of risking culinary gene-lag with techno-veggies.

YIMBY: Yes in My Backyard

"A middle ground is clearly necessary in walking through the current developments that have to do with genetic engineering and genetic information," scientist Alan Kapuler believes. "There are potential dangers involved in genetically altered foods that must be well considered. There are also lovely potentialities for what can be created using the new technology."

Alan envisions the possibility of making perennial crops out of what are now garden annuals. "Those of us who like melons, for example, would be delighted to have melon plants come up from perennial root stock. The same would be true with perennial squash plants, tomatoes, and corn."

Alan is also investigating how to use genetic technology to improve the nutrition of common food plants. "Breeding for nutrition is a science that has barely been touched. Nutritional gardening is a direction to which I am very committed. The technology of genetic manipulation is not intrinsically bad—it depends on the intentions of the creator."

The three Kapuler girls proudly carry freshly picked burdock root into the house to toss into the boiling soup pot. "We know that nutrition in the vegetables is not only a genetic characteristic," Alan adds, "but an environmental characteristic too. I believe you do a better job in your own backyard much of the time.

"In the Oriental religions, rather than the center of the religion being the church, the center of the religion becomes the kitchen," Alan Kapuler muses amid the earthy smells of Linda's cooking infusing their cozy home.

RECIPES FROM SEEDS OF CHANGE FARM

BAKED HARVEST

Serves 4

This is a farm favorite. The layering and baking together marries the flavors of the vegetables and makes for a great meal served over a grain like quinoa or millet. We find the vegetables to be flavorful enough that they need no other spices, and the last-minute fresh greens add a great texture and color to the plate.

1 tablespoon cooking oil, preferably sesame

1/2 cup Southport Red onion, diced

1/4 cup Winter Giant leeks, diced

3 cloves garlic, finely chopped or pressed

1 Delicata squash, peeled, seeded, and cubed

1 Scarlet Nantes carrot, diced

1/2 cup Sakuragima daikon, diced

1 package tempeh or tofu, cubed

1/2 cup Pascal Giant celery

1 cup red cabbage

1/4 cup water

2 cups of fresh greens (kale, spinach, or chard), sliced thin

Oil the bottom of a 2-quart casserole dish. Layer ingredients in the order listed.

Add 1/4 cup water. Cover and bake at 375 degrees for 30 minutes or until squash is tender.

Turn off oven and add greens to the top layer, re-cover, and return quickly to oven. Let sit in oven until greens are bright and tender, about 5 minutes.

Serve with tamari or sesame salt, to taste.

RAINBOW INCA SWEET CORN AND QUINOA WITH PESTO SAUCE

Serves 4

This is a wonderful hearty meal with many nutty flavors and textures. In the Quechua tradition, corn and quinoa were the two staple foods, and we find this a delicious and colorful way to combine them.

2 tablespoons safflower or sesame oil

1 large Walla Walla sweet onion

3 cloves garlic

3 cups Rainbow Inca sweet corn kernels

1 cup quinoa, rinsed well

3 1/2 cups water

1/2 teaspoon salt

1/2 cup Red Ruffled pimento sweet pepper, finely diced

Garnish: 1/4 Red Ruffled pimento sweet pepper, sliced very thin

PESTO SAUCE

1/2 cup almonds or sunflower seeds

4 to 8 cloves garlic, to taste

2 cups large leaf or lemon basil

1/2 cup arugula

1 cup flat Italian parsley

1 cup virgin olive oil

1 tablespoon soy sauce

Heat the oil in a soup pot. Sauté the onion and garlic until clear, then add corn and quinoa. Stir to coat the grains for a few more minutes over a low flame. Add water and salt and bring to a boil.

Cover and simmer over a low heat for 30 minutes, until texture is like a thick stew. Add chopped sweet pepper, and simmer for another 5 minutes. Combine all Pesto

Sauce ingredients together in a blender. Serve in dinner bowls, spooning pesto into the centers. Garnish with sweet pepper slices.

BASIC GRAIN COOKING FOR QUINOA, AMARANTH, MILLET, AND CORN

There is nothing quite as gratifying as eating grains you grew yourself. They have a whole new quality after you've become friends with the plant.

Grains are fluffiest when prepared the following way:

Put on to boil in a kettle more water than you expect to need.

At the same time, brown the grain in an iron pot over a medium flame for 5 to 10 minutes. Stir often with a wooden spoon to prevent burning. When the water is boiling, measure the appropriate amount into the grain pot, and turn the heat down as low as you can. Cover, and cook for the designated time. When done, turn off the flame, fluff grain with a fork, and re-cover and let sit for a few minutes. One cup of grain, measured before cooking, will serve 4 people.

Variations: Sauté chopped onions or other vegetables in a little oil in the pot before adding grain to brown. Nuts can also be sautéed at the beginning to add texture and flavor.

Quinoa: The seeds are covered (naturally) with saponin, so rinse them thoroughly to remove the bitter taste. Run water over quinoa in a bowl or strainer until it runs clear. Cook 1 cup of quinoa with 1 1/2 cups water for 20 minutes.

Amaranth: Use 3 cups of water to 1 cup grain, stirring occasionally to prevent sticking, and cook for 40 minutes.

Millet: Use 3 cups of water to 1 cup of millet, and cook for 30 minutes.

Dried corn: Soak overnight. Then, using 2 cups of water to 1 cup of corn, cook in a pressure cooker for 1 hour.

POPPED AMARANTH

Heat a cast-iron skillet or wok for a couple of minutes. Pour in enough amaranth to cover the bottom of the skillet no more than 1/8 inch deep. Cover the pot, and within 10 seconds amaranth will start to pop. Move the pan to shake the grain, and stir with a wooden spoon to keep it from burning. Within a minute, all the amaranth should be popped. Quickly pour it off and repeat the process. If you should end up with any unpopped seeds, you can pour the whole mix through a strainer, and the unpopped seeds will fall through.

This is a wonderful nutty and nutritional breakfast food, excellent for camping or traveling. In South America, it is often mixed with molasses or honey and pressed to form a candy.

COOL RED RUSSIAN KALE SALAD
Serves 4

In an annual survey of best-tasting vegetables, the one agreed upon by most professional gardeners and seedspeople and growers was Red Russian kale. It's the sweetest-tasting kale we've ever found. Its beautiful leaves can be picked all season long and through much of the winter before they turn bitter. Sautéed in olive oil with garlic and nuts, it makes a great pasta sauce. This is a very nutritious green with many uses.

10 to 20 Red Russian kale leaves
Water
1 Red Ruffled pimento sweet pepper, sliced thin
2 tablespoons olive oil
1 tablespoon red wine or balsamic vinegar
Dash of tamari
1 tablespoon sesame seeds, toasted

Heat a large pan of water to boiling. Slice any tough stems off the kale leaves. Place whole kale leaves in boiling water and stir to cook evenly. In 1 or 2 minutes, when kale becomes bright green and slightly tender, remove leaves from hot water and dip into cold water to stop the cooking process.

Drain and chop kale, and add the sliced pimento. Mix the dressing of oil, vinegar, and tamari, and toss with kale and pimento. Sprinkle with toasted sesame seeds and serve.

SAUTÉED CARROTS AND GOBO (BURDOCK ROOT)
Serves 4 to 6

Root vegetables are great for storing well into the winter, when greens are not available from the garden. This dish is a favorite that kids love especially well. The flavors mingle and enhance each other, and add a sweet spiciness to a winter meal.

1 cup Takinagawa burdock root, julienned
2 tablespoons sesame or other cooking oil
2 cups Royal Chantennay or
Nantes carrots, julienned

Water
Dash of tamari
1 teaspoon fresh grated ginger

Sauté the burdock first in a little oil for 2 or 3 minutes. Add carrots, and sauté for 2 or 3 minutes longer. Add a dash of tamari and enough water to half-cover the vegetables. Cover and cook until almost tender, about 10 to 15 minutes. Add more tamari to taste and a little grated fresh ginger, and cook off the remaining liquid.

TEPARY BEANS O'ODHAM STYLE
Serves 6 to 8

This is the favorite native bean at the farm, one of the great underutilized foods of the Southwest. This traditional recipe comes to us from Native Seeds/SEARCH, which has done a great deal of research on the nutritional qualities and agricultural benefits of this wonderful bean.

2 cups of white or brown tepary beans
About 8 cups of water
1 cup of peeled fresh green chiles (or 2
cups of enchilada sauce)
1/2 teaspoon chiletepin peppers or red chili powder
1/4 teaspoon salt

Sort and wash beans well, then soak overnight. Bring to a boil in a large pot, then drain off the water. Add fresh water to cover the beans, then add 2 inches more of water to the pot. Cover and simmer for 4 hours (or cook in an electric crock-pot on low for 6 to 8 hours). In the final half hour of cooking, add fresh chiles (or sauce), peppers (or chili powder), and salt.

1. "A Brief Review of Selected Environmental Contamination Incidents with a Potential for Health Effects," prepared by the Library of Congress for the Committee on Environment and Public Works, U.S. Senate (August 1980), p. 173.
2. "Study Links DDT and Cancer," *New York Times*, April 22, 1993.
3. National Academy of Sciences, "Diet, Nutrition and Cancer," 1982.
4. Mary S. Godard and Ruth H. Mathews, "Contribution of Fruits and Vegetables to Human Nutrition," *Horticulture Science*, June 1979.
5. National Academy of Sciences, "Effect of Brassica Species Extract and Chemoprevention," *Proceedings of the National Academy of Sciences*, vol. 89 (March 1992), pp. 2394–2398.
6. Jean Carper, *Food Pharmacy* (New York: Bantam, 1988).
7. Dr. James Duke, "Meals That Heal," *HerbalGram*, no. 25 (1991).
8. Jane E. Brody, "Intriguing Studies Link Nutrition to Immunity," *New York Times*, May 21, 1989.
9. John Naisbitt, "The Healing Powers of Food," *New Age Journal*, September/October 1988.
10. Molly O'Neil, "Eating to Heal: The New Frontiers," *New York Times*, February 7, 1990.
11. O'Neil, "Eating to Heal."
12. Alan Kapuler, *Peace Seeds Journal*, vol. 4 (1988).
13. Alan Kapuler, *Peace Seeds Journal*, vol. 5 (1990).
14. National Academy of Sciences, report, "Task Force on Genetic Alterations in Food and Feed Crops" (1973).
15. Doyle, *Altered Harvest*, p. 139.
16. Doyle, *Altered Harvest*, p. 289.
17. Doyle, *Altered Harvest*, p. 141.
18. C. R. Bhatia and R. Rabson, "Nutritional Quality of Cereal Grains, Agronomy Series # 28" (Madison, WI: American Society of Agronomy, Crop Science Society of America, and Soil Science Society of America, 1987).
19. Doyle, *Altered Harvest*, p. 291.
20. Urrutia et al., "1976, Nutritional Quality of Cereal Grains," p. 13.
21. Mortensen et al., "Newman and Eslick, Nutritional Quality of Cereal Grains," p. 16.
22. Mortensen et al., "Newman and Eslick."
23. Bhatia and Rabson, "Nutritional Quality of Cereal Grains."
24. Bhatia and Rabson, "Nutritional Quality of Cereal Grains."
25. Schapiro, "Seeds of Disaster."
26. Lady Eve Balfour, *The Living Soil*, 3d ed. (London: Faber, 1944), pp. 191–192.
27. Lord Tevlot, letter to *Farmers' Weekly*, September 18, 1942.
28. "Soil Laboratory Opens Window on Vibrant Life Beneath a Forest," *New York Times*, April 11, 1989.

29. "Soil Conditions and Food Quality," presented by Dr. Stuart B. Hill, McGill University, 1987.

30. Sharon B. Hornick, Soil Scientist, USDA, as quoted by Joanna Pocavage in "Organic Is More Nutritious," *Organic Gardening Magazine*, November 1991.

31. Dietrich Knorr, Ph.D., "Natural and Organic Foods: Definitions, Quality, and Problems," *Cereal Foods World*, April 1982.

32. Katherine L. Clancy, "Agriculture and Human Health," Sustainable Agricultural Systems, Soil and Water Conservation Society, 1990.

33. Werner Schuphan, "Nutritional Value of Crops as Influenced by Organic and Inorganic Fertilizer Treatments—Results of 12 Years' Experiments with Vegetables (1960–1972)."

34. D. Lairon et al., "Effects of Organic and Mineral Fertilization on the Contents of Vegetables in Minerals, Vitamin C and Nitrates," IFOAM Conference at the University of Kassel, Germany, 1984.

35. Sharon B. Hornick, "Factors Affecting the Nutritional Quality of Crops," *American Journal of Alternative Agriculture* 7, nos. 1 and 2 (1992).

36. Hornick, "Factors Affecting the Nutritional Quality of Crops."

37. *Organic Gardening* 38, no. 8 (November 1991).

38. "A Proposal for Further Study of the Nutritive Value of Organically Grown vs. Conventionally Grown Foods," released by Organic Ag Advisors, Colfax, California, February 17, 1993.

39. J. Leclerc, M. M. Miller, E. Joliet, and G. Rocquelin, "Vitamin and Mineral Contents of Carrot and Celeriac Grown under Mineral or Organic Fertilization," *Components* 3, no. 1 (a publication of UC Sustainable Agriculture Research and Education Program).

40. Gar Hildenbrand, "Nutritional Superiority of Organically Grown Foods," *Healing Newsletter* 5, no. 2 (1989), published by the Gerson Institute.

41. Hildenbrand, "Nutritional Superiority of Organically Grown Foods."

42. Dr. Stuart B. Hill, 1978.

43. "Comparison of Food Quality of Organically Versus Conventionally Grown Plant Foods: 1991," McGill University, prepared by Tina Finesilver, B.SC., R.D.

44. D. B. Long, "Preliminary Considerations and the Methods Used in the Investigations of Nutritional Values at the Soil Association Research Farms." In *Just Consequences*, R. Waller, ed. (London: Charles Knight, 1971), pp. 176–190.

45. E. Aehnelt and J. Hahn, "Animal Fertility: A Possibility for Biological Quality-Assay of Fodder and Feeds?" *Bio-Dynamics*, no. 125, 1978, pp. 36–47.

46. M. C. Linder, "A Review of the Evidence for Food Quality Differences in Relation to Fertilization of the Soil with Organic and Mineral Fertilizers," *Bio-Dynamics*, no. 107, 1973, pp. 1–12.

47. Linder, "A Review of the Evidence for Food Quality Differences."

48. Aehnelt and Hahn, "Animal Fertility."

49. "Natural and Organic Foods: Definitions, Quality, and Problems," by Dietrich Knorr, Ph.D., Department of Food Science and Human Nutrition, University of Delaware.

50. *The Living Earth*, July/September 1988, Ehrenfried Pfeiffer.

51. *The Living Earth*, July/September 1988, Ehrenfried Pfeiffer.

52. Knorr, "Natural and Organic Foods," *Cereal Foods World*, April 1982.

53. California Action Network, Calpirg Report, "Who Chooses Your Food?" (1988).

54. A. A. Kader, "Influence of Preharvest and Postharvest Environment on Nutritional Composition of Fruits and Vegetables," in B. Quebedeaux and F. A. Bliss, eds., *Horticulture and Human Health: Contribution of Fruits and Vegetables* (Englewood Cliffs, NJ, Prentice-Hall, and Alexandria, VA, Amer. Soc. Horticultural Sci., 1987), pp. 18–32.

55. Hornick, "Factors Affecting the Nutritional Quality of Crops."

56. Leslie Kenton, in an address before the Value of Organic Food Conference, Bristol, England, 1988.

57. François Korn, Seed Quest, personal letter to Seeds of Change, May 6, 1993.

58. Korn, personal letter.

59. Judith Gips, Pesticide Action Network, personal interview, May 18, 1993.

60. National Pesticide Telecommunications Network, Texas Tech University, personal interview, May 18, 1993.

61. Trish Crapo, Organic Foods Production Association of North America Reports, May 1993.

62. Crapo, OFPANA Reports.

63. Crapo, OFPANA Reports.

64. "Biotechnology's Bitter Harvest, Herbicide-Tolerant Crops and the Threat to Sustainable Agriculture," Biotechnology Working Group, Rebecca Goldburg, Jane Rissler, Hope Shand, Chuck Hassebrook, March 1990.

65. Martha Brown, *CCOF Statewide News* 9, no. 3 (Summer 1992).

66. Brown, *CCOF Statewide News*.

67. Brown, *CCOF Statewide News*.

68. *Alternative Agriculture*, Committee on the Role of Alternative Farming Methods in Modern Agriculture, Board on Agriculture, National Research Council, Washington, DC, National Academy Press, 1989, pp. 5, 6.

69. *Alternative Agriculture*, p. 8.

70. *Alternative Agriculture*, p. 9.

71. *Alternative Agriculture*, p. 10.

72. *Alternative Agriculture*, p. 21.

73. *Alternative Agriculture*, p. 23.

74. "Weaning Chemical Use: Seeds of Revolt on Farms," *New York Times*, September 11, 1989.

75. *EarthSave* 3, nos. 2 and 3 (Spring and Summer 1992).

76. Molly O'Neil, "Veggie Dishes, But Not the Garden Variety," *New York Times*, June 17, 1992.

77. Alice Waters, personal interview with the author.

78. Mark Miller, personal interview with the author.
79. Charlie Trotter, personal interview with the author.
80. Ted Howard, Pure Food Campaign, January 11, 1993.
81. Scott McMurray, "New Calgene Tomato Might Have Tasted Just as Good without Genetic Alteration," *Wall Street Journal*, January 12, 1993.
82. "A Storm Is Breaking Down on the Farm," *Business Week*, December 14, 1992.
83. "A Storm Is Breaking Down on the Farm."
84. Brown, *CCOF Statewide News*.
85. Representative Albert Gore, Science and Technology subcommittee on Investigations and Oversight, 1984 report.
86. Jane E. Brody, "Arizona Indians Reclaim Ancient Foods," New York Times, May 21, 1991.
87. John Willoughby, "Primal Prescription," *Eating Well*, May/June 1991.
88. Willoughby, "Primal Prescription."
89. Janette C. Brand, B. Janelle Snow, Gary P. Nabham, A. Stewart Truswell, "Plasma Glucose and Insulin Responses to Traditional Pima Indian Meals," *American Journal of Clinical Nutrition*, vol. 51, 1990, pp. 416–420.
90. Brody, "Arizona Indians Reclaim Ancient Foods."

PLANTING
SEEDS
OF CHANGE
THE ENTREPRENEUR
AS SHAMAN

Get your ducks in a row before
you let the cat out of the bag.

Ben Dover,
entrepreneurial shaman

arriage counselors say the main cause of divorce is that the partners discover they have different values. Actually, everything is driven by values. Most businesses are based on only one value: the bottom line, profit. Although I certainly have always viewed Seeds of Change as a commercial proposition, I believe that other values, such as service, can also drive business.

We founded Seeds of Change as a direct response to the environmental crisis of the loss of biodiversity. The essential purpose of the company was environmental improvement, including the advancement of organic agriculture and a safer, healthier food system. The strategy was to effect social change at the end of a hoe.

Ten Thousand Demons

In traditional native cultures, the shaman serves as the bridge between the visible and invisible worlds, joining the realms of matter and spirit. Like a priest or medicine person, the shaman is the magician who brings the etheric into the manifest.

The entrepreneur can play a shamanic role. The entrepreneur holds the vision, the proverbial gleam in the eye, and transposes it from the dream state into the material world. The quest requires a powerful vision, the ability to communicate it vividly and forcefully, and the capacity to move it through the mud of the material world. It also demands the participatory belief of those who share the vision, from funders to workers. In effect, the venture becomes a collective hallucination that must be continuously held until it becomes physically real. It is an immense emotional and spiritual effort, fraught with ten thousand shadows and demons. The traps are relentless and relentlessly clever. They say that to cure an affliction, the shaman must first experience it. It is not a highly sought-after job.

It certainly never occurred to me that filming Gabriel's San Juan garden would lead me to found a seed company, or any kind of company. The idea of entering the world of business at all seemed improbable. My personal interests lay in social change and communications. If anything, I had disdain for the ways of conventional business, which I generally viewed as part of the problem, not the solution. Like Alan Kapuler, I came from a turbulent involvement in the politics of the 1960s and had an anti-capitalist outlook. I've since changed my mind.

From the left, Emigdio Ballon, Gabriel Howearth, Howard-Yana Shapiro, and Richard Pecoraro standing in a field of dry corn and flowers at the Seeds of Change farm, Gila, New Mexico.

At the time Gabriel approached me, I was deeply involved in making the *Hoxsey* movie. Producing the film had started me on an unexpected entrepreneurial path that laid the foundation for creating Seeds of Change as a *value-driven business.* There is one principal element that generally distinguishes a value-driven enterprise. It is bound together by people who are absolutely passionate about the endeavor. Their personal commitment to the shared values is the propellant that projects the venture over the statistical graveyard where nine out of ten new businesses are buried.

Raising money is just slightly easier than raising the dead. But in most cases, capital is essential to start and develop a business, and crossing the mythical shore where the cash meets the flow is itself a shamanic feat. Countless numbers of very worthy value-driven projects never happen simply because it's so incredibly hard to get the money, and very few people are willing, or built, to go through the grueling process of getting the dough. The task becomes doubly difficult for businesses that espouse social values, because the financial community usually views them as flaky.

How Healing Becomes a Crime

I had a strong personal motivation for producing the *Hoxsey* film. After my father died of cancer, I researched the subject intensively, and I discovered that various promising alternative cancer treatments have been systematically obstructed from getting the scientific investigation they seem to merit. The film probed this controversial terrain, using the remarkable story of Harry Hoxsey as the classic case.

I had learned that in 1924 Harry Hoxsey claimed a cure for cancer, a remedy using herbal formulas inherited from his great grandfather. Thousands of patients swore the treatment cured them. But medical authorities branded Hoxsey the worst quack of the century, and so began a dramatic medical war that continues to this day.

By the 1950s, Hoxsey's Texas clinic was the world's largest privately owned cancer center, with branches in seventeen states. Two federal courts upheld the therapeutic value of the treatment. Even Hoxsey's archenemy the American Medical Association admitted it does cure some cases. Yet organized medicine eventually banned the treatment, exiling it to Mexico, where it continues to claim a high success rate today. Why did medical authorities refuse Hoxsey's plea to investigate the treatment? After all, isn't science the impartial evaluation of data?

When I found the Hoxsey story, I realized that, like everything else, medicine is political. Given the dismal failure of conventional cancer treatments—two of three people still die from the disease, a mortality rate that has not improved since the 1950s when Hoxsey was practicing—it seemed unconscionable to deny patients like my father access to information about alternatives and the freedom to try them, especially since they are generally nontoxic and harmless.

I became totally committed to producing *Hoxsey*. It united my twin interests in plant medicine and politics, embedded in a heroic, larger-than-life legend of pure Americana. As an aspiring independent filmmaker, however, I realized I was not independent at all—I was dependent on funding. If I wanted to produce a value-driven project, I would have to raise the cash myself. I would eventually raise over half a million dollars for *Hoxsey*.

Adventure Capital

I teamed up with Catherine Salveson, a bright, courageous nurse interested in herbal medicine, and began to reach out to find a community of value-driven investors. But how do you raise money? I had heard about one person who had raised money for a social venture, a visiting nurse service, so I phoned her to learn about fund-raising. She was perfectly friendly, but when I asked her how she did it, her answer was not what I wanted to hear. Prayer, she replied. I thanked her politely and hung up, disappointed and somewhat angry. I expected hard, practical tips, not some new age jive. "Newage," rhymes with sewage.

Yet, upon further reflection, I didn't come up with any other ideas, so I decided to give prayer a try, with no small embarrassment. I was brought up in a distinctly unreligious household of parents who wanted to assimilate and get away from superstitious Old World religion. Praying was definitely not part of my cultural upbringing, and, technically speaking, I didn't even know what to do.

I sat cross-legged on the floor in the sun as I would to do yoga or meditation, which I had practiced a little bit. I tried to focus on what it meant to ask for something. I found that I was doing something emotionally difficult by asking somebody for money. It is a taboo, I could feel. By asking for money, you are a bum, a mooch, a dependent child. As I pondered this realization, I began to understand that I was not asking for something for myself, but rather I was asking in behalf of a film about alternative health care. I believed in its importance, and I wanted to expose people to information that was useful and not readily available. In that light, I could feel comfortable asking because it was not a selfish request, but one of service.

Because I didn't know people with money, I started to ask around. I was given the name of a local woman who supported good causes. Bracing myself, I called her up. To my amazement, she agreed to a meeting. I laid out my film with great enthusiasm. She said she'd think about it and get back to me. A few days later she called to say yes.

I could hardly believe it. In the course of the conversation, I realized I had been fearful that she would say no, and I was psychologically unprepared for a positive response. I didn't quite know how to accept her generosity, and I clumsily almost discouraged her from going ahead.

This incident showed me that asking for money was only half the game. It's better to give than receive, they say. In our society, we are far better trained to give than to receive. I could see that I also had to be prepared to receive the funding. So I concentrated on the total dynamic of asking, giving, and receiving in what was becoming my funding meditation.

The next ten people I approached said no, but after getting my first yes, I had Pandora's curse of hope. I knew it was possible. One person led to another, and I began to find investors.

In 1982, I first met Josh Mailman, a remarkable visionary who has since emerged as one of the pioneers in the field of socially responsible finance. Josh had a substantial inheritance, and he held very strong political views about spreading the wealth. He had founded a group known as the Threshold Foundation, a collection mainly of young people with inherited wealth who wanted to act responsibly to support projects around spirituality and personal growth. He was truly willing to put his money where his values were, and he exemplified what I came to call "adventure capital." Josh, who had a driving interest in natural medicine, invested in *Hoxsey*, and later became the "fifth Beatle," a crucial investor in Seeds of Change.

The process of raising money was a constant struggle of uncertain survival, both for the film and for myself personally. Week to week, month to month, I never knew how or if I would manage to get the money to keep going. Rejection is the norm. Yet one by one, an exceptional procession of investors emerged who believed in *Hoxsey* deeply.

One of our investors belonged to the Santa Fe Venture Capital Club and insisted we come do a presentation there. I was extremely skeptical, expecting that such a group would basically be interested in conventional kinds of deals with big bottom lines. Venture capitalists do not have a reputation for altruism or personal modesty.

At the crowded meeting, I sat in amazement watching a one-armed man pitch a bowling alley. There was obviously no way anyone would fund his poignant dream. It was a bizarre spectacle. I realized that for many investors, entrepreneurship is a spectator sport, a psychodramatic form of window shopping. If they did provide funding, the venture capitalists generally took a whopping 80-percent share of a business. It seemed less a financial offering than a sacrificial offering. Looking at the one-armed bowler, I couldn't help recalling something about a pound of flesh.

"Capital rules," spoke a coarse whisper in my ear. It was the rasping voice of Ben Dover, who identified himself as my entrepreneurial shaman, the Don Juan of dough. "No," I objected strenuously, "capital *serves!*" Ben surveyed the room of tightly held hands punching calculators. "Look at them—grasping at the physics of greed. Capital rules is the rule of capital. You people who think capital serves always get it upside down, or my name's not Ben Dover!"

To Ben's amazement, two people from the club invested. Despite the extreme hardship, producing *Hoxsey* became a rewarding process of finding a financial family, a money community that was value-driven.

Planting Seeds of Change

I expected to try to produce another film after *Hoxsey*. Then Gabriel showed up at the office one day in 1987 wanting help raising money to obtain the Gila land to create a nonprofit health and agriculture center. I told him it didn't sound practical, because the land was expensive and farming was capital-intensive.

Some time later, he called to say that he had indeed raised the money for the land, along with his friend Andre Ulrych, an affable angel from Aspen who had saved the failing deal with a bridge loan. But Gabriel was far more successful at raising plants than money, and he needed help to raise more funding for farming. I said I couldn't possibly see how to do such an expensive project as a nonprofit center. I asked him about the economics of seeds. Was growing organic seeds a viable commercial enterprise? He put together some production information about yields and prices. Seed growing is very intensive compared with growing produce, and the prices are better. Organic products in general were commanding higher market values, and there was a total lack of organic seeds. Gardening was an established industry and a very large one. The organic aspect could serve as a commercial window into the larger issue of biodiversity, which could appeal to many backyard gardeners.

I had already come to understand the preservation of these seeds as critically important, and it also looked to me as if it could be a viable business. A couple of my *Hoxsey* investors agreed to put up early seed money, and I started to put together a serious business plan. I suggested calling the company Seeds of Change. I committed to help get it started, then I thought I would go back to filmmaking. I never intended to stick around. "I'm not a farmer," I remember saying.

After the business plan and a financial offering were in place, I set up two fund-raising events, one in Los Angeles and one in New York. Gabriel knew quite a few people in L.A., as I did. Many people expressed their excitement and enthusiasm and promised to be there. We went with great optimism. A friend who owned a lovely gallery lent us the space for a Sunday afternoon in February. We spent hours making delicious snacks using foods like quinoa and amaranth, laying them out in a striking display.

Nobody showed up. It was devastating. When we walked down the dark beach in Santa Monica that moonless night, I had a black hole where my heart was.

It was also a serious logistical blow, because spring planting was just around the corner. Unless money came in soon, we would lose an entire year. Suddenly the event in New York had a lot more riding on it.

After leaving New York in 1973, I had virtually nothing to do with the city until I started *Hoxsey* in 1984, when I began to reconnect with a new business community. On a fund-raising trip there in 1985, I got a late-night call from Josh Mailman to come to a party to meet some people. On the fortieth floor of a vertiginous apartment building near swank Sutton Place, a grinning man sat playing a white piano in a mirrored, sleek black apartment. Picture windows overlooked the East River with a view like the one from the starship *Enterprise*. Josh introduced me to Greg Pardes, a glowing buddha of a fellow, whose place it was. Greg was not a funder, as I expected, but a fellow entrepreneur. We became friends instantly.

Greg is the inventor of ReSeal, a patented dispensing system that eliminates the need for preservatives and often for refrigeration. The special valve emits a single dose or portion of a flowable product and then vacuum-reseals itself. The technology holds important implications for a variety of foods, pharmaceuticals, and other products.

From the left, Julie Spelletich, Susan Van Auken, and Jill Perez processing tomatoes for seed at the Seeds of Change farm in September.

Greg, who had a broad interest in nutrition and alternative medicine, was very supportive of *Hoxsey*, and then later of Seeds of Change. He offered to hold the funding reception for us at his apartment and invite a bunch of serious prospects. Gabriel prepared more lovely native foods in Greg's well-appointed kitchen, and I set up the slide show. The doorbell started ringing. Perhaps New York seems an unlikely venue for promoting organic farming, but by the time we finally quieted things down enough to get the presentation going, the room was overflowing.

We walked away that night with enough money to start the project, about $150,000. Greg invested on behalf of ReSeal, and beamed as he asked for a photo of the tractor we would buy with his money. Josh invested. Soon I raised about another $50,000, and I assumed we were on our way. It's the assumptions that get you.

False Start

By the time we were sure we had the money, it was almost April. The agricultural crew Gabriel wanted had dispersed and taken other work. He assured me that we could still pull it off with another crew, and that it was not too late in the season to start.

There were continual farm management problems all summer long. Three hundred miles away in Santa Fe, I didn't find out just how bad it was until it was too late. Several large gardens were lost because they had not been weeded at the right time. Other fields were damaged by a summer-long drought and insufficient irrigation. But somehow one large section of the crops survived.

It was only a few days till harvest when the packs of starving javelinas charged out of the parched mountains and discovered that great organic food all in one place. The pacifist, vegetarian crew at the farm was hog-tied, not knowing what to do during the vicious nocturnal raids by the wild pigs, except to make lots of noise and hold a prayer vigil by day. Desperate, I called up some Harley biker friends in Santa Fe who had approached me previously about hunting at the farm. They rode down, eager and confident. But the javelinas, cannonballs with tusks, proved too fast and mean even against their black leather and guns. The culture clash with the farm crew was radical, the Altamont of organic farming.

Some of the crop was saved, but things had gone very wrong. I had never experienced a failure on this scale, nor one that was so far out of my own control. In retrospect, it was clear that we should have held over the farming for a year instead of starting so late in the season.

Heartsick and mortified over the prospect of losing all my friends' money, I called up Alan Kapuler, who had been an interested adviser to the project at that time. To my surprise, he affirmed the basic concept of the seed company as an excellent idea. He suggested, however, that the person we needed to run the farm was Rich Pecoraro. He said he himself would come fully on board, but only if Rich would. When I spoke to Rich, he agreed. Suddenly we had a deeply strengthened agricultural core. Rich's assessment of our surviving seed inventory found more than we expected.

But the money was gone, and we had big black marks against us. What to do? Even though it was ridiculously late in the seed-selling season, I produced our first seed catalog, establishing the unique magazine format we have used since. From the outset, the goal was not only to sell seeds but also to create awareness about the issues involved. Although the first catalog was too late to sell many seeds, it served as a tool to sell the company.

National Distribution

After founding the Threshold Foundation, Josh Mailman had continued to organize the world of socially responsible funding by starting a group called the Social Venture Network (SVN), a consortium of progressive businesses. Josh agreed I could come as a guest, because Seeds of Change met the social values, if not yet the financial ones, of the group.

I walked into a most extraordinary gathering of the emerging culture of value-driven companies. Among them were Anita Roddick from the Body Shop, Ben Cohen from Ben & Jerry's, and the CEOs of many other maverick businesses committed to social and environmental values. As the meeting was ending on Sunday morning, an acquaintance introduced me to Paul Hawken, co-founder of Smith & Hawken. Paul expressed serious interest in Seeds of Change, and I handed him our catalog. He looked through it approvingly. He had been looking for organic seeds for some time, he told me, and he offered to bring me out to San Francisco to discuss a possible deal.

Drying chiles in the sun at the Seeds of Change farm.

I called up Alan and gave him the news. He was delighted when I asked him to accompany me to San Francisco. The California meeting ended with a deal for Seeds of Change to supply seeds for the winter Smith & Hawken catalog. As we walked around a botanical garden afterward, Alan was already calculating the numbers of packs we needed to produce, more than he had produced in fifteen years combined. Fortunately he had trained a modest growers' network in Oregon, and we had Rich on line at Gila. Alan was certain we could produce enough seeds. I believed him.

I also came in touch with Will Raap, the founder of Gardener's Supply, the other preeminent national catalog for organic gardeners. He too decided to offer Seeds of Change that winter and prepared to place an even larger order. Suddenly we had national distribution through the two most prestigious mail-order catalogs in the field of organic gardening.

Here was a fragile startup company, a shining vision balanced inscrutably between possible success or certain bankruptcy, a high-wire act with no net and a hungry band of snorting javelinas circling furiously below. Under Rich's direction, the farm produced well that season, as did the Oregon growers' network under Alan. Gabriel kept things in order at the farm between Rich's several stints back and forth from Oregon. This time, when harvest came, we had the goods.

I was increasingly overwhelmed, however, trying to keep everything else together. Fund-raising routinely took well over half my time. Then there was running an expanding business with complex and tightly timed biology and marketing. Because we never had adequate money, it was hard to get competent help. It was clear that I had to have a highly capable person actually running the business if it was going to stabilize, much less succeed. That person was Nina Simons, my sweetheart.

I had met Nina in the spring of 1987 when I was completing *Hoxsey*. We fell madly in love almost right away. She was vivacious, adventurous, highly intelligent, and vibrantly alive. Mainly we just got along like peanut butter and jelly.

An ace organizer, Nina had several professional backgrounds, including restaurant management and production management in theater and film. When we first got together, Nina and I formally collaborated selling *Hoxsey* at film festivals in New York and London. We worked together seamlessly. She was instrumental in making key TV sales to HBO and Bravo, as well as to Britain's Channel 4. She was highly effective, and I was deeply grateful. Both her organizational and her marketing abilities were exceptional. When we returned from London, she took a job as director of special projects for the Santa Fe Chamber Music Festival, where she managed complex logistics, budgets, and volatile artistic temperaments. She eventually assumed responsibility for the festival's advertising sales, expanding them dramatically, while also obtaining and implementing large grants. I was just getting Seeds of Change started, writing the business plan in her kitchen.

Two years later, when Seeds of Change seemed as if it was really going to go, I proposed to Nina that she help me run the business. It was a scary prospect because the project continued to be exceedingly unstable financially, and now we would both be log-rolling in the open seas. On the other hand, it was a project worth struggling for, and I knew it had a far higher chance of success with her involvement. Taking a very deep breath and a pay cut, Nina decided to join Seeds of Change, six months after Rich and Alan had done so. We now had the true core of the company necessary to make it work.

Mounds of native squash waiting to be processed at the Seeds of Change farm in the early fall.

By the end of seed-selling season in our second year, our sales reached six figures. We had demonstrated our ability to move our unique product in the national mail-order market. We successfully pioneered the introduction of racks of organic seeds into the natural foods industry. Our own catalog was starting to show reasonable sales and expansion. We were widely and favorably covered by the national media. And we were still a dollar short and a season late.

Financial panic is the entrepreneur's regular late-night visitor, a premature alarm that screeches out with gut-wrenching terror. Usually sometime around 3:00 A.M., the eyes open, widely dilated, to scroll the long tableaux of unmet needs, outstanding bills, tenuous relationships, and hovering, heart-stopping potential fiscal catastrophes. The blessed unconsciousness of sleep grows more distant as the adrenaline kicks in and another anxious dawn rises.

Yet somehow money always came through, just in time to scrape by and make it through the next payroll. Perhaps it's explained by what my friend J. P. calls the Jewish Mother Theory of Worrying. By visualizing all the terrible things that can happen, you actually prevent them from happening. This is a very good theory.

New Partners

A succession of heroic funders stepped in at various junctures to save the day. One was Jeffrey Bronfman, whom I had met through a check he sent for *Hoxsey*. Jeffrey, who is from a branch of the Canadian Bronfman family, which started Seagram's, was uninterested in joining the family business and pursued instead a path as a meditation teacher. He decided to take responsibility for the money he inherited, and attended business school. He also became active in philanthropy with Josh through Threshold, where he became a director.

Jeffrey was an early investor in the company, and he said that he had come to regard Seeds of Change as his favorite investment. "I think it's important for investors to consider what's being produced through the companies that they empower," Jeffrey explained. "There are opportunities for making substantial income and wealth through enterprises that I consider to be perhaps immoral, or socially and environmentally damaging. Is it at the expense of other people, or rivers or other forms of life? What is the service that's being provided through the company that I'm empowering? Will the process that's going to personally provide me with financial benefit be a process that's going to provide greater good for the whole? That's a harder investment to find. Nature doesn't seem to develop itself at the expense of other parts of itself, and the beauty that I saw in Seeds of Change is that people win all the way down the line."

Jeffrey's own work mainly involved the rights of native peoples, a community where he is highly respected. He said he learned the importance of the plants at a ceremony in Mexico, where he was deeply moved by the profound respect indigenous people gave to seeds.

Another key player was Howard-Yana Shapiro. Dressed in black, with a flowing gray beard and a ready grin, Howard looked like a cross between an orthodox rabbi, a Harley biker, and a cracker guarding a still in the woods. He had the largest organic garden in the city of Chicago, and it turned out he was interested in investing.

Howard had already lived several lives—as a college professor with a Ph.D. in philosophy and sixteen years in academia, a Fulbright scholar, NEA award winner, professional sculptor, publisher of the provocative *New Art Examiner*, and a teacher at the Art Institute of Chicago. A Harley enthusiast who owns a large collection of antique choppers, he is a recognized expert on Lewis Carroll and Mexican shamanism. He was then operating Popular Culture, a large custom-construction company whose exemplary work often appeared in venues such as *Architectural Digest*.

But Howard's greatest passions are organic gardening, seeds, and natural foods. As a Ford Foundation fellow in the late 1960s, he was assisting in the accreditation of black colleges in the South, and often stayed in the people's homes because of racism or a lack of other local facilities. "What I realized," Howard recalls, "was that this other society not only had its own social structure, but also the people had their own food. We would sit at the

dinner table and eat collard greens, and then some other food would come on the table—mustard greens, crowder peas, black-eyed peas. There would be five or ten things I'd never seen. When I asked where they got this food, they'd say 'from my grandmother.' Outside the houses were beautiful gardens, and they had saved the seed. The seeds probably came from slaves, from foods brought from Africa or foods they adapted here. From that time on, I realized that every time I spit out a watermelon seed, I ought to get a cup. I started collecting a seed here, a seed there. Soon after that, I started gardening very seriously."

Howard had just bought a small farm outside Santa Fe and was commuting frequently from Chicago. With great gusto, he put a substantial portion of his finances into the budding company. The farm and agricultural people gave him great credibility as a money person who was a serious gardener and operator of heavy equipment. Six months later, he became an employee, happily abandoning his lucrative construction company to realize his dream.

We were fortunate to find other important business and financial connections. Through friends, we met Barbara Whitestone, the business manager for Bob Weir of the Grateful Dead, whose main commitments besides music are to social change and the environment. Barbara is an adept financial manager and organizer who has operated for many years in the realm of socially responsible investing.

Barbara visited us in Santa Fe, and the relationship proved to be a good fit. "Seeds of Change is addressing a very basic need," Barbara noted, "with a long-range vision about a world issue dealing with the planet's survival. People need to invest from their heart. The energy of believing in what you're doing begins a momentum that's beneficial to the company. These things are very important to Bob Weir and me from a long-term view of where this planet is going." Barbara agreed to join our board, and I subsequently formed an advisory council of experienced business people skilled at working with growing companies.

Balancing the Masculine and Feminine

As Nina and I focused on marketing, seed sales shot up 500 percent in a year to well over half a million dollars. Seed rack distribution expanded exponentially in the natural foods industry from fifty to five hundred outlets, while other retail distribution was opening up fast in conventional garden centers. We collaborated with the Smithsonian Institution's special Seeds of Change exhibit by supplying rare native corns and ended up in a successful partnership selling seeds in their museum gift shop. Our own catalog was showing very significant sales, and won a national award for the "design Oscars," placing us in the esteemed company of Smith & Hawken, Mark Miller's Coyote Cafe catalog, and Williams-Sonoma. Soon the catalog would lead to the chance to put our ideas into a book for Harper San Francisco.

I had always viewed Seeds of Change as an information company. Our very product of seeds is composed of information—genetic information—and we established a mandate of public education around the central issues of biodiversity, nutrition, and organic agriculture, of which book publishing was a natural extension. I had been fortunate to link with Steven Schmidt, an original thinker with a deep ten-year background in the publishing industry. Steve encouraged me to pursue a book proposal based on our catalog and my own credentials as a journalist, since *Hoxsey* had won the prestigious "Best Censored Stories" award associated with Bill Moyers. A two-book deal with Harper ensued, as Steve and I put together a Seeds of Change publishing division.

Meanwhile, Nina's performance running the business was exceptional, and I was very proud when the board named her president of Seeds of Change. Although the board had initial concerns about a couple running the company, they recognized that the situation can be a very beneficial one.

Fava beans.

We constantly set up each other's shots. We coordinate masses of planning that would never happen if we didn't live together and routinely hold 3:00 A.M. pillow talk meetings. We pass the ball continually on a thousand invisible matters that keep the company in sync.

We feel that a couple—who love each other as we do—holds a different sense of partnership. We are truly rooting for each other. "The agreement to partner toward a higher goal," Nina believes, "becomes more important than either one of our opinions. Part of what we're doing is seeking to exemplify a balance of the masculine and feminine. The things that make up a good relationship with a friend or a lover or a companion or a family member are the same things that make a good relationship in business."

E-mergence

We now had thirty people working full-time, along with numerous growers and seasonal labor. Our annual budget was over seven figures. Overall, we had been able to continue to attract a magnificent value-driven team, both as talent and as investors.

Despite the immense stress of very hard work, long hours, and financial uncertainty, the team not only endured, but became stronger for it. Alan Kapuler ultimately merged his Peace Seeds catalog with Seeds of Change to create the new Deep Diversity Seed Catalog as a second offering for serious gardeners. Emigdio Ballon, after collaborating long-distance for years, joined the team at the Gila farm, bringing his substantial knowledge and his seed collection.

Meanwhile, however, there had been strife at the farm with Gabriel. He may have held a different vision, one of a more purely educational facility, but he never fully embraced the idea of a business. He appeared uncomfortable with the increasing level of social organization at the farm, and seemed to prefer being on his own, working in the fields late at night, filling in the gaps others missed. Although he continued to make major contributions to the work, we felt his alienation.

The situation finally reached a point of no return. After working very hard for over a year actively to resolve the conflicts and problems, I realized

with sadness that Gabriel would not remain in Seeds of Change. The parting was painful, but we believed it was for the better. We worked out an arrangement for him to continue as a consultant as he prepared to head for Baja once again, where it all started for him many years ago.

In fairness, I also have to say that Seeds of Change has chewed up and spit out several people through its sheer intensity. It is a high-performance game. The work is relentless, the pressure is high, and we have a fiery crew of perfectionists who are utterly devoted. Doing a startup business means that you don't have much of a life. Though the value-driven ideal of the company appeals to many in the abstract, few people can cope with the reality of a needy, chaotic company that is continually demanding, like an infant. Having a life is but a dream.

To Go Where No Seed Has Gone Before

Seeds of Change now has over eighty growers in twenty-seven states. We employ about forty people full-time. Our seed racks are carried in well over a thousand stores, a number that is rapidly rising. Almost a hundred museum gift shops have radiated out from the Smithsonian to carry Seeds of Change, fulfilling our mandate to "go where no seed has gone before." We arranged for Seeds of Change to premiere in 1994 in a pilot with Home Depot, the environmentally conscious mass merchandiser. The seeds humbly saved in the backyards of dedicated collectors like Alan, Gabriel, Emigdio, and Rich are now beginning to find their way into mainstream commerce.

For a biologically driven company, it has been a rapid ascent. It seems a long way from the one-armed bowler, and I hear that Ben Dover is now teaching at a school called Shame-on U. Four years of financial white knuckles finally came to an end.

If you're crazy enough to try to make sense of this singular story of the genesis of a value-driven business, it might go something like this. Seeds of Change was a very good idea for a company. Starting with insufficient capital, the company pressed to attain a level of income that was simply too much too soon. There was always enough success to validate the company but not enough income to sustain it financially. Chronic undercapitalization hobbled its orderly growth. But the shortage of funding evoked the sheer will, determination, and resourcefulness of the people to make it happen, with great economy and efficiency. For a biologically based company, it actually happened very fast, because it was built on the foundation of earlier work. The company finally managed to survive long enough to become successful. The people were driven by values besides money, and they would not have done it only for money.

Companies are people, and the personal relationships among the people constitute the heart of the company. A high level of cooperation made it all work. The people have done vastly more together than they could have done alone. Because of the values at the core of the enterprise, the marketing of the company addressed a culture, not just a product, enlisting even wider support. Working together, a small group of people can have a very real impact in creating a force for social and environmental change.

A value-driven enterprise like Seeds of Change is almost always initiated by people passionate about the field. Only later will business people come on board, generally once the project has shown some viability. The earliest possible collaboration between these two groups would improve the process and lessen the risk significantly.

In a sense, the greatest risk Seeds of Change has faced consistently has been undercapitalization. "Patient capital" is essential for this process to occur in a healthy way, and it has the effect of relieving an immense degree of unnecessary stress on the company's progress. Most startup businesses need at least five years to establish themselves and approach profitability.

For investors, risk is always the four-letter word. Yet risk is high all the way through any startup, whether value-driven or conventional. The commitment of the people is perhaps the single greatest factor in overcoming obstacles. Any startup is very, very difficult. Objectively, it seems as daunting as the growth of a seed. A tiny, virtually weightless seed, buried in the ground, must push through literally tons of soil and rock in its path, growing determinedly toward the light. It must have enough nutrients and water

> I planted some of your seeds, and the tomatoes from varieties of twenty or thirty years ago were a big hit. No one is interested in eating the newer varieties now. **Nancy S., Massachusetts**

and just the right temperature conditions. It must avert predators. The risks are formidable, and planting any seed is a test of faith.

When investors inquire about risk, I often suggest that we need to look at the question from another point of view. What about the risk of the loss of biodiversity? What risk are we running by not supporting a company trying to address this danger? Because all startups are risky business, why not support the ones that are taking on serious social and environmental problems? If we fail, at least we have faltered trying to do something worthwhile.

When Howard Shapiro invested, his friends questioned his sanity in risking his entire "nut" in a dicey startup. But for Howard, the investment came from his heart. "I really felt that I had been given an option to use money that I had made in my work in the most profound way I could. I showed the information to a couple of financial people, but I never read any of the documentation. All I did was wait for these people to say, 'Well—it's a risk.' It didn't matter to me. I don't want a municipal bond. I don't want to finance a bridge over the Delaware River. For me, it was a blessed event. It took me right back to 1968, when I was working for the African-American colleges. I felt that this was the mainstream of that seed that was planted for me then. I told everybody I knew, 'I invested in Seeds of Change.' For me it was like having a baby."

Seeds of Change has managed to keep its freedom and integrity as a company and has been very fortunate not to lose control to an external controlling financial force. In fact, we have tried to strike a genuine balance between investors and the key employees in the company. We feel blessed to have an extraordinary group of investors who are aligned with the higher purpose and values of Seeds of Change. This ideal is not an easy one to attain, and we had a couple of negative experiences while pursuing it, which occurred because of financial strain.

Our board is composed of half core employees and half investors. Or was, I should say. Two of our principal investors have become permanent employees, and now the thin, green corporate line is muddied by fertile soil from the fresh fields of hard labor.

The employee group owns almost a third of the company. This equity acts as a good motivator, and helps to lessen the perception of separation from the investor group. From my point of view as chief executive officer, the key to the company's ultimate success is a highly motivated, harmonious team working closely together toward the same goals. People must recognize their common interests, including financial ones, to achieve the goals of the company.

People within the company recognize and respect the important contribution made by investors and the need for the business to make a profit—sustainable, that is. There now exists a genuine sense of a community of shared values and financial goals, and it has taken several years to reach that equilibrium. Most of the core group, myself included, came from a fairly radical viewpoint about the exploitive history of finance capital.

A Decentralized Intelligence

From early on, we have also operated by an unorthodox social structure. Geography mandated a decentralized intelligence. Our administration and marketing are in Santa Fe, physically separate from our warehouse. The farm is three hundred miles south in Gila, New Mexico, and Alan is in Oregon. We have relied on close communication and a high level of trust that people do not have to be externally motivated to do their jobs. Actually, as far as Alan is concerned, he is not working for Seeds of Change per se. Rather, he is working for the gene pool, and perish the thought that Seeds of Change could ever compete with the gene pool as a motivational force, certainly for Alan.

Internally, we have some measure of hierarchy, but to a high degree we operate by team management. Most of us are antiauthoritarian, yet we have found a chain of command necessary as a mechanism to assure accountability, to know that the job has indeed been done at the end of the day. Short of that, however, we encourage a culture of communication and consensus. People leave their titles at the door, and we are trying to attain a sensible corporate ecology based on relationship, a sociobiology of kinship and mutualism.

One of the earliest lessons in integrating this kind of relationship within the company occurred when we were first setting up the warehouse and customer fulfillment center. The person hired to organize the operation quit just as all the key systems were being installed, from the personnel to the computers, at the height of the irretrievably brief window of seed-selling season. The group of five staff had been working for about a month together when suddenly they were without a boss. Nina and I went to assess the situation and realized that these five people were quite capable of self-management in their individual domains. Maybe they didn't need a boss. We promoted four of the five to managers and encouraged them to work as a team, report to Nina, and see what happened. They rose to the occasion beautifully, and it has worked well ever since.

The Gila farm operates in much the same way. Though Rich is ultimately responsible, the farm group shares quite a bit of responsibility and exercises a lot of internal communication. There is close coordination with the Santa Fe office primarily now through Howard Shapiro, and at the same time there is a great measure of self-management. It is revealing and gratifying that there has been negligible staff turnover in the last three years, despite hard work and not a lot of pay.

The farm crew is unusual altogether. Most have become fairly credible botanists, and they often spend their day off out in the woods collecting seeds. Lee Gearhart was formerly a gardener at the famous Tassajara Zen center in California and has been with Seeds of Change since its prehistory. Susan Van Auken has meticulously managed the farm administration also since its early days. Jim Orlando is a skilled mechanic and gardener who left Vermont in search of a deeper environmental commitment. Will Hoeller, a young Turk who became a disciplined martial artist, has also educated himself into a graduate program in growing diversity. Carlos Perez left farm work in the Bay Area for the Gila farm, where he became a principal manager. The whole group is committed to stewardship of the land and the seeds far beyond any conventional job description.

It is an organic process as much as an ideology. "The goose may be the totem animal for the 1990s," Nina conjectures. "When geese migrate through the sky, they fly in a V formation, and the function of that V formation is that the goose in front actually cuts the wind resistance for the geese that fly behind. So the group formation gives added endurance, and the whole flock is able to fly a much longer distance because they facilitate each other. The one goose that doesn't have reduced wind resistance is the lead goose. That is the goose for whom flying takes a great deal more energy. So when they're migrating, they rotate the lead goose. I think that is a wonderful model for team cooperation."

Seeds of Change has also extended the concept of partnership to our customers. Because one of the lessons of diversity is a social ecology of mutual interests, the essential corporate strategy behind Seeds of Change is to use the estimated market of 100 million backyard gardeners as a mechanism for preserving biodiversity.

A private seed company actually becomes one of the best available vehicles for preserving biodiversity, while also helping to inform and educate large numbers of people about the central issues at stake. Education is essential to the successful sale of our seeds. Once people understand the crucial differences between organic, open-pollinated, diverse seeds and chemically raised hybrids, they are more prone to choose Seeds of Change and simultaneously support these goals.

Prior Art

As a seed company, we refuse to participate in the process of patenting seeds. All the seeds we produce and sell are open-pollinated. They reproduce true to form, and gardeners can save them for themselves if they so choose. We have offered basic seed-saving tips for gardeners in our catalog. The reason we do this is that the gene pool needs to be held in as many hands as possible for the biological well-being of the planet.

Although Alan Kapuler is a professional plant breeder who could easily patent his inventions, he is opposed to the practice. "Patenting mechanical inventions is one thing, but the plants were here before us. To introduce a new gene or rearrange several genes hardly entitles one to property rights over it. To alter one or two genes out of ten thousand should not constitute ownership for plants that were here before we stood erect, grabbed a hoe, and began gardening."

There is an interesting concept in the patent business, an obstacle that can prevent the granting of a patent. The term *prior art* means that the invention was too closely based on an existing entity. Prior art is a very challenging condition for many natural forms, such as plants, making the idea of human ownership patently ridiculous. People did not build the potato, and it is arrogant for plant breeders to think that they did.

It is strategically possible to patent plants and then directly enter them into the public domain, thus making them available to everyone. This practice is common among universities and public institutions, though it is much less prevalent today now that many such institutions are dominated by large corporations that prefer to privatize ownership of the germ plasm.

"Van Gogh loved sunflowers," says Alan brightly. "He painted them again and again. It's amazing that some of the sunflowers that are in van Gogh paintings have been patented by modern seed companies." The best things in life are no longer free, but Alan is working to change that by breeding an exciting new series of sunflowers—open-pollinated hybrids— that he and Seeds of Change are *not* going to patent. "The beauty of flowers is a gift to us all," offers Alan.

Social Responsibility: Product or Byproduct?

As a company we do not view ourselves in isolation but as part of a growing movement of value-driven companies. However, there is a broad and varied range of companies that consider themselves socially responsible. It can mean anything from giving a portion of the profits to environmental causes, to having some degree of employee ownership or worker management, to using recycling programs. It can also entail some degree of progressive commercial relationships, such as buying sustainable ingredients from the rain forest or from indigenous peoples.

But, unfortunately, being socially responsible does not necessarily mean that a company's products are environmentally beneficial or worth producing in the first place. Often the alleged "social responsibility" aspect constitutes secondary by-products rather than actual products of the work. An occasional company is even trying to exploit a green image just for public relations, and we consider them *hippiecrites*.

We set up Seeds of Change to produce a product, seeds, that would directly help offset the loss of biodiversity. Though we also try to run our business in a socially and environmentally responsible manner, the fundamental activity of the enterprise is a direct response to the environmental crisis. Every day when people come to work, their task is directly supporting biodiversity.

Eco-nomics

Business and the environment have traditionally been a match made in hell. Yet these days you don't hear many companies say they're against protecting the environment. It's almost possible to imagine a world in ten years in which companies and nations will work actively toward a sustainable society, just for pragmatic reasons of enlightened self-interest and biological survival. Most of the actual practical solutions are at hand, but implementing them requires altering our values, a philosophical shift wrapped in a change of heart.

Looked at realistically, our environmental problems are grave. Issues such as global warming and global swarming will not be tidily solved by minor lifestyle modifications like recycling and improved fuel emissions standards. We must make fundamental changes in the way we support ourselves on the planet, and the task of restoring the environment demands a worldwide cooperative effort on a massive scale previously unseen except in times of war. But how do we change from a way of life that is systematically devouring our host, the earth, to one that strikes the symbiotic balance that is second nature to the rest of nature?

Because the fate of the environment is tightly lashed to the state of the world economy, environmental problems cannot be solved separately from mainline economics. According to conventional economic models, protecting the environment is too expensive, especially during a depression. The conventional wisdom has held that doing the right environmental thing hurts companies financially. The model says that preventing pollution, reducing waste, conserving biodiversity, and operating sustainably within the resource base are bad for business. If we really believe that, we should be supporting a crash program to colonize Mars.

In reality, not protecting the environment is even more costly, especially in the long term. From an economic point of view, the earth is the source, not a resource, for almost all the wealth of the world. Where does oil come from? Or trees, fish, cement, gold, and soil?

Because of the cybernetic efficiency of high-tech industrial production technologies, powered by a large population based on a culture of consumption, we are fast-forwarding the depletion of natural resources at warp speed. Yet our present gross national product recognizes none of this environmental depreciation as a debit, valuing only total production and not acknowledging the shrinking resource base. Incredibly, the *Exxon Valdez* oil spill actually *added* value to the U.S. gross national product because of the cleanup money it generated. As Vice-President Gore notes, "The partial blindness of our current economic system is the single most powerful force behind what seem to be irrational decisions about the global environment."[1]

In fact, companies that do the right environmental thing can also do well fiscally. Mismanaging the environment is usually just a symptom of mismanagement at large. The businesses that say they can't clean up their environmental act usually also have poor records on worker safety, wages, employee relations, and fiscal management. Polarizing the issue as jobs or profits against the environment is a cynical strategy of myth-management by retrograde interests that are probably themselves on the way to extinction.

Economy and ecology have a natural urge to merge. A rigorous financial discipline is credibly emerging from the conviction that economics is actually a subset of ecology. Reality demands a new "eco-nomics" that derives value from the well-being of the environment itself and assigns negative debit accounting to practices that damage it. It's necessary to factor in the economic value of the extinction of species, the decline of forests, the degradation of water, soil, and air, and the accompanying costs to the public health. Both the United Nations and the U.S. Department of Commerce are starting to include the costs of natural resource depletion as an adjunct to conventional accountings of national wealth. It is an inevitable logic destined to underwrite the ecology of business around the world.

The Business of Restoration

It is essential to turn restoring the environment from a movement into an industry, and business must serve as a vehicle for the transformation. Environmental business is well suited to become the engine of a new economy, creating not only jobs but meaningful work that produces real value. It will also spawn new technologies and substantial wealth.

A good scenario of how to green the economy comes from a partner of ours in Pennsylvania. Coal strip-mining is an industry in decline that will soon be as archaic as the fossils that fueled it. A former foundation of the Pennsylvania economy, King Coal has left a dirty legacy of open wounds all over the region's otherwise verdant rolling hills and rich lands. Acid mine drainage from the abandoned mine sites has killed the state's rivers, which were once brimming with trout. Neither the companies that long ago abandoned the mines nor the government charged with protecting water quality take responsibility. The local population is largely unemployed, broke, and despairing.

The wetlands scientist Doug Kepler grew up in western Pennsylvania and remembers the trout before they disappeared. While wandering in the woods among today's lifeless streams with his young son, Doug winced when his boy said he wished he had a magic wand. What for? To make the streams come alive again and fill with fish. Doug vowed that he was going to spend the rest of his life restoring the watershed of western Pennsylvania.

Doug knew about a magic wand of sorts. He had worked for years for a large engineering firm designing and implementing constructed wetlands for the region's mining industry. Wetlands are a natural biotechnology; they

act as a living filter to clean wastewater, and they have proven a very successful and inexpensive treatment for acid mine drainage.

Doug quit his job to form his own company, Damariscotta, a Native American word for the "place where many fishes gather." He wanted to empower forsaken communities to use this relatively low-cost, low-tech solution to revive their dead waters. He was willing to provide free design expertise and to horse-trade for necessary goods and services. The modest shopping list included the use of a Caterpillar tractor, shovels, labor, and some stands of wetlands plants. He didn't need any five-hundred-dollar Pentagon hammers.

An energetic constellation of volunteers spontaneously combusted around the project. It included Ducks Unlimited, Trout Unlimited, the Audubon Society, the Magic Forests Tourism Bureau, and the League of Women Voters. But the surprise guest was Company B from the 876th Engineers Battalion of the National Guard. The Guard needed to perform training exercises anyway and was ready with bulldozers, backhoes, trucks, and shovels to dig ponds, install channels, and plant cattails. The forty Guardsmen even got to practice using their night-vision gear, and in three weekends the job was done. Materials, fuel, and labor cost about twenty-five thousand dollars.

Six months later, the water quality of Mill Creek exceeded anyone's expectations. The wetlands system was removing 95 percent of the deadly iron and raising the acid pH of the water to seven, a neutral state that supports life. Wood ducks appeared almost immediately, and the first fish are now swimming in the stream. A member of the Guard in an interview with a local paper fought back tears to say that when he joined the Guard, he was seeking to be of service. He couldn't imagine a greater service than he had just performed, one for which his grandchildren will remember him lovingly. He planned to return with his family to go camping. He hoped the Guard would do more environmental projects. In fact, the newly empowered Mill Creek Coalition has already moved upstream to the next site.

For several years, Seeds of Change has been advocating conversion of the military into an ecological task force. With the melting of the cold war, this scenario is actually viable. If the annual military budget of $300 billion were halved, the money saved would service virtually every infrastructure need, from clean water to education. The remaining budget of $150 billion would still give the military multiples more firepower than any other army in the world. According to the Center for Defense Information, a think tank of former high-level military officers, a cut of $100 billion could be easily achieved by 1995, with another $50 billion cut in 1997. Soldiers of the green could be following the Mill Creek Coalition upstream next weekend.

A restored western Pennsylvania watershed will bring back not only the streams and the wildlife, but also the tourists. Though tourism is not without its problems, the residents feel that it beats strip mining and welfare. As the Mill Creek story exemplifies, restoring the environment supplies a broad spectrum of jobs employing everyone from highly trained professionals to ditch diggers.

Restoring the environment of western Pennsylvania is synonymous with reviving the economy. Restoring biodiversity through a seed company like Seeds of Change is a comparable bioeconomic strategy. As a broader vision, it is a program that will permit the United States to play in world markets where countries such as Germany and Japan have already hit the ground remediating. It is telling, for instance, that Japan has targeted the development of environmental technologies as a primary industry for the 1990s. In fact, Japan at present has half the worldwide patents on all natural products, an awesome prospect, considering the potential scope of the field.

Resonance of Change

In the big picture, Seeds of Change is one tiny company. It is a miracle that it has even survived this far. It has done so by virtue of the exceptional commitment and energy of a band of hard-core botanists, biologists, and entrepreneurs who were convinced that this project had to succeed to avert biological disaster. It has also been supported with capital from a group of visionary investors who probably had to straitjacket their financial advisers while they signed the checks. It has progressed without government subsidy or assistance. In fact, it has progressed despite the system.

We believe that our business commitment must go beyond the conventional one of making a profit for our investors. We believe it must also directly serve the environment and the community. If the business is successful, the model may be replicated. These values may ultimately spread more widely throughout the business community. Business and the environment can enter a reconciliation based on shared values of sustainability, diversity, health, freedom, and peace.

In the larger picture, it is high time to devise a coherent global *greenprint*, an enforceable program of sustainable practices to replace the destructive, inefficient methodologies operating today. Just as Seeds of Change has based its business on biodiversity, many more companies and enterprises can be founded on the health and well-being of the biological foundations of the planet, rather than on its destruction.

"We must make the rescue of the environment the central organizing principle for civilization," advocates Vice President Gore, who proposes an environmental version of the Marshall Plan. He notes that the Marshall Plan to restore Europe after World War II from 1948 to 1951 comprised about 2 percent of the nation's GNP, and that a comparable percentage today would supply $100 billion a year, as opposed to a nonmilitary foreign aid budget of $15 billion a year.[2] As Gore points out, this initiative goes beyond national security to global environmental security.

But at times the urgency of the environmental situation is stark and overwhelming. Not all the issues can be addressed on a societal timetable, looking for gradual improvement in ten years. Biodiversity is an issue whose urgency simply cannot be denied or postponed. Every day that passes is a death sentence for countless species. They can't wait ten years for the political wheels to align.

We all know the bad news and the mounting index of environmental horrors. In fact, most environmental problems have been seriously underreported. What if it's even later and things are worse than we've been told? Why bother? Why not stay home and get the patent on a VCR that has a microwave oven in it to make real TV dinners?

There's an intriguing parallel with homeopathy. Homeopathy is a system of medicine that holds that a substance will cure certain symptoms only when given in an infinitesimal dose. Conventional medicine, which is based on large "heroic" doses, has long rejected homeopathy, saying that such a submolecular dose can't possibly produce any real physical effect.

To the contrary, however, scientific trials have repeatedly confirmed that homeopathic doses do have a demonstrable effect. Homeopaths speculate that the submolecular dose appears to create a resonant frequency in the body, much like the resonant power of a tuning fork, or Sonic Bloom's ability to enhance plant growth.

Perhaps companies like Seeds of Change and groups like the Mill Creek Coalition can act as the infinitesimal doses that will serve to set off the resonance of environmental change in the larger society.

The Sacred and the Profane

When the Spanish conquistadores first came to the Americas, they were possessed by the fever of finding gold. After discovering abundant ceremonial gold decorating the Aztec Empire, Cortés began to tell the spiritual leaders of the native peoples that the Spanish had a disease that could be cured only by gold.

Ironically, the Americas' biological diversity of food and other useful plants—corn, tomatoes, squash, beans, potatoes, cocoa, sunflowers, peppers, tobacco, sugar, cotton—were destined to contribute a far greater wealth to the world. One year's crop of the potato alone is worth more than all the gold and silver the Spanish took from the New World.[3] But for the last five hundred years, the worship of gold has outweighed the value of the living treasure, resulting in the ransacking of the natural world.

Indigenous peoples around the world revere and worship nature. They believe that, like human beings, all of nature is alive and has a soul. They do not see themselves as separate from nature or superior to it. They honor nature as a grand mystery by whose beneficent grace they walk the earth in beauty. They recognize their interdependence with all of creation, and they honor it as an inviolate bond between ecology and spirituality. They value nature as they value their own souls. They value the earth as they value their mother.

How do we value the environment? Even if we learn to operate sustainably, is the earth just a dollars-and-cents proposition, a rain forest number crunch in which it makes more financial sense to preserve the habitats than to slash, burn, and graze them?

Restoring the environment is ultimately not just a technological fix. All the technological fixes in the world won't restore the environment until we restore our own spirits by honoring the sacredness of life itself.

When the Europeans arrived in the Americas, they believed they had come upon a wilderness. Vast expanses of densely alive land sang with an endless abundance. The rivers were so thick with fish that one could virtually walk on the water. The skies turned black with birds.

In fact, the land was intensively used, managed, and traveled by large tribes of people. The reason the Europeans perceived it as uninhabited wilderness was that the Native Americans mainly lived lightly in balance with the earth. They often lived so invisibly as to leave signs perceptible only to other close observers of nature. The Indians might as well have been ghosts to the Europeans. Unfortunately, before long, many were. Five hundred years later, the rivers are thick again, and the skies black—but with poisons. The environment is a ghost of its former self, and the final onslaught to extract what's left is at hand.

The degraded condition of the environment today is emblematic of a culture of objectification that treats life on earth as a commodity. The ecological devastation in the Americas today is not a historical accident but a reflection of our disconnection from the natural world and our inner impoverishment. It is completely consistent with the philosophical legacy of Columbus and the fateful encounter he initiated between Europe and the Americas five hundred years ago.

When Columbus left Spain, he held a common European belief that the end of the world was near. In fact, the Europeans were quite sure that Armageddon was coming in exactly 158 years in 1650. Viewing conditions in Europe, one can understand their pessimism. Europe was under the brutal domination of a collection of corrupt monarchies that were literally bankrupt. The peasant masses lived in crowded squalor with starvation and famine as constant companions. Scarcity and disease ruled. The Black Plague had been rampant for two centuries. Torture and execution were the most common forms of public entertainment, in what historians have called a "culture of death."[4] The Inquisition was raging, and 1492 also marked Spain's expulsion of 120,000 Jews.

The Europeans were altogether estranged from nature. Row-crop agriculture and monocultures had radically degraded the topsoil, which was further compacted by large herds of cattle that left the land barren. The oceans were overfished. Hunting was an "obsessive preoccupation," and by the thirteenth century bears and wolves were virtually extinct in Europe.[5]

Philosophically the Europeans regarded nature with dread as a frightful, uncontrolled force to be subjugated. In their view, man was charged as the master and possessor of a soulless, inanimate nature to be conquered, suppressed, and exploited. It was definitely "man" who was charged with this mastery. An element of the Columbian-era Church associated women with witches and nature-worship. "What is woman, other than the ruin of friendship, an inescapable punishment, a necessary disaster, a fascinating evil, a natural temptation, a domestic peril, a desirable danger, a universal evil in fine colors?"[6]

What Columbus encountered in the Americas could hardly have been more different. He found abundance and health. He observed sustainable cultures living in harmony with a bountiful land. He found welcoming people who had only the most primitive weapons. He found biological and cultural diversity and advanced democratic political structures that recognized women as equals.

To the indigenous American peoples, life was a sacred web of interdependent relationships of which humans were stewards. They honored and revered nature in their spiritual practice. They did not believe that anyone could own the land, and possessions were virtually unknown. Agriculture was sophisticated, polycultural, and sustainable, based on a wide diversity of food crops. The Americas ultimately gave the world 60 percent of the foods in global cultivation today. Many primary botanical medicines also came from the Native Americans' knowledge of plant medicine. The Indians had forty words just for different parts of a leaf. Yet Columbus did not bring along even one botanist. In fact, numerous early Spanish explorers literally starved to death rather than eat the plentiful native foods.

More compelling to Columbus was the fact that the Americas would yield three to five times as much gold and silver as existed in all of Europe. "Gold is treasure," he wrote, "and with it, whoever has it may do what he wants in the world, and may succeed in taking souls to Paradise."[7] For all his talk of bearing a Christian God, Columbus neglected to bring a single priest. The possession of material goods replaced all other values. The European greed led to systematic genocide and ecocide. Within a hundred years, 95 percent of the indigenous peoples were extinct. Since 1492, 95 percent of the continent's original forests have disappeared, and the buffalo and the beaver have been virtually exterminated.

From the very beginning of European colonization, the Americas came under the economic control of the first corporation, the Dutch West India Company, soon to be followed by the seminal banking cartels. Subsequent corporations founded by actual pirates like Sir Francis Drake carved up the remaining domain. The common populace who fled Europe as refugees seeking freedom found a contrary terrain. Many immigrants could come only as indentured servants to the New World, where they then found it almost impossible to gain their freedom. Only men who owned land could vote. Slavery soon became institutionalized in the mines and on the sugar and tobacco plantations, whose addictive appetites drove the enslavement of African captives.

The intervening five hundred years since Columbus have witnessed a steady devolution of biological, cultural, and political diversity in the

Americas. The European alienation from nature launched a process of environmental destruction that has extinguished countless life forms, and left soil, water, and air dangerously degraded. The greed that propelled this dreadful process through the clenched hand of business now extends to threaten the entire planet. Environmental issues do not recognize national borders. It is one world, and it has gotten much smaller and a little flatter since the time of Columbus. The business of restoration is now at hand and, with it, the opportunity for business to redeem itself.

Look to the Mountain

Ironically, by the time of the American Revolution, the Founding Fathers had become great admirers of the Native Americans. Benjamin Franklin and Tom Paine actually helped to influence the Constitution and the political structure of the United States based on the Iroquois Confederacy, which they viewed as a very advanced democratic system.

The extinction of biological diversity is inextricably linked with the destruction of cultural diversity. With the loss of native cultures, there is also disappearing the vital and important knowledge of a way of living in balance with the earth and the value system in which it is encoded. To approach the process of restoration, it is essential to learn to see the earth through native eyes.

The Native American educator Gregory Cajete, Ph.D., believes that indigenous education is synonymous with environmental education, because reverence for the earth is central to the indigenous worldview. "Every one of us can trace our roots back to some indigenous source," Dr. Cajete believes. "When I say indigenous, I am reflecting the thought that everyone is of a place, ultimately a place that is one of nature. Through the generations of time, each of us has been sensitized intimately to the nature of the places in which we live. There's a saying that we Pueblo people have: 'That place that the people talk about.' It really is not only a physical place, but also a place of consciousness, a kind of orientation. The idea of sacred orientation to place and space is a key concept of indigenous education."

Freshly harvested Sweetkeeper squash at the Seeds of Change farm in the early fall.

Dr. Cajete, who is also an ethnobotanist and artist, is working with Seeds of Change to develop an educational curriculum based on indigenous knowledge through a nonprofit endeavor we initiated called the Native Scholar Program. The program is designed to preserve the earth-honoring wisdom of native cultures, especially through conserving native seeds and traditional methods of farming. The program is also intended to reorient people to the compass of place and to a connection to the land.

"Native elders reflect constantly on the idea 'Look to the mountain,'" Dr. Cajete observes. "They usually use that phrase in conjunction with suggesting that you need to look at things in a much broader perspective of what you are doing into the next generations and generations thereafter. Indigenous education really is a ten-thousand-, a twenty-thousand-, a thirty-thousand-year strategic plan."

The inspiration for the Native Scholar program came from a traveler from Africa, the minister of agriculture of Dakar-Senegal, who visited the Seeds of Change farm on a farming tour in 1989. While touring the research garden, he suddenly began to cry. He saw growing an African sorghum that Gabriel had collected that he had not seen since his grandmother cultivated it when he was a child. It had since been replaced by a hybrid. He wanted to return to the farm to study varieties and organic farming, which was also supplanted in his home country by chemical agribusiness.

Many traditional methods of farming have great value, and the Native Scholar Program is helping preserve them and integrate them with state-of-the-art contemporary knowledge of sustainable agriculture. Many ancient farming techniques have proved sustainable over long periods of time, according to Dr. Anna C. Roosevelt, an anthropologist at the American Museum of Natural History. "There is a whole range of possibilities that could be carried out based on what ancient people did for thousands of years," Dr. Roosevelt said to the *New York Times*. "In one such technique," the *Times* relates, "Amazonian Indians have learned to manage agricultural plots so that over a period of years they evolve in planned phases from cleared

farmland back into thick forest. The plots move through stages in which wild species of useful plants and trees are encouraged to encroach gradually. These are tapped for a variety of uses, including medicine, insecticides and pesticides. Eventually the forest reclaims a given plot. Meanwhile other plots are in varying phases. The result is that the forest continually renews itself even while sustaining its exploiters."[8]

According to archaeologists, the Amazonian systems sustained large populations for over two thousand years. Dr. Roosevelt says that native peoples have lived there for over ten thousand years and used the forest intensively without destroying it. "What people did in ancient times may be ecologically sensible. At least we know the forest survived."

The National Academy of Sciences found ancient methods exceptional for "re-creating prehistoric abundance." In its report *Lost Crops of the Incas*, the Academy identified complex raised-bed agriculture going back two thousand years and conducted experiments that replicated ancient farming techniques that tripled potato yields. "The combination of raised beds and canals has proved to have remarkably sophisticated environmental effects. For one thing, it reduces the impacts of extremes of moisture. For another, it reduces the impact of temperature extremes. For a third, it maintains fertility of the soil. The prehistoric technology has proved so productive and inexpensive that it is seen as a possible alternative for much of the Third World where scarce resources and harsh local conditions have frustrated the advance of modern agriculture. It requires no modern tools or fertilizers; the main expense is for labor to dig canals and build up the platforms with dirt held in by blocks of sod on the sides," concluded the Academy.[9]

For Emigdio Ballon, with his Quechua heritage, this ancient technology is both high science and high art. "The Indians know many things, but they don't get credit for them," Emigdio sighs. "Machu Picchu was a huge research center of agriculture for the preservation of culture and for the study of the environment." Emigdio is working at the Seeds of Change farm to conduct experiments on aspects of ancient native farming methodologies, and through the Native Scholar Program the farm is additionally preparing to create a "living museum" of traditional farming methods from around the world.

In 1992, the Native Scholar Program sponsored Paul Poncho, a Pueblo Indian farmer from Acoma pueblo in New Mexico, to live and work at the Gila farm for part of the 1992 season. Paul pointed out that Acoma farmed about two thousand acres in 1900, an area diminished to only two hundred today. The tribe would like to renew its agricultural self-reliance and possibly engage in commercial agricultural production. But the larger issue is one of retaining a traditional relationship with the land.

"Corn for Pueblo people became a sacrament of life, a representation of life itself," notes Dr. Cajete. "During the month of August, you find the grand corn dances occurring among Pueblo peoples here in the Southwest because corn, beans, squash, and all of the things that we grew with our hands were the foundation of our life. The reason most indigenous people have ceremonial annual cycles is that you have to do this year in and year out. You have to continue to remember to remember what your relationship is throughout your life and through the generations that will follow. Once you break those cycles, then you begin to forget, and to do the kinds of things that have resulted in what we see today ecologically."

Kokopelli, Bearer of Seeds

Dr. Cajete cites the ancient story of Kokopelli, the seed carrier, as a metaphor of the indigenous worldview. Kokopelli is a hump-backed flute player, the bearer of fertility, good fortune, culture, and music. According to Dr. Cajete, "Kokopelli is a reflection of the nature of reproduction. Each of us really in truth is like a Kokopelli with our bag of seeds, our bag of unique gifts. We are each bringers of seeds, planters of seeds, and each of us has a creative spirit and plays a part in this reproductive process. Similarly, in that world of forty thousand years ago, first men and first women came to understand their relationship to the Earth itself, and came to see the Earth as a feminine being, a procreative being that had life."

I'm so pleased to find Oregon Giant pole beans. Have been searching for them for several years! My mother, who is nearly eighty-three, remembers them as one of the best.
Marianne M., California

A pile of Ruby Gem watermelons at the Seeds of Change farm.

Petuuche Gilbert, the land commissioner of Acoma pueblo in New Mexico, who also participated in the Native Scholar program, shares this view of a living planet. "Even today when our religious people get up in the morning and go to the east end of Acoma with their cornmeal, and turn to the north and say the prayers, they're praying for all things: the rock of Acoma, the land of Acoma, the water, the animal life, the plant life, all people. They're praying for coexistence in that we may all survive peacefully, and that there may be abundance, and good rains."

Petuuche remembers an old man at the pueblo who warned him of changing conditions in the world. The elder recalled herding sheep in his younger days, when the clouds would come from the west in a gently rolling storm bringing rain. But what you see today is scary, he told Petuuche, with a lot of thunder, a lot of wind, a lot of lightning. It's almost as if there's an anger, and it's very disturbing, he confided. He said that this was prophesied to occur, because the envelope around the earth would be torn.

"This is part of our prophesy," Petuuche relates. "It is an indigenous consciousness here, these changes that man has induced. In these last five hundred years, these changes have increased dramatically at a very rapid pace."

The native prophesy is mirrored by developments in Chile near the South Pole, where the "edge of the ozone hole" is beginning to wreak havoc. Fishermen are catching blind salmon, hunters are easily grabbing blind rabbits, and increasing numbers of the nation's 2.5 million sheep are experiencing temporary blindness. Plants are flowering too early or not going to seed, their normal biological cycles so disrupted that greenhouse growing is starting to replace outdoor farming. The rise in ultraviolet radiation is compelling the local population to wear hats and scarves and to cover their faces with protective creams because skin cancer is on the rise. The United Nations Environment Program predicted a 26-percent increase in nonmalignant skin cancers worldwide if overall ozone levels in the stratosphere fall just 10 percent more. The U.S. National Aeronautics and Space Administration found that the ozone layer loss over Antarctica is already estimated at 50 percent, and 40 percent over northern Canada near the North Pole.[10]

Although there is scientific disagreement about the state of global warming, scientists agree that the earth is a degree hotter than it was a hundred years ago. There have been many times the number of natural disasters in the United States in the last few years than at any other time in recorded history, as well as the largest—Hurricane Andrew in 1992. Global warming is believed to be responsible for the increased incidence of hurricanes, wind storms, droughts, and floods. The insurance industry is taking the threat of global warming very seriously, withdrawing coverage in hurricane-prone regions. Greenpeace revealed that, according to an unpublished 1992 Lloyd's of London briefing, from 1966 to 1987 there were no natural disasters for which insured losses topped $1 billion. But from 1987 to 1992 there were fifteen disasters whose insured losses exceeded $1 billion, ten of which were windstorms. Other major global insurance companies have circulated reports linking global warming with rising losses.[11]

"We've created a mass consciousness on this earth that it doesn't make any difference what we do, because the earth is always going to be there for us," said Richard Deertrack of New Mexico's Taos Pueblo at the Seeds of Change Conference in Santa Fe. "We think we can exist without the earth we step on—meaning we think we can exist without the life of the four-legged ones, meaning that we can exist without the green ones. We're beginning to find that is not true. From the point of view of a plant, all human beings look pretty much the same. Whether your skin is white, blue, yellow, or green, we're all on the same planet facing the same dilemma. The native, indigenous people of the world have always said this. That's been our song; that's been our life; that's been our religion. We as men have tried to dominate, and that domination has transferred over into the humans dominating the Earth. That's not the Native American Indian concept of existence. The native American Indian concept of existence is coexistence."

Honoring his kinship with the diversity of life, Richard Deertrack reflected the view of life's interconnectedness that has allowed indigenous peoples to live in a reasonably harmonious balance with the earth for the last fifty thousand years. Richard offered these views at the 1992 annual

Seeds of Change Conference on a panel of Native Americans looking at how to make the next five hundred years better. Perhaps it is time to "look to the mountain," he suggested, with a five-hundred-year plan.

The Bioneers: Restoring the Earth

Seeds of Change started an annual conference, The Bioneers: Practical Solutions for Restoring the Environment, in a further attempt to address the environmental crisis. The event brings together an emerging culture of bioneers in a working group to address the challenge that environmental experts have given us: ten years—the decade of the 1990s—to start seriously reversing the damage we've done to the environment. Can we actually do it? How do we set about restoring the earth?

We have found that practical solutions do already exist for many of our most threatening environmental problems. A leading-edge group of innovators has been persistently defining the forefront of these solutions, creating successful prototypes that demonstrate their viability. The bioneers' working models hold keys to planetary survival that can be perfected, replicated, and spread quickly and economically, with adequate support from the global community.

Subtitled "Brother, Can You Spare a Paradigm?," the conference examines a new approach to problem solving in light of the dawn of the Age of Biology. The hallmark of the bioneers is their reliance on a biological model. The bioneers emphasize imitating nature, using technologies that mimic naturally occurring forms. Their common perspective is an understanding of whole living systems based on dynamic interrelationship rather than on hierarchy and on mechanical models. They employ cooperation instead of domination. They reflect Alan Kapuler's paradigm of the "kindom" of interconnectedness and mutualism.

Part of the solution is also social and political. As a company, Seeds of Change sees itself within a culture of companies that are actively committed to restoring the environment. The conference is helping coalesce this energy into a movement and an industry. Growing numbers of environmentally responsible companies and institutions are supporting the effort,

My grandmother was an Arledge. For many years she had a beautiful garden, from which she would save seeds and give them as Christmas gifts. In 1984 her husband of seventy-three years passed away. Well-meaning "good Samaritans" sold or gave away all her possessions. Amongst them was her seed box. Thank you for offering the Arledge hot chile seed. **Michelle Krieg, Washington** including the Aveda Corporation, Bio-Remediation Services, Earthrise Trading Company, the Odwalla juice company, ReSeal Technologies and Advancements, the Rodale Institute, and the Further Foundation. We believe that a collective corporate effort is essential if we are to effect real change.

"These creatures, long viewed as independent and self-sufficient, nonetheless are endowed to lead a rich social life," according to a *New York Times* report on an analogous phenomenon. "They rarely live alone. They travel in packs, cooperate and are willing to be sacrificed so their fellows may survive. Some aggregate so closely as to mimic a multicellular organism. Others bind themselves together in a cluster for protection against an enemy." This description of the behavior of bacteria prompted one scientist to gush, "We need to understand more about how the properties of the whole arise. We are searching for new principles."[12]

If cooperation is the driving force of life, companies need to express that relationship in real ways, learning to work together in a different mode from the conventional competitive one. Instead of vertical integration—the hierarchical, acquisitive model—perhaps we can practice *horizontal integration*, looking for the overlapping synergy of interests in which everyone benefits.

Gridlock or Greedlock?

But though there are practical solutions available, there are other arcane dimensions to solving our environmental problems. As Jim Hightower dryly points out, "The water won't clear up till you get the hogs out of the creek." It appears that our society today suffers less from political gridlock than from *greedlock*. The concentration of wealth in the United States is the most acute that it has ever been, about equal to what it was in 1929 when the stock market crashed.[13] Concentrated wealth does not seem to benefit the health of the economy or the environment.

The mentality of business must change from the fever of gold and the old ways of the pirates. Josh Mailman founded the Social Venture Network to explore an alternative course of action for business. "For most people, business has created more problems than it has solved. Unlike nations, multinational companies have no boundaries. When three hundred companies control 60 percent of world trade, they become states without boundaries. My desire to build a global web of business activists comes from my impatience with how the global marketplace is failing to respond to global injustice. My father used to have an expression," Josh recalls. "He said, 'Money is like manure. If you pile it up, it stinks. But if you spread it around it can do a lot of good.'"

Ecosystems, Cultural Diversity, and Economics

"If we are serious about our desire to protect the world's most fragile ecosystems and most endangered peoples, then we must ensure that these groups be allowed, both legally and economically, to continue to protect fragile areas as they have done for generations," according to Jason Clay, formerly of Cultural Survival, a group that explores innovative economic strategies for the Third World.[14]

Paying royalties and intellectual property rights to native peoples and lesser developed nations that have conserved these plants is a just and pragmatic course of action. Economic rewards and incentives can help the continued preservation of seed stocks while honoring the cultures and local farmers that have been the guardians of the plants. Over a hundred nations now accept the concept of "farmers' rights," an attempt to recognize the innovations of Third World farmers. Experts say that in the last fifty years, the Third World has given more than half the genes of plants used in the North to develop medicines and crops. The seed companies from the North have sent back patented hybrid seeds, costly chemicals and equipment, and expensive finished products.

According to leaders of countries such as Mexico, Ethiopia, and India, native farmers have carefully selected and bred the varieties that the multinational seed companies then take and patent. One proposed practical solution is that the rich nations whose industries profit from seeds they gather in the Third World pay a mandatory one-percent tax on seed sales. However, the American Seed Trade Association deemed the proposal unacceptable.

I have good news for the seed world. I have found around a hundred different kinds of beans this past year—the old variety of beans that have been kept in the family for 150 years. I live at the foot of the Blue Ridge Mountains in North Carolina and Virginia. It is rich in old seed. I worked hard through the mountains to find the beans. Most of the beans come from around my home, some from Virginia, and two pole beans come from West Virginia. I could not believe I found that many beans. I prayed and looked, prayed and looked. I am a minister, and since I was a young man, many seeds have been destroyed because the old people have passed away, and the beans have died with them. I am scouting for more seed this next year. This might sound like a tale of tales. **Reverend James J. Crouch, North Carolina**

Seeds of Change endorses a proposal of this nature. These seeds will continue to survive only through direct support to the dedicated farmers and gardeners who have maintained these traditional plants. Seeds of Change works directly with native farmers to grow traditional seed varieties, which the company then markets to backyard gardeners. In 1992, Seeds of Change offered several rare kinds of Hopi corn and watermelon grown by the last Hopi farmer known to be raising them. Other groups, such as Native Seeds/SEARCH, also actively support such a strategy. The practice can provide an essential economic strategy for native farmers by paying First World prices for seeds in an otherwise dismal agricultural market. The continuation of these cultural and biological lineages is contingent on an underlying economic basis that is sustainable. In 1993 Seeds of Change contracted with farmers at San Juan Pueblo, where this story began, completing the circle of seeds.

Weaving the Future

"Each seed is encoded with the DNA story," observes Kathleen Harrison, an associate of Seeds of Change who is president of Botanical Dimensions, a group dedicated to preserving medicinal and shamanic plants from the tropics. "Each seed is a long, winding, subtle story. The seeds have crossed human hands and been cultivated by us, and selected by us and bred out, and traded across continents and oceans now, and saved from extinction at the last minute, and lost forever as well. These are all really the voices of the ancestors speaking in each of those seeds. We don't just have all of these species that we're growing at the Seeds of Change farm without the intervention of all the people that came before for thousands and thousands and thousands of years.

"As we collect seeds and we listen, we become aware of the part that the ancestors play in getting them to us. Then we have to be aware that we are the ancestors of the next stage. When we talk about the next five hundred years hopefully being better on this continent, what we're setting up right now is our role as ancestors for our children and those children five hundred years on down the line for whom we will be these distant little voices in the seeds.

Freshly processed seeds of zinnias at the Seeds of Change farm.

"I thought about the word *heirloom* because it comes up so often with the concept of seeds, and I looked it up. *Heir* is as when you inherit something—it is passed down to you from your ancestors. *Loom* in the Old English meant implement, something useful. By the time of Middle English, it literally meant the loom that you weave on. So here we have something that we've inherited in order to weave with. If there are heirloom seeds, then in a way we are taking those and weaving the future with them. Certainly, we are weaving the future of botany, but in a way the future is the whole ecological awareness that is being reborn in the keyhole of history right now."[15]

The collective future is a great concern to the Shuar Indians of Ecuador, according to John Perkins, an author and teacher who collaborates with the Native Scholar program. "The Shuar's belief is that the world is as we dream it—as we create it. Today the Shuar are familiar with the destruction going on in the rest of the world. They told me that this is what we've dreamed: the choked highways, the air pollution, the water pollution, the destroyed rivers and lakes. We wanted this material wealth. They said, 'Only now are you beginning to realize this dream is a nightmare. But it's easy to change that. All you have to do is change the dream, and everything else will change along with it.' They said it can be done in a generation. We need to change the dream. We need to dream an earth-honoring dream."

Though there are obviously multitudes of political and social reforms that could begin to change the face of the world virtually overnight, we can all change the dream ourselves in the here and now. Our philosophy at Seeds of Change is characterized by direct action and personal responsibility. Nobody here waited for the bus. One of the things I ended up liking about business is the freedom it can afford. We identified a market of gardeners, and we're working with them as a mechanism for environmental improvement and social change. As long as our company can show a profit, we are free to live out our destiny.

The formation of Seeds of Change was preceded by a loose collection of backyard bioneers who simply took it upon themselves to start saving and growing diversity. The company gathered that energy and mobilized it into a larger social force. In effect, Seeds of Change considers itself a non-governmental organization in service to the environment. We have declared ourselves a free zone and a global center of diversity. You can do the same thing in your backyard, and start linking with other kindred spirits.

Inner Tan

Seeds of Change has changed my life. For a while I thought it was an interim project between films, an important endeavor I wanted to assist and support. Then it revealed itself as an urgent quest, a life-and-death struggle that demanded everything I had to give, and more. The process of creating the company shattered any limits I thought I had in terms of my own endurance, pain threshold, and ability to produce.

In the end, I surrendered. I love Seeds of Change, and I believe it's one of the important companies in the world today. I love working with a global army of gardeners in direct action on behalf of life and its magnificent diversity.

I also fell madly in love with the people. It's an astonishing team, and an honor to be part of the circle. Working together is a blessing in itself.

In my life, I've been moved to action mainly by a sense of service, by the urgency of the destruction around us and the terrible pain and suffering it is causing. I've tried to respond where I felt it was needed most, and where I could contribute best. As to whether we'll have any real impact, it's hard to say. As someone once commented, "I'm not here to be successful—I'm here to be faithful."

Part of the destruction is so very trivial. Five hundred years after the traumatic European encounter, Columbus Day is just a celebration of shopping. The culture of consumption must be one of the first things to go. We are shopping the planet to extinction. It's simply not possible to give the entire world the level of consumption the First World has. The planet cannot support it. Who needs all this stuff, anyway?

The real treasure is the living treasure, the gift of life. The Mayan word *gene* means "spiral of life." The spiral can't be owned, only passed on between generations. Now is the time to rescue the treasure, to restore the environment, to re-enchant the earth.

I'm not actually very ambitious. I've never really wanted a career. We're all wage slaves, forced to work by a compulsive, acquisitive society unwilling to stop and be still, perhaps afraid to live with its own mortality. When asked what he thought of Western civilization, Gandhi is reputed to have said, "It would be a good idea."

While in prison for fomenting an anarchist plot, Paul LaFargue, son-in-law of Karl Marx, wrote a pamphlet called "The Right to Be Lazy." He described most of the trouble in the world as the consequence of the frenetic miasma of compulsive activity that human beings are mindlessly spinning. The world would be a better and far less troubled place, said LaFargue, if we just did less and cultivated our laziness more.

I am in complete agreement. I would like to work on perfecting my innate lazy nature, sitting up against an adobe wall in the waning light of the summer sun, working on my inner tan. Pitching woo with Nina, dreaming the world, and contemplating the diversity of weeds in my garden.

1. Gore, *Earth in the Balance*, p. 183.
2. Gore, *Earth in the Balance*, p. 304.
3. Manfredo Macioti, "West to East: America's Gifts to the Old World," *Impact of Science on Society*, no. 167 (1992): 225–239.
4. Kirkpatrick Sale, *The Conquest of Paradise: Christopher Columbus and the Columbian Legacy* (New York: Knopf, 1990), p. 28.
5. Sale, *Conquest of Paradise*.
6. Sale, *Conquest of Paradise*, p. 249.
7. Sale, *Conquest of Paradise*, p. 181.
8. William K. Stevens, "Complex Farming Found in Amazon," *New York Times*, April 3, 1990.
9. *Lost Crops of the Incas*, pp. 8–9.
10. Isabel Vincent, "Edge of the Ozone Hole a Scary Place to Live," *Seattle Times*, May 4, 1992.
11. Jeremy Leggett, Scientific Director, Greenpeace International Climate Campaign, letter to the editor, *New York Times*, May 18, 1993.
12. Gina Kolata, "Bacteria Are Found to Thrive on Rich Social Life," *New York Times*, October 13, 1992.
13. G. William Domhoff, *The Power Elite and the State: How Policy Is Made in America* (New York: Aldine de Gruyter, 1990).
14. Jason Clay, "Genes, Genius, and Genocide," *Cultural Survival Quarterly* 14 (4).
15. Kathleen Harrison, president of Botanical Dimensions, in a speech at the 1992 Seeds of Change Conference, Santa Fe, NM.

WHAT TO GROW

One of the advantages to growing some of your own food is that you can explore and sample varieties that you won't normally find in your supermarket. By planting these exotic varieties you will be adding diversity to your diet and participating in the effort to support diversity in the food chain and in the genetic pool of life of the planet. While there are hundreds of uncommon varieties in the Seeds of Change catalog, here is what we recommend to first-time gardeners.

An Exotic Salad Garden

Arugula

Peacevine Cherry Tomatoes

Rouge D'Hiver Lettuce

Lemon Cucumbers

Green Wave Mustard Greens

Hearty Late Season Greens

Giant Swiss Chard

Red Russian Kale

Herbs

Bouquet Dill

Genovese Basil

Italian Flat-Leaf parsley

Lemon Balm

Edible Flowers

African Marigold

Nasturtium

Borage

Licorice Mint

One final pointer from Alan Kapuler: Plant what you want to eat, what you want to smell, what you want to see.

SOW YOUR OWN SEEDS
Getting started in the garden

Gardening is not only the most popular and fastest-growing hobby in the United States, it is among the most rewarding. Working with soil and sun, seeds and water, participating in the cycle of life, and putting fresh food on the table provide stress release, emotional fulfillment, and culinary delight for millions of Americans and others around the world every year. Following are a few tips you can use if you want to join the ranks of backyard biodiversity gardeners.

HOW TO GROW
The basics: Space... Soil...
Seeds... Water... Sun... Bugs...

It is a good idea to start small. As you gain experience you can always expand your garden in years to come. If you live in the city, you can grow in pots or boxes. There are many good books that can give you ideas. **Soil** not only holds the seed and provides a foundation from which the plant can grow, it also feeds the seed and the plant it becomes. You can get good organic soil and soil boosters from most garden centers or from catalog houses. Ultimately, you may want to build your own compost pile and your own soil. There are over 500 varieties of seeds for edible plants in the Seeds of Change catalog, and you can find Seeds of Change seeds in many health food stores and garden centers. Growing instructions are on the pack and in our catalog. **Water** is a critical factor for the success of your garden, especially when seeds are first planted and germinating. Watering should be done in the morning or evening, and not during the heat of day. You will have to water less if you get lots of rain. Generally, your soil should not get bone dry, nor should you flood it when you water. **Sun** is the other critical factor for the success of your garden. Some plants like more or less sun, but they all need some. Most seed packs indicate if a plant needs full sun or partial shade. **Bugs** are mostly good and you may want more of the right ones in your garden. There are good, organic methods for dealing with pests. Ultimately, good healthy plants in good healthy soil will be fairly well resistant to pests and will attract beneficial insects and birds.

In general, if you have questions or doubts, ask your local gardening center or catalog supplier or another gardener, or call Organic Gardening magazine. You will find that gardeners love to share their experience and to help each other out.

SOURCES

For gardening suppliers & information: Gardener's Supply, 128 Intervale Road, Burlington, VT 05401-2850 (802) 863-1700, or Peaceful Valley Farm Supply, PO Box 2209, Grass Valley, CA 95945 (916) 272-4769

For books and magazines on organic gardening: Rodale Press, 33 E. Minor Street, Emmaus, PA 18049 (215) 967-5171

For a catalog of organic seeds: Seeds of Change, P.O. Box 15700, Santa Fe, NM 87506-5700

For beneficial insects: Rincon Vitora Insectries, PO Box 95, Oak View, CA 93022 (805) 643-5407

RESOURCES
AVAILABLE FROM
SEEDS OF CHANGE

P.O. Box 15700
Santa Fe, NM 87506-5700
(505) 438-8080
fax: (505) 438-7052
The Seeds of Change Catalog
The Deep Diversity Catalog
Information about the Native
Scholar Program and the
Seeds of Change Conference
produced by the Gila Interna-
tional Center of Diversity.

A complete list of *The
Peace Papers*—scholarly papers
written by geneticist, microbi-
ologist, and research director
for Seeds of Change, Dr. Alan
Kapuler.

Information about Reali-
dad Productions and films
by Kenny Ausubel, including
*Hoxsey: How Healing Becomes a
Crime, Hope and a Prayer: Atti-
tudinal Healing with Dr. Bernie
Siegel,* and *Los Remedios: The
Healing Herbs.*

SUPPLIERS: SEEDS
AND NURSERIES

Companion Plants

7247 North Coolville Ridge Rd
Athens, OH 45701
(614) 592-4643
Catalog, $2 or free if you call.
Among the widest diversity of
herbs as plants and seeds in the
country, including: medicinal,
ornamental, culinary, aromatic,
dye plant, everlasting, traditional, and ceremonial herbs.

Ethnobotanical Catalog of Seeds

J. L. Hudson, Seedsman
P.O. Box 1058
Redwood City, CA 94064
Well-researched, highly infor-
mative catalog including the
Zapotec Collection, lists of
books, societies, and other
sources, essays. Germination
instructions.

Forest Farm

990 Tetherow
Williams, OR 97544
(503) 846-6963
Extensive collection of perennial shrubs and trees mainly
for the temperate zone.
Catalog, $3

Plants of the Southwest

Route 6, Box 11A
Santa Fe, NM 87501
(505) 471-2212
Selling ancient and adapted
southwestern vegetable varieties: native grasses, wildflowers, trees, and shrubs, as
well as seeds of native plants.
Catalog full of landscaping and
cultural information. Specialists in xeriscaping.

Southmeadow Fruit Gardens

Box SM
Lakeside, MI 49116
(616) 469-2865
Excellent farm for fruit tree
growing and smart experimentation. They experiment with
hardy native fruits for attract-
ing wildlife such as birds and
deer, for example. Many are
dual purpose, used as fences
and also for human consumption. Many are little known,
rarely planted by fruit lovers,
and difficult to find.

SUPPLIERS: TOOLS, SOIL
AMENDMENTS, PEST
MANAGEMENT

Bozeman Bio-Tech

1612 Gold Avenue
P.O. Box 3146
Bozeman, MT 59772
(800) 289-6656
Natural products for least-
toxic, long-term protection
from insect pests.

Gardener's Supply

128 Intervale Road
Burlington, VT 05401
(802) 660-3500,
fax: (802) 660-3501
The finest mail-order company for innovative gardening
solutions, tools, and supplies.

IFM

333 Ohme Gardens Road
Wenachee, WA 98801
(800) 332-3179
Integrated management products and services for natural
agriculture.

Necessary Trading Company

One Nature's Way
New Castle, VA 24127-0305
(703) 864-5103,
fax: (703) 864-5186
Dispenses organic fertilizers
and soil conditioners, natural
pest management systems, and
information on nearly everything one needs to know about
nontoxic farming for the home
gardener as well as for large-
scale sustainable production.

Peaceful Valley Farm Supply

Organic Growers' Source Book and Catalog
P.O. Box 2209
Grass Valley, CA 95945
(916) 272-4769
Effective state-of-the-art organic growing supplies and the information and tools needed to apply them. They offer seed, fertilizer, pest control, and season-extending products in home-scale sizes as well as commercial quantities. The tool selection ranges from hand tools and market garden and small-farm tools to farm equipment.

Rincon Vitova Insectaries

P.O. Box 1555
Ventura, CA 93002
(805) 643-5407
Respected supplier of beneficial insects.

ORGANIZATIONS: FARMING AND GARDENING

Bio-Dynamic Farming and Gardening Association

P.O. Box 550
Kimberton, PA 19442
(215) 935-7797,
fax: (215) 983-3196
A nonprofit corporation dedicated to the advancement of the practices and principles of biodynamic agriculture. To this end, they support a bimonthly magazine, *Biodynamics*, publish books, offer an advisory service, sponsor conferences and lectures, and support training and research projects.

Ecology Action of the Midpeninsula

5798 Ridgewood Road
Willits, CA 95490
(707) 459-3390
Developers of the smallest, least demanding "mini-farm" that will sustainably maintain a family, and larger community market plots.

Healthy Harvest Society

1424 16th St. NW, Suite 105
Washington, DC 20036
(202) 462-8800
Supports the common goal of preservation and long-term sustainability of the earth and its soil for production of foods free of toxic pesticides. Major programs are information and research, organic farming and farm development, developing organic markets, food and nutrition policy. Publishes a bimonthly newsletter and a *Directory of Sustainable Agriculture*.

International Alliance for Sustainable Agriculture (IASA)

Newman Center, University of Minnesota
1701 University Avenue, SE
Minneapolis, MN 55414
(612) 331-1099,
fax: (612) 379-1527
Nonprofit, tax-exempt organization founded in 1983 by farmers, consumers, researchers, business leaders, government officials, and various groups who shared a vision of bringing about the worldwide realization of sustainable agriculture—food systems that are ecologically sound, economically viable, socially just,

and humane. It depends on members for support.

Publishes a quarterly newsletter, *Manna*, and numerous other publications, including the book *Breaking the Pesticide Habit*, by Terry Gips. The Alliance has successfully helped develop a number of landmark initiatives, from a $3.3 million sustainable agriculture program in Minnesota to the Circle of Poison Prevention Act and the Valdez Principles for corporate environmental responsibility.

Permaculture Institute of North America

4949 Sunnyside Avenue North, Room 345, Seattle, WA 98103
Permaculture, modeling natural ecosystems, harmoniously integrates landscape and people to provide food, energy, shelter, and other needs in sustainable ways.

Rodale Institute

222 Main Street, Box KS
Emmaus, PA 18098
(215) 683-6383,
fax: (215) 683-8548
Rodale Institute is a nonprofit educational and research organization based in southeastern Pennsylvania that works closely with farmers, scientists, and extension personnel in the United States and around the world to develop new gardening and farming methods that protect the land, improve productivity, and reduce or eliminate the need for costly chemical fertilizers and pesticides. Publishes *The New Farm* magazine. The New Farm Li-

brary also offers practical how-to books with farmer-proven techniques for reducing chemical inputs and replacing them with natural on-farm resources such as cover crops and manure. Rodale Press publishes *Organic Gardening* magazine and numerous other works.

Rodale Institute Research Center

611 Siegfriedale Road
Kutztown, PA 19530
(215) 683-6009,
fax: (215) 683-8548
The 333-acre Rodale Institute Research Center is one of the world's leading centers for the study of organic horticulture and sustainable agriculture. At any given time, visitors can observe a variety of research and demonstration projects in process, from compost and tillage trials to studies of field cropping systems designed to enrich and protect the soil.

ORGANIZATIONS: FOOD AND NUTRITION ISSUES

EarthSave Foundation

706 Frederick Street
Santa Cruz, CA 95062-2205
(408) 423-4069
Founded by John Robbins, author of *Diet for a New America* and *May All Be Fed*, Earth-Save's message is that a plant-based diet profoundly affects the whole web of life on earth for the better. An animal-based diet, and the factory farming that underlies it, causes enormous depletion and pollution of the natural world, suffering for the animals, and danger to

our own health. A great source of disturbing facts and positive solutions.

National Resources Defense Council

1350 New York Avenue NW,
Suite 300
Washington, DC 20005
(202) 783-7800
Uses legal and other tools to influence policy affecting the conservation of biological diversity in the United States and abroad. Principal areas of activity include forest management, grasslands and deserts management, the Endangered Species Act, exotic species management, and, internationally, the overexploitation of wild plants/forests and economic development projects that affect ecosystems. Funded by members and foundations.

Oregon Tilth

P.O. Box 218
Tualatin, OR 97062-0218
(503) 692-4877,
(503) 691-2514
Worldwide organic certification organization of farmers, packers, processors, brokers, and distributors.

OT's purpose is to educate farmers, gardeners, legislators, and the general public about the need to develop and use sustainable growing practices that promote soil health, conserve natural resources, and prevent environmental degradation, while producing a clean and healthful food supply for all.

Pure Food Campaign

Jeremy Rifkin
1130 17th Street, No. 630
Washington, DC 20036
(202) 466-2823
Organizing growers, producers, dairy farmers, and health food stores into a campaign to support the boycott on genetically engineered food products.

CULTURAL AND BIOLOGICAL DIVERSITY

Botanical Dimensions

Kathleen Harrison
5000 Bohemian Highway
Occidental, CA 95465
(707) 874-1531
Ethnobotanical gardens for preserving plants sacred to native peoples worldwide. Unique publication on shamanic and tropical folkloric plants, *Plantwise*.

Native Seeds/SEARCH

2509 N. Campbell Avenue,
No. 325
Tucson, AZ 85719
(602) 327-9123
Native Seeds/SEARCH (Southwestern Endangered Aridlands Resource Clearing House) is one of the country's first regional seed banks, founded to keep ancient desert plants and traditional farming methods from disappearing forever. Its seed bank contains over 1200 collections. Publishes *The Seedhead News* quarterly and *Seedlisting*, which offers for sale hundreds of crop varieties and many of their wild relatives, semiannually. Seeds are free to Native American gardeners.

Seed Savers Exchange

Rural Route 3, Box 239
Decorah, IA 52101
(319) 382-5990,
fax: (319) 382-5872
The definitive network dedicated to cataloging and preserving diversity of nonhybrid vegetable seeds.

HerbalGram

American Botanical Council
P.O. Box 201660
Austin, TX 78720
(512) 331-8868
fax: (512) 331-1924
The first-rate magazine published by the American Botanical Council documents medicinal plants. Edited by Mark Blumenthal, it provides a fascinating glimmer of the botanical basis of natural pharmacology.

LAND TRUSTS

Rural Advancement Foundation International

101 Hillsboro Street, Room 5
Pittsboro, NC 27312
(919) 542-1396,
fax: (919) 542-2460
Dedicated to the preservation of family farms, conservation of genetic diversity, and safe food.

PLANT SOCIETIES

Missouri Botanical Garden

4344 Shaw Avenue
Saint Louis, MO 63110
(314) 577-5100
One of the largest and finest botanical gardens in the United States. The Missouri Botanical Garden operates the world's most active research program in tropical botany. Scientific research at the garden focuses on exploration and study of the tropics, which encompass the earth's least known, most diverse, but most rapidly vanishing ecosystems.

Institute of Economic Botany

Dr. Michael Balick
New York Botanical Garden
200 St. and Southern Blvd.
Bronx, NY 10458
(718) 817-8763
fax: (718) 220-1029
The primary mission of the IEB is understanding the relationship between plants and people. Projects and field activities are currently carried out in eighteen countries. An example: IEB scientists working with herbal healers in Central America collect and identify medicinal plants, then ship bulk samples to the National Cancer Institute for study as potential therapies for AIDS and cancer. Write for publications.

The Society of Ethnobiology

Office of the Secretary-Treasurer
Brien Meilleur
Amy Greenwell Ethnobotanical Garden
Bishop Museum Project
P.O. Box 1053
Captain Cook, HI 96704
A scholarly society that publishes two issues of a journal yearly and holds an annual meeting. The society is devoted to the study of native uses of plants and animals worldwide and includes paleobotany, paleozoology, and other studies of these materials in the past.

IMPORTANT RESOURCE PUBLICATIONS

Suppliers of Beneficial Organisms in North America

This free booklet available from the Department of Pesticide Regulation includes ninety-five suppliers of more than 126 biological pest controls. Write the to the department, Attn: Beneficial Organisms Booklet, P.O. Box 94287, Sacramento, CA 94271-0001. Or call (916) 654-1141.